AF679932

Final Report of the Forty-fifth Antarctic Treaty Consultative Meeting

ANTARCTIC TREATY
CONSULTATIVE MEETING

Final Report of the Forty-fifth Antarctic Treaty Consultative Meeting

Helsinki, Finland
29 May - 8 June 2023

Volume I

Secretariat of the Antarctic Treaty
Buenos Aires
2023

Antarctic Treaty Consultative Meeting (45th : 2023 : Helsinki)
Final Report of the Forty-fifth Antarctic Treaty Consultative Meeting. Helsinki, Finland, 29 May – 8 June 2023.
Buenos Aires : Secretariat of the Antarctic Treaty, 2023.
284 p.

ISBN 978-987-8929-27-9

1. International law – Environmental issues. 2. Antarctic Treaty system.
3. Environmental law – Antarctica. 4. Environmental protection – Antarctica.

DDC 341.762 5

Published by:

Secretariat of the Antarctic Treaty
Secrétariat du Traité sur l'Antarctique
Секретариат Договора об Антарктике
Secretaría del Tratado Antártico

Maipú 757, Piso 4
C1006ACI Ciudad Autónoma Buenos Aires
Argentina
Tel: +54 11 3991 4250
ats@ats.aq

This book is available for free in digital format from www.ats.aq and for purchase in hard copy from https://www.amazon.com.

ISSN 2346-9897
ISBN 978-987-8929-27-9

Contents

VOLUME I

Additional documents derived from this meeting, including opening and closing remarks, reports from Depositaries, Observers and Experts, a list of participants, and other materials, are available in the Final Reports section of the ATS website. Management plans adopted at this meeting are available as attachments in the Antarctic Treaty database.

Acronyms and abbreviations

ACAP	Agreement on the Conservation of Albatrosses and Petrels
ACBR	Antarctic Conservation Biogeographic Region
ASMA	Antarctic Specially Managed Area
ASOC	Antarctic and Southern Ocean Coalition
ASPA	Antarctic Specially Protected Area
ATS	Antarctic Treaty System or Antarctic Treaty Secretariat
ATCM	Antarctic Treaty Consultative Meeting
ATCP	Antarctic Treaty Consultative Party
ATME	Antarctic Treaty Meeting of Experts
BP	Background Paper
CCAMLR	Convention on the Conservation of Antarctic Marine Living Resources and/or Commission for the Conservation of Antarctic Marine Living Resources
CCAS	Convention for the Conservation of Antarctic Seals
CCRWP	Climate Change Response Work Programme
CEE	Comprehensive Environmental Evaluation
CEP	Committee for Environmental Protection
COMNAP	Council of Managers of National Antarctic Programs
EIA	Environmental Impact Assessment
EDI	Equity, Diversity and Inclusion
EIES	Electronic Information Exchange System
HCA	Hydrographic Committee on Antarctica
HSM	Historic Site or Monument
IAATO	International Association of Antarctica Tour Operators
IBA	Important Bird Area
ICAO	International Civil Aviation Organization
ICG	Intersessional Contact Group
IEE	Initial Environmental Evaluation
IGP&I Clubs	International Group of Protection and Indemnity Clubs
IHO	International Hydrographic Organization
IMO	International Maritime Organization
IOC	Intergovernmental Oceanographic Commission
IOPC Funds	International Oil Pollution Compensation Funds
IP	Information Paper
IPCC	Intergovernmental Panel on Climate Change
IUCN	International Union for Conservation of Nature
MPA	Marine Protected Area
NCA	National Competent Authority
RCC	Rescue Coordination Centre
SAR	Search and Rescue
SCAR	Scientific Committee on Antarctic Research
SC-CAMLR	Scientific Committee of CCAMLR
SGCCR	Subsidiary Group on Climate Change Response
SGMP	Subsidiary Group on Management Plans
SOLAS	International Convention for the Safety of Life at Sea
SOOS	Southern Ocean Observing System
SP	Secretariat Paper
ToR	Term of Reference
UAV/RPAS	Unmanned Aerial Vehicle / Remotely Piloted Aircraft System
UNEP	United Nations Environment Programme
UNFCCC	United Nations Framework Convention on Climate Change
VSSOS	Vessel-Supported Short Overnight Stay
WMO	World Meteorological Organization
WP	Working Paper
WTO	World Tourism Organization

PART I

Final Report

1. ATCM XLV Final Report

Final Report of the Forty-fifth Antarctic Treaty Consultative Meeting

Helsinki, Finland, 30 May – 8 June 2023

(1) Pursuant to Article IX of the Antarctic Treaty, Representatives of the Consultative Parties (Argentina, Australia, Belgium, Brazil, Bulgaria, Chile, China, Czechia, Ecuador, Finland, France, Germany, India, Italy, Japan, the Republic of Korea, the Netherlands, New Zealand, Norway, Peru, Poland, the Russian Federation, South Africa, Spain, Sweden, Ukraine, the United Kingdom of Great Britain and Northern Ireland, the United States of America, and Uruguay) met in Helsinki from 30 May to 8 June 2023, for the purpose of exchanging information, holding consultations, and considering and recommending to their Governments measures in furtherance of the principles and objectives of the Treaty. The Meeting was held in person with a virtual audience.

(2) The Meeting was also attended by delegations from the following Contracting Parties to the Antarctic Treaty which are not Consultative Parties: Belarus, Canada, Colombia, Estonia, Malaysia, Monaco, Portugal, Romania, Slovakia, Switzerland, Türkiye and Venezuela.

(3) In accordance with Rules 2 and 31 of the Rules of Procedure, Observers from the Commission for the Conservation of Antarctic Marine Living Resources (CCAMLR), the Scientific Committee on Antarctic Research (SCAR) and the Council of Managers of National Antarctic Programs (COMNAP) attended the meeting.

(4) In accordance with Rule 39 of the Rules of Procedure, Experts from the following international organisations and non-governmental organisations attended the Meeting: the Antarctic and Southern Ocean Coalition (ASOC), the International Association of Antarctica Tour Operators (IAATO), the International Hydrographic Association (IHO), the International Union for the Conservation of Nature (IUCN), the United Nations Environment Programme (UNEP), and the World Meteorological Organization (WMO).

(5) The Host Country Finland fulfilled its information requirements towards the Contracting Parties, Observers and Experts through the Secretariat, Circulars, letters and a dedicated website.

Item 1: Opening of the Meeting

(6) The Meeting was officially opened on 30 May 2023. On behalf of the Host Government, in accordance with Rules 5 and 6 of the Rules of Procedure, the Head of the Host Government Secretariat, Ms Tiina Jortikka-Laitinen, called the Meeting to order and proposed the candidacy of Ms Päivi Kaukoranta as Chair of ATCM XLV. The proposal was accepted and Ms Päivi Kaukoranta was elected as Chair of the ATCM XLV in accordance with Rule 6.

(7) The Chair warmly welcomed all Parties, Observers and Experts to Helsinki. The Chair expressed her hope that Parties could interact productively for the good of Antarctica and for the Antarctic Treaty.

(8) Delegates observed a minute of silence in honour of friends, colleagues and service members who had been active in the Antarctic community and had passed away in the previous year.

(9) The Chair noted that ATCM XLV would be carried out in person and with a virtual audience.

(10) The Russian Federation noted that the Host Country had not issued visas for some members, including its Head of Delegation, thus creating unequal conditions for the

Russian delegation. The Russian Federation stressed that with respect to the meeting of the Contracting Parties, Article IX referred to all Contracting Parties named in the preamble, and expressed its hope that all Parties would be able to attend the Meeting in the future in accordance with the Treaty and on an equal basis.

(11) Ms Johanna Sumuvuori, Deputy Minister for Foreign Affairs, welcomed delegates to Finland, which was hosting the ATCM for the first time. Noting its status as an Arctic nation and world leader in icebreaking capability, Ms Sumuvuori stated that Finland's role in the Arctic was part of a national strategy with relevance to the whole of the country. She drew on Finland's experience in the Arctic Council, which stressed the importance of environmental protection and keeping the Arctic free of geopolitical tension. She stated that the Russian illegal invasion of Ukraine had violated the Principles of the UN Charter and the Organization for Security and Co-operation in Europe (OSCE) and had hampered Arctic cooperation. She praised the Antarctic Treaty as a great success of international treaty-based cooperation. She emphasised that the Antarctic Treaty was a strong instrument for environmental protection, cooperation, scientific research and peace. She observed that one Consultative Party threatened this cooperation through preventing another from fulfilling its Antarctic ambitions. She noted that Finland stood in solidarity with Ukraine. Ms Sumuvuori stressed that climate change issues had grown in prominence and noted with satisfaction that an entire day of the Helsinki meeting was dedicated to the climate change. She underlined that scientific information was extremely important in finding solutions to the challenges the world faced. She summarised the mission of the Helsinki meeting in the slogan "From Urgency to Action" and urged Parties to find solutions for the future and send a powerful message to ongoing intergovernmental processes.

(12) Ms Terhi Lehtonen, State Secretary for the Ministry for the Environment, noted the role of the Antarctic Treaty in maintaining peace for the region and the Environment Protocol in providing a comprehensive framework for environmental protection in Antarctica. She noted that the joint CEP/ATCM session on climate change would be time for a much needed discussion and that climate change impacts from the polar regions would have a dramatic impact on the rest of the world. She noted that Finland encouraged collaboration between the Parties and the United Nations Framework Convention on Climate Change (UNFCCC), and that the Parties should work together on sustainable development for all of society. She expressed a hope that this Meeting would send a strong message on global action for climate change to the rest of the world.

(13) Ms Helena Gualinga, a Finnish-Ecuadorian climate and environmental activist, drew the Meeting's attention to her homes in the Amazon Rainforest and Finland, noting that, while their environments may seem different, their ecosystems were deeply interconnected. Ms Gualinga stated that what happened in the poles did not stay in the poles, highlighting the destructive flooding in the Amazon during the COVID-19 pandemic. She stated that her advocacy work was motivated by her desires to build a better world, and to ensure that future generations would be able to enjoy the beauty of the natural world that she had grown up enjoying. She also stated that young people should have a say in the decisions being made regarding climate change and environmental damage. Ms Gualinga reaffirmed that young people were counting on those attending the Meeting to stand by their side and leave them a justified and sustainable legacy.

(14) The Chair thanked the speakers for their messages and Ms Gualinga for her touching words and the message from young people.

(15) The Russian Federation responded to comments by Ms Johanna Sumuvuori by stating that her comments regarding Ukraine were political and unrelated to the Meeting. The Russian Federation recalled similar discussions in ATCM XLIV, emphasised that the

statement presented a challenge to the Antarctic Treaty system and appealed to Parties to refrain from politicising the ATCM. It stated that its special military operation aimed to remove security threats from Ukraine and to demilitarise the area. The Russian Federation reiterated that the Host Country had not made it possible for some of the Russian Federation's delegation, including its Head of Delegation, to obtain visas for the Meeting. The Russian Federation suggested that the Host Country had breached the Revised Rules of Procedure for the ATCM (2016), and expressed its hope that this would not become a systemic issue and that all Parties would be able to attend the Meeting in the future.

(16) Ukraine stated that the Antarctic Treaty existed within the context of the United Nations system of treaties and rules and that, when one Party breached these rules, that Party could not say it was merely politicisation. It reported that the bombing of the Ukrainian national Antarctic programme's head office by a ballistic missile had deeply impacted Ukraine's Antarctic activities. Ukraine also noted that many of its scientists were unable to engage in Antarctic activities because they were fighting for their homeland and families.

(17) Many Parties reiterated their condemnation of the Russian Federation's unprovoked war on Ukraine and reaffirmed their unwavering support for Ukraine's sovereignty and territorial integrity. Many noted the Russian Federation's violations of international law and norms, and stated that the Russian Federation must stop its war and withdraw all military forces from Ukraine. Some Parties also condemned the support of the war by Belarus. Many Parties noted that this war between Consultative Parties impacted all of the national Antarctic programmes operating on the continent. It was also noted that the comments of Ms Johanna Sumuvuori simply stated the facts that a Consultative Party had invaded another Consultative Party, and that invasion had impacted the Ukrainian Antarctic Programme, and accordingly could not be considered politicisation of the Meeting. Many Parties noted that international cooperation, which was a cornerstone of the Antarctic Treaty system and the work of the ATCM, was being directly challenged by the Russian Federation's actions.

(18) China stated that the ATCM was not an appropriate platform for discussing geopolitical issues, and cautioned the Meeting not to go beyond its mandate. China emphasised that Parties should remain focussed on cooperation and only discuss issues of relevance to Antarctica.

Item 2: Election of Officers and Creation of Working Groups

(19) Dr Muthalagu Ravichandran, Head of Delegation of India, Host Country of ATCM 46, was elected Vice-Chair. In accordance with Rule 7 of the Rules of Procedure, Mr Albert Lluberas Bonaba, Executive Secretary of the Antarctic Treaty Secretariat, acted as Secretary to the Meeting. Ms Tiina Jortikka-Laitinen, head of the Host Country Secretariat, acted as Deputy Secretary.

(20) The Meeting noted that the meeting of the Committee for Environmental Protection (CEP) was led by its Chair Ms Birgit Njåstad of Norway.

(21) Two Working Groups were established:

- Working Group 1: Policy, Legal and Institutional Issues;
- Working Group 2: Operations, Science and Tourism.

(22) The following Chairs of the Working Groups were elected:

- Working Group 1: Mr Theodore Kill from the United States;

- Working Group 2: Ms Sonia Ramos Garcia from Spain and Dr Phillip Tracey from Australia.

Item 3: Adoption of the Agenda and Allocation of Items to Working Groups

(23) The following Agenda was adopted:

1. Opening of the Meeting
2. Election of Officers and Creation of Working Groups
3. Adoption of the Agenda and Allocation of Items to Working Groups and Consideration of the Multi-year Strategic Work Plan
4. Operation of the Antarctic Treaty System: Reports by Parties, Observers and Experts
5. Report of the Committee for Environmental Protection
6. Operation of the Antarctic Treaty System
    a. Request from Belarus to become a Consultative Party
    b. Request from Canada to become a Consultative Party
    c. Implementation of IMO Polar Code
    d. Climate Change
    e. General matters
7. Operation of the Antarctic Treaty System: Matters related to the Secretariat
8. Liability
9. Biological Prospecting in Antarctica
10. Exchange of Information
11. Education Issues
12. Multi-year Strategic Work Plan
    a. Policy, Legal and Institutional priorities
    b. Science, Operations and Tourism priorities
13. Safety and Operations in Antarctica
14. Inspections under the Antarctic Treaty and the Environment Protocol
15. Science issues, future science challenges, scientific cooperation and facilitation
16. Implications of Climate Change for Management of the Antarctic Treaty Area
17. Tourism and Non-Governmental Activities in the Antarctic Treaty Area, including Competent Authorities Issues
18. Preparation of the 46th Meeting
19. Any Other Business
20. Adoption of the Final Report
21. Close of the Meeting

(24) The Meeting adopted the following allocation of agenda items:

- Plenary: Items 1, 2, 3, 4, 5, 6a, 6b, 6c, 6d, 18, 19, 20, 21.
- Working Group 1: Items 6e, 7, 8, 9, 10, 11, 12a.
- Working Group 2: 12b, 13, 14, 15, 16, 17.

(25) The Meeting also decided to allocate draft instruments arising out of the work of the Committee for Environmental Protection and the Working Groups to a legal drafting group for consideration of their legal and institutional aspects.

Item 4: Operation of the Antarctic Treaty System: Reports by Parties, Observers and Experts

(26) Pursuant to Recommendation XIII-2, the Meeting received reports from depositary governments and secretariats.

(27) The United States, in its capacity as Depositary Government of the Antarctic Treaty and its Environment Protocol, reported on the status of the Antarctic Treaty and the Protocol on Environmental Protection to the Antarctic Treaty (IP 4). Since the last report, there had been two accessions to the Antarctic Treaty. Costa Rica had deposited its instrument of accession on 11 August 2022, and San Marino had deposited its instrument of accession on 14 February 2023. The Antarctic Treaty had entered into force for Costa Rica and San Marino, respectively, on the dates of deposit of their instruments of accession. There had been no actions with respect to the Protocol on Environmental Protection to the Antarctic Treaty and its Annexes. The United States noted that there were currently 56 Contracting Parties to the Treaty and 42 Parties to the Protocol and recalled that the Antarctic Treaty area was reserved for peace and science.

(28) Australia, in its capacity as Depositary for the Convention on the Conservation of Antarctic Marine Living Resources (CCAMLR), reported that, since ATCM XLIV, Ecuador had acceded to the Convention on 24 July 2022. It noted that there were currently 37 Parties to the Convention (IP 14).

(29) The United Kingdom, in its capacity as Depositary of the Convention for the Conservation of Antarctic Seals (CCAS), reported that it had not received any requests to accede to the Convention, or any instruments of accession, since ATCM XLIV (IP 3 rev. 1). The United Kingdom reminded Contracting Parties to CCAS that the Exchange of Information for the reporting period of 1 March 2022 to 28 February 2023 was due by 30 June 2023. The United Kingdom encouraged all Contracting Parties to CCAS to submit their returns on time.

(30) Australia, in its capacity as Depositary for the Agreement on the Conservation of Albatrosses and Petrels (ACAP), reported that there had been no new accessions to the Agreement since ATCM XLIV, and that there were currently 13 Parties to the Agreement (IP 13). Australia encouraged Parties to join the Agreement.

(31) CCAMLR presented IP 2 *Report by the CCAMLR Observer to the Forty Fifth Antarctic Treaty Consultative Meeting*, which reported on the 41st Annual Meeting of the Commission for the Conservation of Antarctic Marine Living Resources (CCAMLR-41) held in Hobart, Australia, from 24 October to 4 November 2022. CCAMLR reported that the Commission had developed its krill management approach and had agreed on a new climate change resolution. The Commission reported that the incidental mortality of birds in longline fisheries during 2022 was the lowest on record. The Commission had not reached consensus regarding the approval of revised management plans for Antarctic Specially Protected Areas (ASPAs) 152 and 153, which had been forwarded to it in accordance with Decision 9 (2005). The Commission agreed to hold an extraordinary meeting on spatial planning and Marine Protected Areas (MPAs) in Santiago, Chile, from 19 to 23 June 2023. The 42nd Meeting of the Commission would be held in Hobart, Australia, from 16 to 27 October 2023. CCAMLR noted that Ukraine (Mr V. Tsymabliuk) would serve as Chair for the Commission in 2023 and 2024.

(32) The Meeting thanked CCAMLR for its report, noted the significance of the upcoming special meeting of CCAMLR on Marine Protected Areas, and welcomed the Commission's new resolution on climate change.

(33) SCAR presented IP 10 rev.1 *The Scientific Committee on Antarctic Research Annual Report 2023 to the XLV Antarctic Treaty Consultative Meeting*, which summarised its

recent work to promote scientific knowledge, understanding and education on Antarctica and its position as the main exchange point for the Antarctic science community. Through its hosting of the Antarctic Environments Portal (IP 75), SCAR provided impartial information based on the best available science to support informed discussion on issues relevant to the CEP and wider stakeholders. It reported on the launching of its new five-year strategic plan for 2023-28 (IP 47) and on key activities including the organisation of workshops and academic events on the conservation and management of Antarctica and the Southern Ocean. SCAR's 10th Open Science Conference (OSC) was held online in August 2022, and the XXXVII SCAR Delegates Meeting was held in September 2022 in Goa, India, in hybrid format. Luxembourg was admitted as a new Associate Member, Professor Steven Chown was awarded honorary membership, and Dr Marcelo Leppe (Chile) and Prof Burcu Özsoy (Türkiye) were elected as Vice Presidents. SCAR also noted: its policy and outreach efforts such as advice to CCAMLR and side-events at UNFCCC COP27 in Egypt; communication outputs for experts and for the general public and a number of scientific group activities; that it had awarded five early-career fellowships; its preparations for a fifth International Polar Year in 2032-33; and the ongoing promotion of equality, diversity and inclusion actions by its dedicated Action Group.

(34) The Meeting thanked SCAR for its report, recalling the importance of SCAR's role in providing objective and independent advice, and thanked SCAR for the ongoing hosting and management of the Antarctic Environments Portal.

(35) COMNAP presented IP 7 *The Council of Managers of National Antarctic Programs (COMNAP) Annual Report 2022/23*. COMNAP reported that, since ATCM XLIV, Canada became a Member in July 2022. COMNAP also reported that its 32 Member and five Observer national Antarctic programmes were enabling and leading key international research initiatives including through research for, logistics related to, and extraction and return to home institutes and repositories of, the planet's oldest ice to inform critical climate models. COMNAP noted that vital to this provision of critical Antarctic data were the national Antarctic programmes' infrastructure, assets and the expertise of programme personnel. COMNAP AGM 2022 had endorsed a draft policy entitled "Welcoming the Power of Diversity within our Membership" with a commitment to contribute to positive change and ensure that everyone who works in Antarctica feels safe, respected and welcomed. COMNAP reported that its work over the past several years on COVID-19 preparedness and response throughout the global pandemic resulted in no deaths in the Antarctic Treaty Area and was an exemplar for international collaboration. COMNAP continued to develop and share best practice on a range of topics of importance to national Antarctic programmes. The ATCM was reminded of internationally collaborative projects that could only be achieved through the collective action of the COMNAP Membership as well as of the 5th Antarctic Search and Rescue Workshop, the 20th COMNAP Symposium and work on natural hazards and response.

(36) The Meeting thanked COMNAP for its report, noting the strong cooperation between national Antarctic programmes in support of science and safe operations in Antarctica, and the important safety measures COMNAP had implemented through the global pandemic.

(37) In relation to Article III-2 of the Antarctic Treaty, the Meeting received reports from other international organisations.

(38) WMO presented IP 16 *Annual Report of the World Meteorological Organization (WMO)*. WMO reminded Parties that its work covered a range of activities relevant to the Antarctic Treaty system, relating to different aspects of science, observations and infrastructure. It reported on information related to several research and modelling activities undertaken through the World Climate Research Programme, including

Antarctic CORDEX and Antarctica 2300 Projections of ice sheet contributions to sea-level rise, as well as the activities of the Climate and Cryosphere Core Project and the World Weather Research Programme's Year of Polar Prediction in the Southern Hemisphere. Noting the collaborative nature of its work, including with SCAR, WMO called attention to its ongoing efforts to establish networks with relevance to the work of Parties, as well as its work with UNEP co-sponsoring the IPCC. WMO noted that its report drew attention to WMO's Unified Data Policy. It also highlighted its contributions to Antarctic maritime safety services, its regional meteorological warning services, and its work to make accessible ice navigation information for mariners. WMO noted its high-level publications relating to Antarctic and climate-related science and expressed its appreciation for the positive and mutually beneficial engagement with Parties.

(39) ASOC presented IP 115 *ASOC Report to the ATCM*, which summarised ASOC's activities to promote Antarctic conservation over the past year. ASOC and its members supported workshops on Antarctic science and policy, and engaged in public outreach activities, including the first World Krill Day. ASOC invited the Antarctic community to participate in the next World Krill Day on 11 August 2023. ASOC also participated in meetings relevant to the work of the ATCM and CEP to promote Antarctic conservation, including meetings of the UNFCCC Conference of the Parties and meetings of the International Maritime Organization. ASOC and its members supported a range of policy-relevant science on climate change, fisheries, marine protected areas, krill, and vulnerable marine ecosystems. Finally, ASOC contributed to intersessional discussions at the online ATCM and CEP fora, and attended the recent workshop on tourism in Paris. ASOC concluded by noting that there was an urgent need to use the tools of the Protocol effectively by establishing new protected areas, regulating tourism and shipping, reducing the footprint of human activities, and protecting vulnerable species. ASOC echoed the comments of Vice Minister Sumuvuori in urging Parties to move beyond discussion to action.

(40) IAATO presented IP 55 *Report of the International Association of Antarctica Tour Operators 2022-23*, reporting on its activities during the previous year. IAATO highlighted its mission to advocate and promote the practice of safe and environmentally responsible private sector travel to Antarctica. It reported that its membership currently comprised 109 Operators and Associates. After experiencing reduced activity during the COVID-19 pandemic and a modest resumption of operations in the 2021/22 season, operators had in the 2022/23 season seen a significant recovery in operations, with a total number of 104,897 visitors. During the 2022/23 season there had been three tourism incidents, which had resulted in the death of four individuals travelling with IAATO Operators. IAATO noted that these incidents were felt not only by the Antarctic operators but all Antarctic stakeholders and thanked them for their support. IAATO noted that at its recent annual meeting, it had adopted a new five-year strategic plan and agreed upon measures to support its mission, including evolving its operational procedures for wildlife viewing, expanding geofenced whale slow-down areas, and the engagement of a third party vendor to assist in implementation of IAATO's climate pledge. It highlighted that many of these activities were based on collaboration, which would be crucial moving forward as IAATO continued to evolve its procedures. It further noted that all Parties were invited to join the open sessions of these meetings, which provided an opportunity to help promote wise management of Antarctic tourism. IAATO reported that it had engaged in a number of meetings and collaborations with Observers and Experts, and that it continued to provide air and vessel support to national Antarctic programmes.

(41) The Meeting thanked WMO, ASOC and IAATO for their reports.

Item 5: Report of the Committee for Environmental Protection

(42) Ms Birgit Njåstad, Chair of the Committee for Environmental Protection, introduced the report of CEP XXV. The CEP had considered 44 Working Papers and 69 Information Papers, noting the consistency in workload from the past few years. Ms Njåstad noted that 39 of 42 Members had attended CEP XXV.

(43) The Chair of the CEP advised that there had been no new accessions to the Protocol since the last meeting and that the CEP still comprised 42 Members.

Strategic Discussions on the Future Work of the CEP (CEP Agenda Item 3)

(44) The Chair of the CEP advised that the Committee had discussed the outcomes of an informal workshop held in Helsinki just before the start of CEP XXV, which had considered the CEP's strategic priorities and Five-year Work Plan. The Committee had noted the value of the Five-year Work Plan as a central tool for framing the work of the CEP, and Members had highlighted that discussions on CEP strategic priorities had been important and constructive, resulting in relevant reflections and exchanges on how to promote the effectiveness and enhance the work of the Committee.

(45) The Chair of the CEP reported that, although much had been accomplished in the past 25 years, Members had noted that significant work remained to reach the objectives of the Environment Protocol. The Committee had agreed to establish an ICG to continue these discussions and develop a revised Five-year Work Plan for discussion and adoption at CEP 26. The Committee had also encouraged Members, on the basis of the outcomes of the informal CEP workshop, to continue developing a framework that could guide the CEP in its efforts to frame and monitor knowledge needs in the future. The Committee had welcomed the offer from Norway to act as ICG convenor.

(46) The Chair of the CEP noted that the Committee had updated its Five-year Work Plan to incorporate actions arising from CEP XXV.

(47) The Meeting reaffirmed the importance of the CEP in providing independent advice and recommendations to the ATCM, based on the best available science. It welcomed the CEP's continued work and initiative to review its Five-year Work Plan and its functions, and reaffirmed that it was a separate body to the ATCM, charged with providing advice to the ATCM and encouraged the CEP to continue its strategic work.

(48) Some Parties suggested that the ATCM consider how to continue to strengthen the flow of advice from the CEP to the ATCM, including considering if it would be appropriate to discuss separating the two meetings in time in order to ensure adequate time for the Parties to consider the Committee's advice in advance of its deliberations, and if resourcing of the Committee should be considered. Some Parties highlighted that the review of the Five-year Work Plan would be an opportunity to consider how to most effectively connect the Committee's advice to the ATCM. Some Parties also raised a question on possible interlinkages between the CEP Five-year Work Plan and the ATCM Multi-year Strategic Work Plan. Several Parties noted the urgency of accounting for climate change in the future work of the Committee.

(49) In response to questions raised, the CEP Chair noted that the scheduling of CEP meetings warranted consideration and could be incorporated into both CEP and ATCM discussions. She also noted that Parties' views on the matter would be important to CEP discussions. The CEP Chair acknowledged that interlinkages between the CEP Five-year Work Plan and the ATCM Multi-year Strategic Work Plan were likely, and such issues could be discussed intersessionally and in upcoming meetings in context of the continued discussions on strategic priorities and Five-year Work Plan.

Operation of the CEP (CEP Agenda Item 4)

(50) The Chair of CEP advised that, on the basis of experiences gained in the last several years, the Committee had discussed and agreed to revise its procedure for intersessional consideration of draft CEEs, clarifying procedures with regard to timely notification of planned submission, clear communication procedures in the submission process and enabling timely availability of translated documents.

(51) The Chair of the CEP noted that the Committee had agreed to advise the ATCM that it had updated its procedure for CEP consideration of draft CEEs (Appendix 2 of the CEP Report). It also had agreed to draw the ATCM's attention to the provisions reflecting the Secretariat's role to facilitate the handling and translation of draft CEEs.

(52) The Chair of the CEP reported that the Committee had also considered and agreed to a proposal to update the Committee's Rules of Procedure to include guidance on procedures for the nomination and election of the CEP Chair and Vice-Chairs. The Committee had also noted several gendered references in the CEP Rules of Procedure and had agreed to update those references to gender-inclusive language. The Committee had forwarded the revised version of the CEP Rules of Procedure to the ATCM for approval through a Decision.

(53) The Meeting commended the CEP for the update of the Rules of Procedure to incorporate procedures for nominating and electing the CEP Chair and Vice-Chairs, noting that this would ensure clarity and transparency. The Meeting welcomed the updated Rules of Procedure to use gender neutral and inclusive language, which it considered a timely step forward. It further encouraged the CEP to consider whether documents underlying the new procedures required updating, and to inform the ATCM if harmonisation across documents was necessary.

(54) The Meeting adopted Decision 1 (2023) *Revised Rules of Procedure for the Committee for Environmental Protection (2023).*

Cooperation with other Organisations (CEP Agenda Item 5)

(55) The Chair of the CEP reported that the Committee had received annual reports from its Observers. The Committee had nominated CEP representatives to attend the meetings of other organisations over the coming year.

(56) The Chair also reported that the Committee had noted the importance of the Observers to the work of the CEP and had noted the spirit of cooperation and community that had been expressed and developed in recent years among Observers.

Climate Change Implications for the Environment: Strategic approach (CEP Agenda Item 7)

Strategic Approach

(57) The Chair of the CEP recalled that a report and advice from CEP discussions and agreements under Item 7 had been presented to Parties during the joint session on climate change in the previous week. The CEP Chair noted that, under this Item, the Committee had considered SCAR's update on the 2022 Decadal Update of its Antarctic Climate Change and the Environment (ACCE) report. The Committee had commended SCAR on its continued commitment to providing updates based on the best available science. The Committee had noted that scientific information from SCAR was fundamental in its work to understand and address environmental management in Antarctica in the light of climate change, and that it provided an even greater impetus to efforts to implement the Climate Change Response Work Programme (CCRWP) as a matter of priority.

(58) The Chair of the CEP reported that the Committee had also considered a report on COMNAP's perspectives on the implementation of the ACCE recommendations. The Committee had noted the important role of national Antarctic programmes in managing the implications of climate change for human activities and the environment in Antarctica.

(59) The Chair of the CEP further reported that the Committee had welcomed and acted on Finland's invitation to draft a paragraph for the proposed Helsinki Declaration on Climate Change and the Antarctic, which would enable the Committee to underline its commitment to the goals of the Declaration.

(60) The Meeting expressed appreciation to the CEP for submitting an operative paragraph on its climate work for inclusion in the Helsinki Declaration, noting that much of the Meeting's substantive work related to climate change originated from the CEP.

Implementation and Review of the Climate Change Response Work Programme

(61) The Chair of the CEP noted that the Committee had considered a report from the Subsidiary Group on Climate Change Response (SGCCR), which outlined the work and outputs of the SGCCR during the intersessional period. It had agreed to advise the ATCM that it continued work to implement the CCRWP, and noted that, during its meeting, the CEP had discussed numerous actions that had been delivered or which concerned ongoing research that was relevant in the context of the CCRWP. The Chair noted that this list of actions illustrated that the Committee was progressing on a broad range of topics through the CCRWP. She further noted that the Committee had agreed to endorse six priority activities to be advanced during the next intersessional period. It also had continued its preparation of the next Joint CEP/SC-CAMLR Workshop, and had adopted Terms of Reference for this workshop and a way forward to work with SC-CAMLR to prepare to implement the workshop. The Committee had further agreed to request support from the Secretariat and that Parties consider funding options for the workshop, recalling that a mechanism was in place for the CEP to request funding on a case-by-case basis.

(62) The Meeting thanked the CEP for its ongoing excellent work in implementing the CCRWP as a matter of priority, in accordance with Resolution 4 (2015), and encouraged broad participation in this work among Members. The Meeting thanked the SGCCR for its substantial work during the intersessional period, acknowledged the substantial list of issues remaining to be advanced during the coming intersessional period, and asked what the ATCM could do to support the SGCCR. It also welcomed the ongoing close work between the CEP and SC-CAMLR across the areas of shared interest, and noted that the upcoming workshop with SC-CAMLR on climate change could be an important means of connecting work across the Antarctic Treaty system.

(63) Many Parties also highlighted the Committee's task of supporting work to assess the status of climate vulnerable Antarctic species, highlighting the continued need to deploy tools of the Protocol in the context of climate change.

(64) Responding to a question, the Chair of the CEP clarified that remediation had been identified as a priority under the climate change work strand because the need to initiate remediation efforts could be influenced due to increasing risks related to climate change.

Environmental Impact Assessment (EIA) (CEP Agenda Item 8)

Draft Comprehensive Environmental Evaluations

(65) The Chair of the CEP reported that the Committee had considered the draft CEE submitted by Argentina for the Redevelopment of Petrel Station, Dundee Island, Antarctica (WP 61 rev. 1) and the report of an ICG led by New Zealand to review the draft CEE (WP 32). The Committee had welcomed Argentina's commitment to respond to the issues raised by the ICG and by the Committee during discussion.

(66) The Chair of the CEP noted that the Committee, based on its discussions of presented documents and information provided in the meeting, had agreed to advise the ATCM that: the draft CEE largely conformed to requirements of Article 3 of Annex I to the Protocol on Environmental Protection to the Antarctic Treaty, although there was a need to address some elements of Article 3 in greater detail; and that, if Argentina decided to proceed with the proposed activity, there were aspects for which further information should be provided in the final CEE. In particular, the Committee had suggested that further details should be provided regarding the description of the proposed activity, particularly including more detail, both of the construction and operational activities including for tourist and non-governmental purposes; alternatives to the proposed activity; the initial environmental reference state; the methodology used to forecast the impacts of the proposed activity; a more comprehensive assessment of cumulative impacts that might arise with the proposed activities, existing activities, and other known planned activities in the area; a more comprehensive assessment and description of the mitigation measures; the environmental monitoring programme before, during and after construction activities; and gaps in knowledge relevant to the proposed activities. The Committee had also agreed to advise the ATCM that, due to the scale and complexity of the proposed activities outlined in the CEE for the Redevelopment of Petrel Station, impacts on the environment were likely to have more than a minor or transitory impact on the environment and that a CEE was the appropriate level of environmental impact assessment for the proposed activity. The Committee had noted that the conclusion of the draft CEE did not align with the EIA and identified mitigation measures, and had suggested that a consideration of mitigation measures would be needed to support the conclusion of the CEE. The Committee further agreed to advise the ATCM that the draft CEE was generally clear, well-structured and well-presented although, due to the scale and complexity of the proposed activities, suggestions had been made to enhance the presentation and clarity of the document.

(67) The CEP Chair noted that the Committee had observed that there was not yet a standard method for addressing and incorporating comments into a final CEE in accordance with Article 3.6 of Annex I to the Environment Protocol. The Committee had therefore agreed to request the Secretariat to review how comments and responses had been reflected in final CEEs in the past as a basis for future CEP discussion.

(68) Argentina expressed its gratitude to the Committee for its work and advice, and in particular, to New Zealand for its efforts in convening the ICG. It noted that it would take full account of the advice in preparation of its final CEE.

(69) The Meeting thanked Argentina for its work. It also thanked New Zealand for its efforts in convening the ICG. The Meeting noted and agreed to the CEP's advice on the draft CEE, and noted Argentina's intentions to follow up on these issues in its preparation of the final documents.

(70) In response to questions raised by Parties, Argentina stated that the purpose of the redevelopment of the Petrel Station was to support scientific activities by providing logistical support for new science capabilities. This was intended also to complement activities at Marambio Base. Argentina also highlighted that it would only receive visitors under the same modality in which they were received in other Antarctic stations and according to guidelines.

Other EIA Matters

(71) The Chair of the CEP reported that the Committee had considered a report summarising informal intersessional discussions on improving the effectiveness of the EIA system. The Committee had underlined the importance of improving the EIA process as a fundamental component of the Environment Protocol and crucial for environmental protection. The Committee had welcomed the proposal to schedule further work on improving the effectiveness of the Antarctic EIA system, particularly regarding consistency, cumulative impact assessments, monitoring, and thresholds for when EIA documents should be amended or a new EIA conducted when an activity changed. The Committee had also encouraged Members to share information associated with the operation of their EIA processes for the benefit of Members. It had also agreed to request a summary of previous EIAs from the Secretariat to assist in improving EIAs with particular regard to cumulative impact assessments. The Committee had agreed to a draft Resolution on Improving the Effectiveness of Antarctic EIA.

(72) Many Parties reiterated that environmental impact assessment was a core foundation of the Environment Protocol's comprehensive framework for environmental protection in Antarctica, and welcomed work to continue to strengthen EIA processes and practices. Several Parties also noted the importance of developing EIAs with particular recognition of cumulative impacts. Some Parties highlighted the role of national competent authorities in ensuring appropriate assessment procedures.

(73) In response to a request from the Meeting, SCAR agreed to investigate the scope of providing further information on the issue of cumulative impacts, drawing on subject-specific expertise of the scientific community within SCAR and building on the work of the Secretariat in preparing a comprehensive summary of previous CEP discussions on assessing cumulative impacts.

(74) The Meeting adopted Resolution 1 (2023) *Consideration of Mitigation Measures in Environmental Impact Assessment.*

Area Protection and Management Plans (CEP Agenda 9)

Management Plans

(75) The CEP Chair reported that the Committee had considered one draft management plan for a proposed merger of two ASPAs and one management plan for a proposed new ASPA, both of which had been reviewed by the Subsidiary Group for Management Plans (SGMP) in the intersessional period.

(76) The CEP Chair noted that the Committee had agreed to the merger of Antarctic Specially Protected Areas (ASPAs) 152 and 153 and the draft management plan for the newly merged area and had agreed that the plan would be re-submitted to SC-CAMLR for approval in accordance with Decision 9 (2005), with the intent to then forward it to ATCM 46 for adoption.

(77) The CEP Chair reported that, following changing prohibited zones to restricted zones, the Committee had also agreed to the establishment of and the management plan for a new ASPA in parts of the Western Sør Rondane Mountains, Dronning Maud Land, East Antarctica. Many Members had expressed disappointment that consensus was not reached on including prohibited zones within the ASPA. Many Members urged Parties to respect the robust scientific rationale for using prohibited zones in the Area and refrain from entering these areas without full consultation with other Parties.

(78) The Meeting noted the CEP's advice regarding the proposed ASPA in the Western Sør

Rondane Mountains. Many Parties expressed their disappointment that the ASPA's small and scientifically-based prohibited zones had been changed to restricted zones in order to achieve consensus at the CEP. These Parties noted the importance of prohibiting access in this case, in keeping with the strong scientific rationale for future research, in accordance with Annex V(3)(a). Some Parties emphasised that the technologies needed to research the proposed prohibited zones best were perhaps not in existence yet and that it would be unfortunate if human activity impacted these vulnerable areas in the interim. Some Parties also noted that autonomous and remote monitoring techniques were acceptable for scientific research and that direct human activity was not necessary for monitoring.

(79) Many Parties emphasised that it was important for the CEP and Parties to use all the tools available under the Environment Protocol and highlighted that Annex V of the Environment Protocol expressly provided for the designation of ASPAs as inviolate areas and for the inclusion of prohibited areas within an ASPA. Some Parties called for the ATCM to agree the proposed ASPA with "prohibited areas" instead of the suggested "restricted zones", highlighting that many CEP Members had considered that the scientific rationale for "prohibited zone" was robust.

(80) China supported the advice of the CEP on the establishment of the ASPA following the changing prohibited zones to restricted zones, and raised the general issue with regard to the idea of establishing prohibited areas. China noted the benefits of allowing scientific research and monitoring, and emphasised that the potential designation of prohibited zones may have legal conflict with the freedom of scientific investigation, the review requirement and the inspection rules of the Antarctic Treaty.

(81) Many Parties stressed that there was no conflict between the provisions allowing for scientific freedom in the Antarctic Treaty and the Environment Protocol, including Annex V, and noted that, instead, the instruments operated in concert with each other.

(82) Some Parties expressed their regret that the issue regarding prohibited zones arising from the original proposal was not referred to the ATCM for discussion and decision. These Parties emphasised that the CEP should endeavour to provide advice within its mandate to the ATCM and recalled that its advice should reflect the views expressed. Several Parties noted that the CEP did not need to reach consensus before advising the ATCM. The Committee's advice to the ATCM should be based on the best scientific and technical advice related to the achievement of environmental protection.

(83) IUCN supported the Parties' initiative of proposing the designation of prohibited zones within ASPAs and stressed their value as a conservation strategy. IUCN reminded the Parties that, under the IUCN categories of protected areas, prohibited zones could contribute to the protection of unique values at specific locations without impacting research or monitoring activities.

(84) Following these discussions, the Meeting agreed to the establishment of a new ASPA in the Western Sør Rondane Mountains, Dronning Maud Land, East Antarctica, noting the change of prohibited zones to restricted zones.

(85) The CEP Chair reported that the Committee had considered 15 revised ASPA management plans and one revised management plan for an ASMA. These 16 plans had undergone pre-meeting review by the SGMP in accordance with its new terms of reference agreed to at CEP XXIV and were thus handled quickly and efficiently by the Committee in its Meeting.

(86) The CEP Chair further noted that the Committee had also considered a draft management plan for two new protected areas: i) Danger Islands Archipelago (North-eastern Antarctic Peninsula) and ii) Farrier Col, Horseshoe Island, Marguerite Bay. The Committee had

reaffirmed that it recognised that the outstanding values of these sites warranted protection and referred them to the SGMP for review.

(87) The CEP Chair noted that the Committee had also considered the prior assessment of one proposed new protected area in the Argentine Islands and Kyiv Peninsula, Antarctic Peninsula, applying the Guidelines *A prior assessment process for the designation of ASPAs and ASMAs*. The CEP Chair further noted that, while the Committee had expressed general support for the prior assessment, the Committee had also noted the need for better clarity on some key issues. The Committee had encouraged the proponent to consider the Committee's comments to continue developing a clearer framework for the area's protection. In response to a question, the CEP Chair clarified that the general support was a reflection of the support for the assessment, but not necessarily support at this stage for designating the area as an ASPA.

(88) The CEP Chair noted that the Committee had further considered a proposal to de-designate ASPA 144 Chile Bay (Discovery Bay). The Committee had observed that the Area's primary objective as a control area for fauna restoration was no longer valid and that no significant presence of other values would support continued special protection. Based on the thorough assessment, the Committee had agreed that ASPA 144 could be de-designated. The Committee had again underscored that such decisions to de-designate an area should not be taken lightly and had noted that the area would remain subject to the comprehensive general protections of the Environment Protocol that apply to all areas.

(89) The Meeting adopted the following Measures on Protected Areas:

- Measure 1 (2023) *Antarctic Specially Managed Area No 1 (Admiralty Bay, King George Island): Revised Management Plan.*
- Measure 2 (2023) *Antarctic Specially Protected Area No 108 (Green Island, Berthelot Islands, Antarctic Peninsula): Revised Management Plan.*
- Measure 3 (2023) *Antarctic Specially Protected Area No 117 (Avian Island, Marguerite Bay, Antarctic Peninsula): Revised Management Plan.*
- Measure 4 (2023) *Antarctic Specially Protected Area No 122 (Arrival Heights, Hut Point Peninsula, Ross Island): Revised Management Plan.*
- Measure 5 (2023) *Antarctic Specially Protected Area No 123 (Barwick and Balham Valleys, Southern Victoria Land): Revised Management Plan.*
- Measure 6 (2023) *Antarctic Specially Protected Area No 132 (Potter Peninsula, King George Island (Isla 25 de Mayo), South Shetland Islands): Revised Management Plan.*
- Measure 7 (2023) *Antarctic Specially Protected Area No 137 (Northwest White Island, McMurdo Sound): Revised Management Plan.*
- Measure 8 (2023) *Antarctic Specially Protected Area No 138 (Linnaeus Terrace, Asgard Range, Victoria Land): Revised Management Plan.*
- Measure 9 (2023) *Antarctic Specially Protected Area No 144 (Chile Bay (Discovery Bay), Greenwich Islands, South Shetland Islands): Revoked Management Plan.*
- Measure 10 (2023) *Antarctic Specially Protected Area No 145 (Port Foster, Deception Island, South Shetland Islands): Revised Management Plan.*
- Measure 11 (2023) *Antarctic Specially Protected Area No 147 (Ablation Valley and Ganymede Heights, Alexander Island): Revised Management Plan.*
- Measure 12 (2023) *Antarctic Specially Protected Area No 149 (Cape Shirreff and San Telmo Island, Livingston Island, South Shetland Islands): Revised Management Plan.*
- Measure 13 (2023) *Antarctic Specially Protected Area No 156 (Lewis Bay, Mount*

Erebus, Ross Island): Revised Management Plan.

- Measure 14 (2023) *Antarctic Specially Protected Area No 165 (Edmonson Point, Wood Bay, Ross Sea): Revised Management Plan.*
- Measure 15 (2023) *Antarctic Specially Protected Area No 168 (Mount Harding, Grove Mountains, East Antarctica): Revised Management Plan.*
- Measure 16 (2023) *Antarctic Specially Protected Area No 170 (Marion Nunataks, Charcot Island, Antarctic Peninsula): Revised Management Plan.*
- Measure 17 (2023) *Antarctic Specially Protected Area No 172 (Lower Taylor Glacier and Blood Falls, McMurdo Dry Valleys, Victoria Land): Revised Management Plan.*
- Measure 18 (2023) *Antarctic Specially Protected Area No 179 (Parts of Western Sør Rondane Mountains, Dronning Maud Land, East Antarctica): Management Plan.*

Historic Sites and Monuments

(90) The CEP Chair noted that the Committee had considered an assessment of future storage and display options for artefacts from HSM 68. The Committee had noted that the proponents preferred long-term storage and safekeeping of these objects outside Antarctica and had recognised that the decision to relocate the items had been difficult. The Committee had agreed to update the Conservation Status on HSM 68 to reflect this change. The Chair of the CEP further noted that the Committee had also reported the utility of developing further guidance for managing and conserving HSMs that may need to be relocated outside Antarctica, highlighting the provisions of Article 8.4 of Annex V of the Environment Protocol. Concerning HSMs, the CEP Chair noted these need not be reviewed by the ATCM.

(91) The CEP Chair stated that the Committee had also considered and discussed future protection of the wreck of the *Endurance* following its discovery on 5 March 2022. The Committee noted its continued work to consider the appropriate level of protection for the wreck and the progress in developing a Conservation Management Plan for the underwater site.

Other Annex V Matters

(92) The CEP Chair reported that the Committee had considered the report of the work by the SGMP under its ToR 3 and 4. The Committee had also adopted the SGMP work plan for 2023-24.

(93) The Committee had also noted ongoing work on promoting an awareness of palaeontological heritage, welcomed the valuable contribution to preserving paleontological heritage, and encouraged further engagement.

(94) The Chair of the CEP noted that the Committee had emphasised the vulnerability and importance of Antarctic inland water bodies and the need for their increased protection and discussions on the topic in the future.

Conservation of Antarctic Flora and Fauna (CEP Agenda Item 10)

Quarantine and Non-native Species

(95) The Chair of the CEP reported that the Committee had considered issues and concerns about the implications of the large worldwide outbreak of Highly Pathogenic Avian Influenza (HPAI). The Committee had acknowledged the potential risks of HPAI spread

in Antarctica and its great dangers to Antarctic bird colonies and mammals. The Committee had welcomed all information shared on valuable national experiences and examples of procedures for preventing the introduction or spread of HPAI in the Antarctic. It had welcomed the contributions as particularly useful in the context of future collaboration between competent authorities and in promoting preventive procedures among national programmes and other stakeholders. The Committee had encouraged Members to use the Competent Authorities Sub-forum to exchange information to facilitate coordination and collaboration to meet this urgent challenge.

(96) The Chair of the CEP noted that the Committee had considered that an outbreak of avian flu in Antarctica was likely and could be a detrimental threat to Antarctic wildlife. The Committee therefore advised the ATCM that it had agreed to encourage Parties and other stakeholders to develop and implement procedures for surveillance, prevention and response to the introduction, spread, or potential outbreaks of HPAI; encourage Parties to share information on HPAI detections in Antarctica, including the location of suspected and confirmed outbreaks, species, and approximate number of individuals affected, and the symptoms observed; and request that SCAR provide updates to the CEP on the potential impacts of HPAI to native birds and mammals in Antarctica.

(97) The Meeting noted with serious concern the Committee's statement about the likely outbreak of HPAI. Several Parties highlighted HPAI's potential to have devastating consequences in Antarctica and emphasised the need for action. They noted the need to minimise risk of human introduction of HPAI, while noting that such an outbreak was most likely to take place via the natural migration of birds to Antarctica. The Meeting welcomed the actions by the various national Antarctic programmes, SCAR and IAATO to ensure that, as far as possible, HPAI did not impact wildlife and humans. Parties welcomed ongoing advice from the CEP as well as SCAR, COMNAP and IAATO on preventing its introduction and spread.

(98) The Committee had considered the findings of a review of IMO and Antarctic Treaty system guidelines and agreements concerning ship biofouling and ballast water management. The Committee had noted that risks associated with marine non-native species were a high-priority issue for the CEP. The Committee had called on Members to enhance their understanding of such risks and thanked Observers for providing up-to-date advice.

(99) The CEP Chair noted that the Committee had considered the review and agreed to request COMNAP and IAATO to provide advice by CEP 27 (2025) on their members' ship biofouling and ballast water management practices. The Committee had encouraged monitoring for non-native marine species to enhance understanding of risks and to inform consideration of marine biosecurity measures in line with identified needs in the Five-year Work Plan, CCRWP and Non-native Species Manual. The Committee had also agreed to bring the CEP's ongoing work on ship biofouling and ballast water management to the attention of SC-CAMLR.

(100) The Meeting welcomed the CEP's work on the issue of biofouling and ballast water management.

(101) The Committee had also noted information from several Members regarding findings and the presence of non-native species at and near their stations in Antarctica. The Committee had drawn attention to the concerning spread of non-native species and the call to review domestic procedures and take collaborative action to prevent the spread of non-native species, particularly in King George Island. The Meeting noted this information with concern and encouraged appropriate the CEP's continued focus on this issue as a matter of priority, particularly in the context of climate change.

Specially Protected Species

(102) The CEP Chair noted that the Committee had considered management initiatives by Members to protect the emperor penguin, including listing the species as specially protected under domestic legislation. Most Members had again expressed disappointment that the Committee had been unable to list the emperor penguin as a Specially Protected Species during CEP XXIV. These Members had noted that the best available science, previously presented by SCAR, as well as other available scientific data, demonstrated that the emperor penguin was vulnerable and warranted designation in accordance with Annex II to the Environment Protocol and agreed procedures.

(103) The CEP Chair reported that China had noted that conclusions it had drawn from the draft Antarctic Specially Protected Action Plan for Emperor Penguins (ATCM XLIV-WP 34) did not support the designation of the emperor penguin as a Specially Protected Species.

(104) The CEP Chair also reported that Members had agreed that domestic legislation might contribute to the protection of Antarctic species under threat. Further, Members had also agreed to report recent research results on the status of the emperor penguin and thanked SCAR for its ongoing contributions in this regard.

(105) The Committee had also considered the results of a study on the impacts on emperor penguins of low sea ice extent, noting that land-fast sea ice was crucial for emperor penguins as a breeding and moulting platform. Many Members had noted that changes in sea ice threatened the emperor penguin species. Many Members had indicated a need to take a precautionary approach and consider the species as one under threat. Most Members had encouraged continued work toward the designation of the emperor penguin as a Specially Protected Species at the earliest opportunity.

(106) The Meeting thanked the Committee for its update. Many Parties expressed disappointment that no progress had been made regarding special protection for the species, noting that the best available science, which had been updated and presented at CEP XXV, indicated that the population was expected to decline significantly because of climate change. Several Parties emphasised that the emperor penguin clearly fulfilled the requirements to be designated as a specially protected species under Annex II of the Environment Protocol.

(107) Some Parties recalled that the Protocol placed a duty on Parties to preserve Antarctica as a natural reserve for peace and science, noting that the threshold for protection under the Environment Protocol was significantly different to the approach taken by CCAMLR. Therefore, they considered that the Meeting had a role to play in ensuring that stressors on species due to climate change were not exacerbated by human activity, making action on climate-vulnerable species relevant to the Meeting's work.

(108) Several Parties called for emperor penguins to be designated as Antarctic specially protected species at ATCM XLV, drawing on the views expressed by the majority of CEP Members that the best available science, previously presented by SCAR, as well as other available scientific data, demonstrated that the emperor penguin was vulnerable and warranted designation in accordance with Annex II to the Environment Protocol and agreed procedures.

(109) China noted the relevant science needs identified in the CEP Five-year Work Plan, and expressed its view that assessing the status of Antarctic species not only required focusing on their vulnerability to climate change, but also required assessment of the population trends and distributions and other threats and pressures resulting from human activity. It highlighted that as a management body, the ATCM could only directly manage human activity, not natural processes like climate or environmental change in Antarctica.

(110) WMO responded to China's comment by recalling that, although natural variations in climate were significant in the Antarctic context, climate forcing due to greenhouse gas emissions predominated. WMO indicated that Parties could manage or influence climate change and referred Parties to the IPCC's Sixth Assessment Review and SCAR's ACCE report.

(111) In response to WMO, China emphasised its view that, while the Meeting could take action to reduce greenhouse gas emissions through national Antarctic programmes in order to address climate change from its source, the overall reduction of greenhouse gas emissions was the mandate of the UNFCCC, not the Antarctic Treaty.

(112) IUCN reminded Parties that the "near-threatened" category assigned to emperor penguins did not indicate that the population was stable. Acknowledging that more data was needed in light of the changes to the species that climate change was producing in Antarctica, IUCN underscored the need for action to protect the emperor penguin in the context of the precautionary principle. It expressed its interest in actively participating in discussions regarding actions around the conservation of the emperor penguin.

(113) Some Parties noted that the CEP was not required to achieve consensus in its advice to the ATCM. Those Parties emphasised that the CEP provided advice to the Parties in connection with the implementation of the Environment Protocol. They noted that the ATCM was the correct forum for these negotiations.

(114) Some Parties encouraged further work towards designating the emperor penguin as a Specially Protected Species at the earliest opportunity, and in the interim, encouraged continued and increased efforts to advance the actions in the draft Action Plan.

Environmental Monitoring and Reporting (CEP Agenda Item 11)

(115) The CEP Chair recalled that, as environmental monitoring was an obligation under Article 3.2 of the Environment Protocol, the Committee had discussed and considered issues relating to environmental monitoring and how to enable better assessment of possible environmental changes and identifying impacts of human activities. The Committee had emphasised the importance of ongoing information-sharing related to monitoring and collation of data related to human impacts in Antarctica and the value of monitoring as a basis for EIAs. Having considered a number of aspects relating to the issue, the Committee had agreed to establish an ICG to discuss the development of an international framework for environmental monitoring.

(116) The Committee had also considered a proposal from SCAR to develop a mechanism for providing information relevant to the State of the Antarctic Environment Reporting (SAER). The Committee had welcomed SCAR's proposal to develop a mechanism for SAER, noting its relevance to the CEP's work, including with respect to environmental monitoring and providing advice to the ATCM. Members highlighted this initiative's usefulness for the CEP's entire work agenda, including developing a systematic approach to environmental monitoring and further developing the Antarctic Protected Area System. The Committee had noted that it would be useful to receive an example report from SCAR to fully assess the practicality and usefulness of its proposed mechanism for providing information on SAER.

(117) The Committee had also considered information from SCAR on the establishment of the Antarctic Near-shore and Terrestrial Observing System (ANTOS). The Committee had warmly welcomed the goals of ANTOS, recognising it as a valuable monitoring tool with significant potential. Members had expressed their willingness to engage in ANTOS and outlined various ways their national Antarctic programmes and research projects contributed to and would continue to contribute to the system.

(118) The Committee had also welcomed several other papers on environmental monitoring and reporting.

(119) The Meeting thanked the CEP for its substantial advice on environmental monitoring and some Parties strongly endorsed the value of monitoring as part of the EIA process.

General Matters (CEP Agenda Item 13)

(120) The CEP Chair reported that the Committee had considered a paper relating to gender-neutral language in the Antarctic Treaty system and a proposal that the CEP request the Secretariat to review all relevant CEP documents that pertained to current and future cooperation to ensure the use of gender-neutral language across these documents. The Committee had: acknowledged the importance of using a gender-neutral approach to language; agreed to advise the ATCM that it encouraged Members and Observers to continue promoting equity, diversity and inclusion (EDI) in their Antarctic activities; and agreed to use gender-neutral and respectful inclusive language in spoken and written documentation, reporting and other forms of communication. The Committee had tasked the Secretariat to review all relevant documents.

Election of Officers (CEP Agenda Item 14)

(121) The CEP Chair reported that the Committee had re-elected Anoop Kumar Tiwari from India as Vice-Chair for a second two-year term and congratulated him on his reappointment. He was also reappointed as convenor of the SGMP. The Committee had also elected Patricia Ortúzar from Argentina as Chair of the CEP and congratulated her on her appointment.

(122) The Meeting warmly thanked Birgit Njåstad for her excellent leadership throughout her two terms as CEP Chair and welcomed Patricia Ortúzar's election as CEP Chair.

Preparation for Next Meeting (CEP Agenda Item 15)

(123) The CEP Chair noted that the Committee had adopted the Preliminary Agenda for CEP 26, reflecting the agenda for CEP XXV.

Item 6a: Operation of the Antarctic Treaty System: Request from Belarus to become a Consultative Party

(124) Belarus presented IP 5 *Republic of Belarus in the System of the Antarctic Treaty. Justification of the status of the Consultative Party of the Antarctic Treaty*. Referring to its application submitted in 2019, Belarus presented further information about its compliance with the requirements for Consultative Status and provided additional information on its Antarctic activities since the submission. Belarus noted that, since it had had become a Contracting Party to the Antarctic Treaty in 2006, it had actively developed national legislation for activities in Antarctica and participated in scientific work and international collaboration in Antarctica, including constant membership of the CEP, membership of COMNAP since 2015, and associate membership of SCAR since 2018. Belarus underlined the activity of its scientific expeditions and its intention to become a full member of SCAR in the near future. Belarus highlighted some of its significant work in Antarctica, including 15 seasonal expeditions with more than 90 Belarusian and six foreign scientists, and the continuing international cooperation in transport and logistics between Belarus and the Russian Federation. It noted that the construction of a Belarusian research station had been carried out in 2015 near Vechernyaya Mount in East Antarctica, and that the station had been inspected by an

Australian delegation in 2020 with positive outcomes. Further environmental protection improvements had been implemented at the station in 2021-23. Belarusian scientific programmes in Antarctica were being carried out with the participation of research institutes of the National Academy of Sciences of Belarus and the Belarusian State University in cooperation with scientific organisations, scientists and specialists from other countries. Belarus noted that it had 14 agreements on scientific and technical cooperation in Antarctica with governments and organisations from nine countries participating in the Antarctic Treaty system. The scientific activity of Belarusian scientists in the Antarctic since 2007 had led to the publication of several books and dozens of scientific articles, many as a result of international collaboration. Belarus restated its commitment to the fundamental principles of the Antarctic Treaty and the Environment Protocol. It reaffirmed that, based on the information presented in its papers, its activities met the necessary criteria under Article IX of the Antarctic Treaty for Consultative Party status as well as Decision 2 (2017).

(125) The United States, in its capacity as Depositary Government of the Antarctic Treaty and the Environment Protocol, confirmed that Belarus had complied with the guidelines set out in Decision 2 (2017).

(126) The Consultative Parties thanked Belarus for its presentation. Some Parties supported the application and some Parties stated that Belarus had not met the requirement under Article IX (2) for the need to have conducted substantial scientific research activity in Antarctica. There was no consensus on Belarus' application for Consultative Party status.

Item 6b: Operation of the Antarctic Treaty System: Request from Canada to become a Consultative Party

(127) Canada presented IP 12 *Update on Canada's Engagement in the Antarctic*, in which Canada reviewed its long history of Antarctic research and engagement. Referring to its application for Consultative Party status in the Antarctic Treaty system submitted in 2021, Canada presented an overview of its past and ongoing activities in Antarctica and its collaboration with the other Parties to the Treaty. It noted that its researchers had authored approximately 1500 science journal articles on Antarctic and Southern Ocean science, and highlighted Canadian scientific achievements in the three science groups of SCAR, including in the fields of research on ground ice, the mapping of Antarctic ice, research on ozone depletion in the Antarctic, and predictions and modelling of Antarctic sea ice conditions. Researchers based at Canadian universities had participated in several international expeditions in the season 2022/23 and would continue to do so in the coming season. Since the previous ATCM, Canada had been approved as a full member of COMNAP and it continued to attend the meetings of CCAMLR as an observer. Canada also informed the Meeting that the Canadian Antarctic Research Program Framework continued to focus on high level themes and areas of focus, including glaciological and geological research, the study of the impact of Antarctic climate change on the global climate system, opportunities in Antarctica for observing space weather and the universe, and a cross-cutting theme of anthropogenic effects on the Antarctic environment and their mitigation. Canada stressed the usefulness of its Arctic research infrastructure and knowledge in cross-polar research and stated its commitment to supporting joint polar research. It added that the advancement of the Canadian Antarctic Research Program would provide new directions and funding for collaborative research activities in Antarctica.

(128) The United States, in its capacity as Depositary Government of the Antarctic Treaty and the Environment Protocol, confirmed that Canada had complied with the guidelines set out in Decision 2 (2017).

(129) Canada noted that it understood that there had not been any change beyond the positions expressed in 2022 and therefore it notified the Meeting about its request to postpone the consideration of its application to become a Consultative Party until 2024.

(130) The Consultative Parties thanked Canada for its presentation. They noted that Canada's application would be placed on the agenda at ATCM 46.

Item 6c: Operation of the Antarctic Treaty System: Implementation of the IMO Polar Code

(131) The ATCM Chair introduced the Co-Chairs of the special session on the Implementation of the IMO Polar Code, Fausto López Crozet, National Director for Antarctic Foreign Policy, Ministry of Foreign Affairs, International Trade and Worship (Argentina), and Dr Anita Mäkinen, Alternative Permanent Representative of Finland to IMO.

(132) Minna Kivimäki, Permanent Secretary of the Ministry of Transport and Communications (Finland), thanked Argentina for its collaboration in organising the special session, as well as invited experts and Parties for their contributions. She highlighted the Polar Code as a successful example of multilateral decision-making, noting its status as the first goal-based instrument adopted by IMO. Emphasising the Code's goals of ensuring safe shipping and the protection of polar environments, she noted that since the Code's entry into force in 2017, seafarers in polar waters had benefitted from clear rules and guidance on tackling the unique demands of traversing polar seas. She also acknowledged shortcomings of the Polar Code, which were highlighted in WP 46 and the other papers submitted to the session. She drew Parties' attention to paragraph 11 of WP 46, which advised Parties to continue promoting the Polar Code and its implementation to ship owners and operators calling into their ports, as well as vessel designers, shipyards and other stakeholders in their national maritime clusters.

(133) Fausto López Crozet welcomed Finland's initiative to host the special session. He recalled that ATCM XLIV had agreed that Parties would hold a special session at ATCM XLV to share experiences from the domestic implementation of the Polar Code, and improve and support its harmonised implementation. He also noted this issue's relevance to the ATCM Multi-year Strategic Work Plan. He observed that the adoption of the Polar Code by IMO had been a milestone in the effort to reduce risks associated with complex navigation in polar waters. Recalling Resolution 8 (2009), in which Parties had expressed their wish for IMO to develop mandatory shipping codes for vessels operating in Antarctic waters, he stressed the need to continue relevant dialogues. Noting that international cooperation was a fundamental pillar of the Antarctic Treaty system, Mr López Crozet highlighted the importance of positive collaboration between Parties, IMO, and the Arctic Council as essential to protecting ships and people on board in the harsh environments of polar waters. He emphasised that Parties played a central role in implementing the Polar Code. He indicated the importance of this in Argentina given its strong Antarctic activity and its SAR responsibility in the highly navigated Antarctic Peninsula area. He noted challenges in implementation, including issues related to compliance, training, and expansion to certain types of vessels not currently covered by the Code's requirements. He emphasised the importance of continued movement toward harmonised implementation and effective application of the IMO Polar Code in the ATCM Multi-year Strategic Work Plan.

(134) Loukas Kontogiannis, Head of Marine Pollution Section (IMO), gave a keynote presentation on the harmonised implementation of IMO's International Code for Ships Operating in Polar Waters. He noted that the challenges posed by operating conditions in the polar regions necessitated a comprehensive framework to ensure safety, and indicated that the Polar Code had played a crucial role in this regard. He indicated that

work at IMO on polar matters had continued since the Polar Code's entry into force in 2017 and highlighted issues being addressed during the second phase of work. These included extending the application of chapters on safety and voyage planning to non-SOLAS ships, namely to fishing vessels of 24 metres in length and over, pleasure yachts of 300 gross tonnage and over not engaged in trade, and cargo ships between 300-500 gross tonnage. He also noted recent progress related to search and rescue, including new guidance on estimating the maximum expected time of rescue, which took into account the availability of nearby ships for assistance in case of emergency. He emphasised the importance of harmonised implementation of the Polar Code, including enhancement of the ability of flag administrations and coastal states to enforce the code through common understanding of its provisions as well as capacity building. He noted that such harmonisation aligned with key principles of the Antarctic Treaty system, including international cooperation and environmental stewardship.

(135) Robert Hindley of Aker Arctic, a Finnish vessel design company, and Vice-admiral David Burden (Argentina) discussed challenges and opportunities in implementing the Polar Code. Based on their experience collaborating on the design of Argentina's new polar logistics vessel, they highlighted several areas relevant to Polar Code implementation, including operations, maintenance, government relations, and design considerations. They noted the value of defining an "operational envelope" in the early stages of work, identifying the area, conditions, duration, and functions of a ship's operation. They also identified the importance of balancing the need to ensure reliability and compliance with mandatory rules with the opportunity to embrace innovative design and take advantage of new technological solutions in implementation. They noted the value of dialogue between ship designers and operators as a way to strike this balance. They emphasised operational assessment as a key aspect of such dialogue, including identifying whether risk would be mitigated through procedures or equipment and ensuring that decisions in this regard would be traced in a verifiable way between ship design and its subsequent periods of operation. Noting key messages coming from their collaborative work, they highlighted the need to improve processes for verifying conformity to the Polar Code and ensuring consistency in implementation, as well as the importance of robustness throughout the process.

(136) Isto Mattila of the Laurea University of Applied Sciences gave a presentation on the EU-funded project *Artificial Intelligence-based Virtual Control Room for the Arctic* (AI-ARC). He noted that climate change had led to decreasing sea ice and therefore increasing ship traffic, which necessitated improved maritime safety conditions. The AI-ARC project aimed to create a system for data sharing and to establish a communication network for monitoring on maritime safety. Highlighting the importance of data, Mattila noted that the EU had been addressing information sharing within its remit. He indicated that AI-ARC services could be used to analyse the current status of the maritime area and detect anomalies. This would improve safety conditions for actors that had previously been able to rely only on other vessels in cases of emergency due to a lack of existing infrastructure. Mattila encouraged enhanced international cooperation to increase safety at sea and encouraged the creation of symbiotic services.

(137) Norway introduced WP 46 *Harmonised implementation of the IMO Polar Code*, prepared jointly with Argentina and Finland, which proposed that Parties strengthen their efforts to implement the IMO Polar Code in a harmonised way. It suggested that the success of the Polar Code would ultimately depend on its harmonised implementation and enforcement, which would avoid complications arising from regulatory differences in diverse flag and port states. Norway recalled that these goals had been previously discussed in the Arctic Council as well as at the first International Conference on Harmonized implementation of the Polar Code in Helsinki in February 2018, and

highlighted the relevance of the Arctic Shipping Best Practice Information Forum, currently chaired by Norway. While acknowledging differences in risk levels in Arctic and Antarctic waters, the importance of cooperation and exchanging best practices to facilitate a harmonised implementation of the Polar Code was underlined. Norway encouraged Antarctic flag states operating in polar areas to participate in a future session of the forum dedicated to sharing experiences on the Polar Code seen from both polar areas.

(138) The Meeting thanked Finland and Argentina for arranging the session, as well as invited experts and the authors of WP 46 for their important work. Parties discussed similarities and differences between the Arctic and the Antarctic in terms of shipping safety, navigational conditions and the environment, and reiterated the importance of sharing information and best practices. Many Parties also highlighted challenges to search and rescue operations in Antarctica, indicating the importance of vessels of opportunity in ensuring adequate emergency response time.

(139) The Russian Federation pointed out that the applicability of the Polar Code to both Southern and Northern polar regions does not mean equivalence of Arctic and Antarctic programmes of States, and does not indicate direct value of experience gained in the Arctic for Antarctic activities. The Russian Federation recalled the specific legal regime of Antarctica and stated that there is no need/relevance in cooperation with Arctic Council States or with the Arctic Council itself.

(140) The Meeting recognised the need to continue prioritising the harmonised implementation and effective enforcement the IMO Polar Code in the Multi-year Strategic Work Plan and advised Parties to keep promoting the Polar Code and its implementation to shipowners and operators calling their ports, as well as vessel designers, shipyards and other stakeholders in their national maritime clusters. Most Parties also supported the recommendation to discuss possible ways for Parties to cooperate with Arctic Council States and other major Flag States for sharing information and best practices in implementing the Polar Code.

(141) Spain presented IP 67 *Implementing the Polar Code: Gaps and Challenges*. It reported that, since the entry into force of the Polar Code, the Spanish maritime administration had only certified one vessel, the oceanographic vessel *Sarmiento de Gamboa*. Spain encouraged all actors to: share their experiences and concerns in applying the Polar Code; take steps to develop common standards for evaluating risks involved in polar navigation; and actively cooperate in the promotion of the Polar Code in all relevant multilateral bodies and working groups.

(142) Chile presented IP 69 *Implementation of the International Code for Ships Operating in Polar Waters in vessels flying a Chilean flag and their control in Chilean jurisdiction waters*. Chile reported that it had fully implemented the Polar Code, with all recommended provisions adopted as mandatory by February 2021. It also recalled a regional workshop that had been held in 2019 to provide relevant training. It recommended that all Parties implement the Polar Code and support the drafting of the Polar Waters Operations Manual (PWOM) to contribute to safe navigation and protection of the Antarctic environment.

(143) Australia presented IP 92 *Australian experience with implementation of the International Code for Ships Operating in Polar Waters (Polar Code)*. Australia noted that it had encountered challenges similar to those expressed by other Parties and welcomed opportunities to share experiences and best practices on Polar Code implementation in the Antarctic. Noting its responsibility for search and rescue operations in a large and partially remote area of East Antarctica, Australia expressed particular interest in sharing experiences with Parties and operators active in the remote regions of continental

Antarctica, particularly the East Antarctic region. Australia also pointed out that its experience applying the Polar Code to date had focused on designing, constructing and operating Australia's new Polar Class 3 icebreaker RSV *Nuyina*.

(144) The Russian Federation presented IP 127 *Применение Полярного кодекса Российской Федерацией* [*Implementation of the Polar Code by the Russian Federation*], which reported on implementation of the Polar Code by the Russian Federation. Recalling that activities in Antarctica require permits, the Russian Federation referred to its current authorisation procedure, which was in force under its federal laws. The Russian Federation noted that its competent authorities had been responsible for compliance with the requirements of the Polar Code since it had entered into force. Due to the existence of domestic legislation and other IMO mechanisms, no amendments had been necessary. The Russian Federation informed that there was no specific statistics of vessels operated in Antarctica within the context of the Polar Code requirements.

(145) IAATO presented IP 58 *Implementation of the IMO Polar Code: A Practical Perspective*. IAATO noted it continued to contribute to discussions of IMO on the Polar Code, and regularly engaged with discussions with flag states, classification societies, and managers to help strengthen understanding and find solutions to some of the challenges identified by Parties, and highlighted in the presentations. Responding to points raised during discussion, IAATO highlighted the importance of harmonising interpretation and training, and the challenge of making the connection between equipment and decision-making procedures in port-state control / mitigation measures. IAATO also acknowledged the importance of vessels of opportunity in reducing emergency response time, noting that an IAATO vessel had evacuated a fishing vessel's crew member as directed by MRCC Chile.

(146) ASOC presented IP 119 *Improving safety and environmental protection of shipping in the Antarctic Treaty Area*. It highlighted the latest international developments of relevance to vessels operating in the Antarctic Treaty Area including the new IMO guidelines for safety measures for large pleasure yachts, the forthcoming IMO mandatory requirements for navigation and planning for non-SOLAS ships, and parallel discussions at the IMO Maritime Safety Committee. ASOC noted existing knowledge gaps regarding sea ice patterns, weather conditions and marine mammal activity, and highlighted the geographic and climatic conditions that influenced search and rescue activities. It urged Parties to work actively, including through IMO, to develop a plan for action and to include indigenous knowledge in enhancing implementation.

(147) The following paper was also submitted under this agenda item and taken as presented:

- IP 8 *Preliminary Survey Responses Regarding Implementation of IMO Polar Code: National Antarctic Programme vessels* (COMNAP).

Item 6d: Operation of the Antarctic Treaty System: Climate Change

(148) The Chair of ATCM XLV, Ms Päivi Kaukoranta, opened the joint ATCM-CEP session on climate change. She highlighted that, over the past 50 years, the west coast of the Antarctic Peninsula had been one of the most rapidly warming parts of the planet and that, due to the temperature increase of 3°C in this area, once stable ice shelves were now retreating. The Chair noted that this warming was not only restricted to the land but was also observed in the Southern Ocean. Consequently, the physical and living environment of this pristine region was threatened and, as temperatures continued to increase, so did the risks of species extinction or irreversible loss of biodiversity. The Chair stated that, along with increasing their knowledge on climate change, the ATCM and CEP had significantly strengthened their efforts to work on the issue. The Chair recalled the 2010 Antarctic Treaty Meeting of Experts (ATME) on Climate Change organised by Norway

in response to SCAR's ACCE report. She noted that the ATME had led to the establishment of the CCRWP in 2015, and the SGCCR in 2017. Since then, the ATCM and the CEP had continued to progress work on climate change responses including, for example, through Resolution 8 (2021) *Antarctica in a Changing Climate*, and through work to update the CCRWP. She noted that, through the Paris Declaration, Parties had reaffirmed their commitment to work together to better understand changes to the Antarctic climate and implemented actions consistent with the Paris Agreement's goals. These actions were with a view to limiting the adverse impacts of climate change on the Antarctic environment and dependent and associated ecosystems, protecting ecosystems, and improving Antarctica's resilience to climate change.

(149) The Meeting thanked the Chair and recalled that ATCM XLIV had welcomed SCAR's ACCE Decadal Synopsis and Recommendations for Action, adopted Resolution 4 (2022) and Decision 4 (2022) on this subject, and agreed to hold a full-day joint session of the CEP and the ATCM, with SCAR and COMNAP, to consider the implementation of the ACCE recommendations at ATCM XLV.

(150) Dr Petteri Taalas, the Secretary General of WMO, made a virtual presentation on Antarctic climate challenges. Dr Taalas underscored that climate change posed one of the greatest risks for the global economy. He noted that the probability of a 2.5°C warming was very high and that this would lead to record high temperatures around the globe. With respect to issues impacting Antarctica, Dr Taalas noted five climate research challenges: the amplification of surface warming; the Antarctic sea ice trigger, which had seen sharp declines in sea ice extent in the region; extreme weather including heatwaves and atmospheric rivers; the melting of Antarctic ice shelves and the loss of Antarctic ice sheet mass; and sea-level rise.

(151) Simon Stiell, Executive Secretary of the UNFCCC, made a virtual presentation to the Meeting. He noted the immediate dangers to Antarctica and the expertise among the Parties working to address it. He stated that climate change posed a global threat and that the countries lying below sea level would experience the most dire consequences of climate change. He referred to recent studies indicating that the earth, including Antarctica, was reaching an important threshold of an average global warming of 1.5°C. Mr Stiell called for strengthened climate action for the sake of Antarctica and its ecosystems as well as for all humankind. He encouraged all participants to develop ambitious visions and concrete assessments at the upcoming 28th session of the COP 28 to the UNFCCC to be held from 30 November to 12 December 2023. He stated that international cooperation and collaboration were essential to reaching an average of net zero carbon emissions by 2040. Mr Stiell encouraged Parties to invest in resilience building and to prepare the public for an increase in extreme weather events. Mr Stiell concluded by urging Parties to prevent an irreversible loss of ecosystems and to take a holistic view of climate change rather than focussing only on areas within domestic legislation.

(152) Dr Valérie Masson-Delmotte, Co-Chair of IPCC Working Group 1, gave a presentation on science emerging from the IPCC in relation to the Antarctic environment. Dr Masson-Delmotte outlined the work of the IPCC, explaining that it drew upon the contributions of over 1000 lead authors, scientists and reviewers. She added that the IPCC had referenced more than 85,000 peer-reviewed scientific publications as a basis for its work. Dr Masson-Delmotte stressed the seriousness of climate change impacts on Antarctica and the Southern Ocean including its physical environments, biodiversity and ecosystems. She underscored the interconnectedness of the global climate, and that climate impacts in Antarctica would have a broader effect on global communities, especially in relation to sea-level rise and food security. Dr Masson-Delmotte highlighted the urgency of mitigating climate change and urged Parties to take action to avoid the

worst impacts of both in Antarctica and beyond. These actions included ensuring the carbon reduction and carbon neutrality of national Antarctic programmes' operations, increased learning and outreach on climate change in Antarctica, and ensuring governments were informed on the consequences of climate. She concluded that decisions made at meetings such as the ATCM would reverberate worldwide and that every year mattered in plight to reduce CO_2 emissions.

(153) The Meeting thanked Dr Masson-Delmotte for her presentation, the work of the IPCC and the conclusions she had drawn in relation to climate change and Antarctica. Some Parties noted that the ATCM acknowledged the seriousness of the issue of climate change and had been working on addressing and understanding the impacts of climate change for many years. Some Parties noted the interconnectedness of the climate change crisis and the biodiversity crisis. Some Parties noted the urgency and need to take further action to protect the Antarctic environment and its ecosystems. They also emphasised the importance of education and outreach in building the public's understanding of the risks posed to Antarctica by climate change. Further, some Parties noted that increased research, monitoring and information exchange were essential to addressing the complex and interconnected climate change issues. Several Parties pointed out that the outcomes of this Meeting, such as the Reaffirmation of the Environment Protocol and the Helsinki Declaration, were important in reaffirming the ATCM's commitment to addressing climate change and its impacts.

(154) China noted that it was pointed out on page nine of the IPCC AR6 Report that modelled scenarios and pathways used were quantitative projections rather than predictions or forecasts, and global modelled emission pathway, including those based on cost effective approaches, contained regionally differentiated assumptions and outcomes, and had to be assessed with the careful recognition of these assumptions. It was also highlighted in the Report that most of those assumptions did not contain explicit assumptions about global equity, environment justice or intraregional income distribution. China noted that it looked forward to efforts to close knowledge gaps in this respect.

(155) Parties asked Dr Masson-Delmotte a variety of questions including: how IPCC panellists had responded to SCAR's ACCE Decadal Synopsis; how Parties could engage with those not engaged from Antarctica; which was the single most important priority Parties should be advancing in relation to climate change; the main implementation gaps that the Parties could address; and if there was good awareness of the ATCM addressing climate change.

(156) In response, Dr Masson-Delmotte reaffirmed that cooperation and collaboration were key to addressing the challenges of climate change. In this regard, she provided the example of the newly formed partnership between the IPCC and Intergovernmental Science-Policy Platform on Biodiversity and Ecosystem Services (IPBES) during the IPCC's 6th Assessment Cycle. She also emphasised that environmental monitoring was critical for identifying information and implementation gaps. She also highlighted the IPCC's conclusions that marine protected areas were a valuable tool in increasing the resilience of the ecosystems threatened by impacts such as ocean acidification. Dr Masson-Delmotte reiterated the importance of critically examining and being transparent about greenhouse gas emissions from national Antarctic programmes, and encouraged Parties to consider providing information about their potential emission reductions. Dr Masson-Delmotte further indicated that SCAR's ACCE Decadal Synopsis was welcomed by the IPCC.

(157) Professor Steven L. Chown addressed the Meeting on behalf of SCAR. He began by presenting a record of atmospheric carbon dioxide which showed an alarming rise of 108 parts per million since the signing of the Antarctic Treaty in 1959. He then referred to SCAR's ACCE Decadal Synopsis, and drew two main conclusions from its 18 recommendations. First, he noted that Antarctica was not a side event in climate change

discussions, but central to understanding changes in the Earth system. He noted the contributions of the Antarctic region to global mean sea-level rise and the climate system had critical consequences for society. Professor Chown stressed that Antarctica was also important because of its extraordinary biodiversity. He highlighted that Antarctica was central to climate change impact research, ranging from observations and understanding of the cryosphere to identifying potentially irreversible tipping points and to understanding the impacts of change on biodiversity, including through the introduction of non-native species. Second, Professor Chown emphasised the urgency of collaborative implementation, communication and action by the Parties to the Antarctic Treaty. He underlined that ensuring humankind's understanding of the Antarctic was a joint responsibility of all the Parties and that properly facilitated international scientific collaboration was vital. He also highlighted the importance of making new findings and data openly available to the scientific community and others. In conclusion, Professor Chown reaffirmed SCAR's willingness to provide the Antarctic Treaty community with the most recent and best available scientific information.

(158) The Meeting thanked Professor Chown for the presentation and echoed his call for action. Several Parties also asked Professor Chown questions on various topics he introduced.

(159) In response, Professor Chown further highlighted the usefulness of the Parties' ongoing efforts to foster international scientific collaboration. He reiterated the importance of ensuring that Antarctic concerns were conveyed by the governments of the Parties to all relevant decision-making bodies such as the UNFCCC. He also noted that international collaboration in science was valuable at all levels and did not always require large infrastructure. Such collaboration could be promoted through the exchange of data, findings, individuals and knowledge itself.

(160) The Chair of the CEP, Ms Birgit Njåstad, made a presentation on the CEP's advice to the ATCM in relation to CEP XXV discussion on climate change, the ACCE report, and other relevant documents. Ms Njåstad highlighted that the Committee took action on the understanding that climate change was already having an impact in Antarctica and that, in the future, it would likely be the most important factor threatening the values of this unique natural reserve. She pointed out that climate change had relevance to, and was imbedded in most of, the CEP discussions, and that the CEP often also had to acknowledge that the knowledge base could be too weak to support clear and concrete management action. She highlighted that consequentially more research and monitoring was crucial to enable understanding and forecast on the environment and how it could change. She noted that climate change had been a top priority issue for the CEP over the years, coming into light with the discussions on CEP strategies and priorities in 2006 in the CEP Edinburgh workshop. She also noted that climate change discussions in the CEP had evolved over the years and that the Committee had worked continually to better organise and prioritise its efforts, leading to the adoption of the CCRWP in 2015. She recalled that the CCRWP identified gaps and needs related to climate issues, and that the CEP had prioritised 35 actions and tasks required to fill these gaps and needs. These included non-native species, ocean acidification, terrestrial environments and near-shore marine environments, species and habitats at risk, as well as the built human environment. In relation to these issues, the Committee had during CEP XXV discussed the need to update its Non-native Species Manual, biofouling from ship operations, threats to terrestrial biodiversity, changing sea ice and its implications for habitats and species, and the status of the emperor penguin. Ms Njåstad reported that the CEP had continued to work on the implementation of the CCRWP, and had discussed and endorsed the following six priority activities to be advanced by the SGCCR in the next intersessional period: support work to assess the status of climate-vulnerable Antarctic

species; develop guidance on climate change considerations in documents for establishing and managing protected areas; keep the Non-native Species Manual updated with current developments; intensify coordination on climate change response in the marine realm with SC-CAMLR: de-contamination of past sites of activities in the Antarctic area; and assess the risk of climate change for Antarctic existing and projected infrastructure. She reported that the Committee had agreed to advise the ATCM that it had adopted terms of reference for the next joint CEP/SC-CAMLR workshop and provided an operative paragraph reflecting the CEP's commitment to climate change for the Helsinki Declaration on Climate Change and the Antarctic.

(161) The Meeting thanked Ms Njåstad for her presentation and for her excellent leadership as CEP Chair. It highlighted that the work of the CEP and its SGCCR were instrumental to the work of the ATCM, and provided essential tools to advance the goal of creating resilience and mitigating the impacts of climate change in Antarctica. The Meeting supported the CEP's continuing advice on climate change and recognised its fundamental value in strengthening the work of the ATCM. It also noted that the Environment Protocol stipulated that the CEP work closely with relevant organisations, and welcomed the relationship the Committee had developed with SCAR and COMNAP. Some Parties noted the challenge of synchronising domestic actions and management plans with a global approach, and welcomed the identification of priority actions, as provided by the CEP. Some Parties emphasised the need to commit to widely disseminating work and research on climate change and seek for synergies to advance more efficiently towards conservation efforts. Parties stressed that keeping Antarctica frozen should be a global concern, encouraged large-scale collaboration, and emphasised that the protection of Antarctica required tackling collective challenges together.

(162) COMNAP Executive Secretary, Michelle Rogan-Finnemore, introduced WP 29 *Implementation of ACCE Imperatives: A COMNAP perspective*. She noted the paper's recommendations that emphasised the critical need to communicate externally the urgency and importance of ensuring collaborative efforts to maintain the Antarctic region close to its current state. COMNAP's advice to the ATCM emphasised that the Antarctic Treaty Area was a critical source of information vital to informing global climate models, and urged Parties to advance scientific collaboration in Antarctica and effectively communicate the importance of Antarctica to the wider public. She also suggested that polar research strategies could prioritise progress against filling remaining knowledge gaps, and stressed that clear messaging across a variety of channels was important. COMNAP encouraged Parties to work together to develop key messages that could be distributed to society, noting that, while the Meeting clearly valued Antarctica, there remained a need to convince the world of the value of Antarctica, and the impact global actions were having on Antarctica and the surrounding marine area.

(163) The Meeting thanked Ms Rogan-Finnemore for her presentation and COMNAP for its work to facilitate international research and cooperation. It noted the pivotal role that national Antarctic programmes play in the facilitation of science and in efforts to address the management implications of a changing climate, and reiterated the importance of communicating information about Antarctica and the changing global climate system to the outside world.

(164) Ms Njåstad mentioned that WP 29 had been discussed at CEP XXV and that its recommendations had been supported by the Committee.

(165) Some Parties highlighted their national Antarctic programme's practices and procedures in relation to climate change mitigation and adaption including through scientific collaboration. They also drew the Meeting's attention to relevant documents, such as IP 64 on decarbonising Antarctic stations (Uruguay, ASOC), IP 59 on the *Antarctica InSync* project (Germany, Australia, France, Italy, Norway, the United Kingdom and the United

States), and Resolution 4 (2017) on the concept of the Green Expedition. The Meeting also noted the importance of long-term planning to ensure that Antarctic infrastructure was developed in readiness for climate change impacts such as extreme weather events.

(166) With respect to COMNAP's call for greater communication with wider audiences, Parties highlighted the important role of education and outreach, especially to young people and future generations.

(167) The Parties agreed to:

- Continue to support national Antarctic programmes to engage in research that was internationally collaborative, filled gaps in knowledge and reduced uncertainty in regard to a changing Antarctic region. This included support for long-term monitoring efforts that often required long-term sustainable investment;

- Develop jointly, with the CEP, key messages for the global community in regard to a changing Antarctica based on best available research, including that those changes were globally significant, what impacts those changes would have to global society, and how the Parties could stop or mitigate changes through their global actions;

- Work with their national Antarctic programmes, and through COMNAP, SCAR and ATCM Experts, to deliver and promote those key messages through the range of education, outreach and communications fora and through a range of media including art and social media;

- Continue support to couple global communications with local management policies that enabled ongoing and long-term efforts to facilitate Antarctic research, while continuing to assess the impact on the Antarctic Treaty Area of direct human activities there;

- Through COMNAP, continue work to assist national Antarctic programmes to assess risk of change in climate to Antarctic infrastructures, and impacts to operations, logistics and science delivery and support;

- Continue to support national Antarctic programme efforts to decarbonise or reduce fossil fuel use, safely, as part of their Antarctic activities in line with domestic policies and through sharing of best practice through COMNAP;

- Review CEP guidance and advice in regard to existing biosecurity practices (Non-native Species Manual), especially to adapt current "response protocols" to better respond to marine non-native species introduction in a changing ocean (Biofouling and Ballast Water Management), and update accordingly; and

- Assess or reassess which sites of their past activities were most likely to be affected by a changing climate and to prioritise their clean-up efforts based on their assessment. This should be coupled with a review of CEP guidance and advice in regard to clean-up of sites of past activity *(ie*, the CEP Clean-Up Manual) especially considering areas that may be affected by changing environmental conditions near those sites of past activity.

(168) SCAR introduced WP 42 rev. 1 *SCAR updates on Antarctic Climate Change and the Environment*, which provided an update on its 2022 ACCE Decadal Synopsis. SCAR affirmed that the research and policy recommendations provided in the ACCE Decadal Synopsis remained current. Recognising the urgency of action on climate change, SCAR

reiterated its commitment to provide regular advice to the ATCM on the best available science. This included science representing current understanding of, and projections for, climate change and its impacts both in Antarctica and on the Earth's system. SCAR noted that this commitment was also made clear in its new strategic plan, as outlined in IP 47. SCAR encouraged Parties to consider recommendations to further advance the research and policy advice contained in the ACCE Decadal Synopsis.

(169) The Meeting thanked SCAR for its paper, as well as for the recommendations brought forward in the 2022 ACCE Decadal Synopsis. The Meeting further expressed its appreciation to SCAR for its ongoing provision of independent scientific advice to the ATCM, which had relevance to all of the Meeting's decision making, including on protected areas, tourism and invasive species. Several Parties noted the relevance of SCAR's recommendations to the work of the CEP, including the CEP's Five-year Work Plan and the CCRWP. Several Parties noted the excellent progress by the Parties implementing the recommendations of SCAR's report, noted that they were in the process of implementing many of these recommendations, or in undertaking work on related scientific priorities such as sea ice, and encouraged this work to continue in accordance with Resolution 4 (2002). The Meeting also referred to past work of relevance to the ATCM, including Resolution 8 (2021) *Antarctica in a Changing Climate*.

(170) Some Parties highlighted the importance of Antarctic science to delivering on the goals of the Paris Agreement, including through ambitious Nationally Determined Contributions (NDCs), and therefore to ensuring the resilience of Antarctica.

(171) The Chair of the CEP noted that the CEP had also considered WP 42 rev. 1. The Committee had noted that science information from SCAR was fundamental in its work to understand and address environmental management in Antarctica in light of climate change, and provided even greater impetus to efforts to implement the CCRWP as a matter of priority. The Committee also commended recent efforts by Parties to fulfil the need for multinational, large-scale, well-resourced and coordinated research efforts, such as the International Science and Infrastructure for Synchronous Observation (Antarctica InSync). It expressed its support for all the recommendations in WP 42 rev. 1, underscoring, in particular, the need to connect this work to the Five-year Work Plan and CCRWP, including the list of science needs that the CEP was working on.

(172) WMO stated that it and its World Climate Research Programme would continue to support SCAR and Parties with relevant updates, and especially to prioritise implementation of the recommendations outlined in WP 42 rev. 1. It emphasised that the ACCE report provided crucial, Antarctic-focused updates to the IPCC reports, and that it provided a timely call for action.

(173) IAATO reported that it had taken steps to understand, account for, and reduce its community's emissions, as reported in ATCM XLIV - WP 41. It noted the importance of collaboration and information sharing to finding solutions, and that air and sea gateways had an important role to play. It highlighted that tourism provided a unique opportunity to talk about Antarctica and climate change to an engaged audience.

(174) The Meeting agreed to invite SCAR to continue to provide regular updates on Antarctic Climate Change and the Environment.

(175) The Meeting agreed to encourage Parties to:

- Continue their efforts to implement the 2022 ACCE Decadal Synopsis recommendations with urgency, particularly in communicating internationally the critical importance of meeting and exceeding targets for the reduction of greenhouse gas emissions, and the need for resources to address research priorities to understand global impacts, as well as impacts on Antarctica;

- Continue to engage with the research community to deepen understanding of the key messages emerging from research as well as to determine what science and what types of information would best support the development of robust policies and actions; and

- Consider how to provide regular assessments of progress against the recommendations and priority actions identified by the 2022 ACCE Decadal Synopsis and the 2023 joint CEP-ATCM session on climate change.

(176) Finland introduced WP 43 *The Recommendations of SCAR on Climate Action in the Antarctic: The Finnish Perspective*, which provided Finland's perspective on SCAR's recommendations in the ACCE report. It set out several recommendations focused on outreach and communication, research needs and coordination, and actions and policy proposals. Finland noted that countries were collectively not on track to reach the Paris Agreement's long-term goal, and that this put all coastal regions at risk. It noted the importance of outreach and communication in order to make these risks understood. On research needs and coordination, Finland highlighted the importance of finding synergies between both of the poles, including for enhanced scientific cooperation. Finland also noted that both the ATCM and UNFCCC needed to base their decision-making on recent scientific evidence, and therefore encouraged cooperation between SCAR and the IPCC. Finland further emphasised the need for international collaboration to reduce environmental impacts, acknowledging that there were many current examples. Highlighting policy and action, Finland stressed that greenhouse gas emissions would need to peak immediately or in 2025 if Paris Agreement goals were to be kept in reach.

(177) The Meeting thanked Finland for the paper, which provided useful insights that complemented SCAR's work. Many Parties and SCAR expressed their support for the recommendations in the paper, highlighting in particular the value of cooperation in an operative and holistic way. It was noted that this would be relevant not only for strengthening cooperation between Parties, but also for reducing carbon footprints. Some also noted that pooling of resources might be more appropriate in the Antarctic Peninsula, where there was a higher concentration of stations. Regarding collaboration between the Arctic and the Antarctic, some Parties cautioned that differences between the poles corresponded to different management needs, and that these differences should be accounted for when considering future collaboration.

(178) Portugal highlighted that the ICG on Education and Outreach provided a platform for networking and information exchange between Parties, Observers, and Experts. To advance action on outreach and communications on climate change in Antarctica, it proposed to add a topic in the ATCM on informal education and outreach, focused on key messages on climate change from Antarctica, in the next intersessional period. It invited contributions from all interested parties and noted that deliverable outputs could be provided to the next ATCM.

(179) Norway introduced WP 31 *Network of Observation Systems*, which explored the state of coordinated observing efforts in Antarctica and suggested actions toward improvement. Norway observed that well-supported, long-term monitoring of the physical and living environment was essential to understanding ongoing environmental changes in Antarctica. Norway advised movement toward further coordinated, comprehensive and complementary observation networks, which it suggested would facilitate well-founded use of limited resources by Parties. Norway described the Troll Observing Network (TONe) as one of many holistic observational networks developed by stations and national programmes. It emphasised that, although the cost of research was growing, so

too was the cost of having gaps in knowledge and observations. To enable well-founded investments, Norway recommended that the ATCM invite SCAR to give Parties an overview and assessment of Antarctic long-term observation efforts to enhance their use and robustness, as well as to identify gaps in observation needs. It further recommended that the ATCM consider mechanisms for, and encourage further exchange of, information on technological solutions for observation efforts in Antarctica, and in this manner strengthen the long-term capacity for a pan-Antarctic observation effort.

(180) The Meeting thanked Norway for submitting WP 31. It noted that the paper reflected key messages that had been presented throughout the joint CEP-ATCM session, including the needs for long-term, well-supported monitoring efforts and for integrated, coordinated approaches to scientific research on climate change. Parties also noted the paper's relevance to discussions that had taken place during CEP XXV, as well as the CEP's plans to make progress on developing a harmonised approach to environmental monitoring by identifying and analysing existing monitoring activities and available data. The Meeting encouraged Parties to ensure that data collected in Antarctica would be made available to the international scientific community, which would facilitate better understanding of climate change impacts and enable informed decision-making.

(181) The Russian Federation stated that observation and monitoring were elements to achieve environmental protection management, whose efficiency could only be achieved through a holistic and comprehensive approach. The Russian Federation argued that such an approach required general strategy and involvement of relevant ATS bodies, in particular analysis from SCAR where scientific expertise was needed, and that the ATCM should be informed by the CEP. The Russian Federation noted that recommendations presented in the document did not fully reflect this.

(182) SCAR emphasised the increasing importance of remote observation systems facilitated by new technologies. It noted a number of initiatives that aimed to coordinate efforts across Antarctica and the Southern Ocean including the Antarctic Near-shore and Terrestrial Observing System (ANTOS) (WP 49 rev. 1) and the Southern Ocean Observing System (SOOS). SCAR indicated that it would consider what further information it could provide on current observation efforts and systems, noting that this would also be relevant to the CEP's work towards the development of an international framework for environmental monitoring, and that information shared by Parties would be helpful in obtaining a holistic picture of observation efforts and in closing gaps in knowledge.

(183) Norway introduced WP 39 *DML-RINGS and Enderby Land RINGS – opening extensive international collaboration to close critical data gaps for sea-level projections*, prepared jointly with Australia, Belgium, China, Finland, Germany, India, Japan, Sweden, the United States and SCAR. It also referred to IP 73 *Addressing critical knowledge gaps identified by the IPCC in Antarctica's future contribution to sea level rise by international collaboration,* prepared jointly with SCAR. Norway highlighted the importance of accurate projections of the future evolution of the Antarctic ice sheet to mitigating potential risks to people in coastal and low-lying areas. It introduced RINGS, a SCAR action group established in 2012 to develop a coordinated framework to facilitate complementary and comprehensive airborne surveys in the coastal zone of the Antarctic Ice Sheet. New RINGS initiatives in Dronning Maud Land (DML) and Enderby Land had been made possible by broad collaboration between various national Antarctic programmes in order to help close data gaps.

(184) The Meeting thanked the proponents of WP 39 and several Parties expressed interest in contributing to this effort moving forward. The Meeting encouraged Parties to:

- take note of the important SCAR RINGS initiative and its role in increasing the science community's ability to constrain the uncertainties relating to Antarctica's contribution to future sea-level rise;

- make appropriate efforts to enable regional surveys and supplemental ground-based and vessel-based work in an internationally coordinated manner, looking at the Dronning Maud Land RINGS and Enderby Land RINGS initiatives as useful examples; and

- support and contribute to the Dronning Maud Land RINGS and Enderby Land RINGS as appropriate.

(185) COMNAP expressed that the RINGS initiative was a prime example of national Antarctic programmes coming together to contribute assets to filling a scientific data gap. It highlighted the paper's statement that in Dronning Maud Land alone, approximately 100 flight hours would be carried out in support of the initiative, which represented a significant resource contribution. COMNAP noted that it would discuss regional support to RINGS in other areas of Antarctica at its Annual General Meeting in June 2023.

(186) Norway introduced WP 35 *Addressing management implications of loss of sea-ice*, prepared jointly with the United Kingdom. Norway noted that SCAR's ACCE report had indicated loss of sea ice as an ongoing change that would present new challenges for the management of areas of high human activity in the Antarctic. It highlighted that, since 2017, the four lowest sea ice extent minimums had been recorded, with 2022 and 2023 setting new records in this regard. Norway highlighted that declining sea ice might lead to an expanded visitation season in Antarctica, which could expose new areas, species, and habitats to increased human disturbance. Norway recalled that, according to the Environment Protocol, Parties should take steps to avoid or minimise the risk of human activity leading to unintended and unforeseen impacts on vulnerable species and habitats. It therefore suggested that further information about vulnerable areas, species, and habitats might be useful to discussions related to management of human activities, especially in the Antarctic Peninsula region. The proponents further emphasised the ambition to scale up these efforts, as record sea ice lows could indicate widespread issues to come.

(187) The Meeting thanked Norway and the United Kingdom for their paper. It noted, with concern, the rapid and significant changes to Antarctic sea ice, which demonstrated the vulnerability of Antarctic ecosystems to climate change. Several Parties reiterated the need to take steps to avoid or minimise the risk of human activity leading to unintended or unforeseen impacts on vulnerable species and habitats, and stressed the importance of undertaking proactive action based on the precautionary principle. The Meeting expressed support for the recommendations in WP 35, and for the ambition to scale up this effort.

(188) China noted the importance of defining "vulnerability" for future assessment, as well as elaborating on measures to distinguish the influence of climate change and the influence of human activities; the value of considering spatial and temporal scales; the relevance of CEP discussions on research and monitoring using both remote sensing and on-site research; and the need to clarify what was meant by avoiding human activity, and whether all human activity was implied by this.

(189) SCAR noted that the Antarctic Environments Portal had published three relevant summaries on Antarctic sea ice that could be used to inform these discussions. It also highlighted that collaborative, interdisciplinary research, such as that proposed under the UN Decade of Ocean Science and Antarctica InSync, would be an important contribution.

(190) IAATO acknowledged the importance of the Antarctic Peninsula in this regard and noted that among IAATO's annual contributions to the ATCM was a paper reporting on operator use of Antarctic Peninsula landing sites and ATCM Visitor Site Guidelines (IP 53). IAATO further noted that it had a process for creating guidelines for sites where ATCM site guidelines were not yet in place, which were shared with Parties as appropriate. It welcomed collaboration with Parties on the development of new site guidelines and review of those that IAATO had developed.

(191) The Meeting agreed to request the CEP, with the support of SCAR, to provide advice on how human activity could avoid or mitigate unintended or unforeseen negative impacts on vulnerable species or habitats affected by local or regional sea-ice loss. In the first instance, the Meeting:

- invited SCAR to provide a first level assessment of vulnerabilities in space and time, exposed by changing sea-ice extent in the Antarctic Peninsula region; and
- asked the CEP to consider potential management implications for the Antarctic Peninsula region, noting that it experienced high and increasing levels of human activity.

(192) SCAR indicated that it would endeavour to provide further information on changing sea ice extent and associated vulnerabilities in future updates, recognising especially the importance of such information to the work of the CEP.

(193) WMO presented IP 93 *Antarctica 2300 (ISMIP6) Projections.* The paper outlined the World Climate Research Programme's Ice Sheet Model Intercomparison Project (ISMIP), which aimed to provide process-based projections of ice sheet contribution to sea-level rise for the 21st Century. WMO explained that ISMIP6 Antarctica 2300 Projections was a continuation of the successful ISMIP6 project, and would extend previous simulations to 2300. It highlighted projections indicating that Antarctic ice sheets were likely to reach tipping points by the end of the century and that these would have intergenerational consequences. WMO emphasised the importance of understanding near-term impacts and risks of sea-level rise not just for coastal communities but also the Antarctic coastline including on infrastructure, historic sites and ecosystems. WMO also noted that its paper supported WP 42 rev. 1 (SCAR) and IP 95 (SCAR, COMNAP).

(194) ASOC presented IP 64 *Decarbonizing Antarctic Operations: best practices for renewable energy deployment at Antarctic research stations,* prepared jointly with Uruguay. The paper outlined the importance of decarbonising Antarctic operations and highlighted recent progress in this area. Uruguay and ASOC recommended that Parties and other Antarctic operators: conduct feasibility studies to decarbonise their operations, bases and activities with the aim of achieving a net zero condition and allocate funds to this objective; collaborate with public and industry stakeholders to implement established renewable energy sources and energy efficiency practices; and agree on developing a manual that outlines the best practices for reducing carbon emissions in Antarctic operations, with a specific focus on using renewable energy and improving energy efficiency at research facilities.

(195) ASOC presented IP 117 *Irreversible near-term consequences of Southern Ocean acidification with current CO2 emissions pathways*, and IP 120 *Increasing evidence of critical sea-level rise with emissions above 1.5°C Paris agreement limit.* These papers highlighted how climate change and ocean acidification were impacting, and would continue to impact, the Antarctic region. With regard to IP 117, ASOC highlighted the

closeness of the Southern Ocean to irreversible acidification thresholds, which seriously threatened marine ecosystems and fisheries. With regard to IP 120, it noted that sea-level rise in particular would impact vulnerable millions living in coastal areas. ASOC reported that an increasing number of sophisticated studies were converging on 1.5°C to 1.8°C as critical thresholds for the stability of Antarctic systems. It concluded that greater efforts were needed to support continued monitoring and modelling, as well as communicating this research, including at COP28 in Dubai, as one output from the joint session on climate change at ATCM XLV.

(196) Portugal presented IP 38 *ATCM-CEP Joint Session on Climate Change: Portugal's research and policy activities on climate change*, which summarised research and policy activities undertaken by Portugal related to climate change. Portugal noted that its paper recognised the implications of climate change worldwide, and also noted with appreciation the reports of IPCC, SCAR and WMO. Portugal highlighted the relevance of science for policy making; its commitment to fighting climate change, including its focus on wind and solar energy; and its contributions to education and outreach. Portugal noted that much work was needed on education and outreach by Parties, Observers and Experts, including the need to note the level of urgency for actions and the need for greater access to scientific evidence. It also acknowledged David Vaughan from the United Kingdom and Andrés Barbosa from Spain, who passed away in the previous year, for their excellent contributions to scientific research.

(197) Finland introduced WP 38 rev. 1 *Helsinki Declaration on Climate Change and the Antarctic*, which presented the proposal and process for developing a Declaration on Climate Change and the Antarctic. Finland recalled that, following discussion on the ATCM Discussion Forum, it had led intersessional discussions to formulate a Joint Declaration emphasising the necessity of urgent climate action in Antarctica.

(198) Following further discussion, the Meeting adopted Resolution 2 (2023) *Helsinki Declaration on Climate Change and the Antarctic*.

(199) The following papers were also submitted under this agenda item and taken as presented:

- IP 25 *Logistical Challenges due to Changing Environmental Conditions: Experiences from the Korean Antarctic Program 2022-23* (Republic of Korea).
- IP 72 *Australia's Antarctic climate science* (Australia).
- IP 94 *The Climate and Cryosphere (CliC) Project of the World Climate Research Programme (WCRP)* (WMO).
- IP 95 *Understanding Future Sea-level Change Around Antarctica* (SCAR, COMNAP).
- IP 97 *Policy-relevant science highlights from the Antarctic CORDEX project* (WMO).

Item 6e: Operation of the Antarctic Treaty System: General Matters

(200) Finland introduced WP 36 *Towards gender-neutral language in the Antarctic Treaty System*, prepared jointly with the United Kingdom, Spain, Germany, New Zealand, Norway and France. Finland noted the significant increase in the participation of women in Antarctic science, research and governance, and recalled that, on several occasions, Parties had emphasised the importance of equality and inclusiveness in their Antarctic programmes. The co-sponsors therefore proposed the further promotion of gender equality through the use of gender-neutral language in activities concerning Antarctica and in the operation of the Antarctic Treaty system.

(201) The Meeting thanked the proponents for their valuable work promoting gender-neutral language in the Antarctic Treaty system. Most Parties noted the relevance of inclusion and diversity for this topic. The Meeting noted the collective responsibility and importance of ensuring that the Antarctic Treaty system promoted equality, inclusion and diversity.

(202) Some Parties noted that their government agencies had integrated gender-neutral language into policies and legislation. Parties also volunteered to help the Secretariat adopt gender-neutral language into the official Treaty languages. Australia suggested that the Parties consider commissioning a survey to determine how inclusivity and diversity were measured across national Antarctic programmes.

(203) The Russian Federation pointed out the importance to reflect specificities of all official languages. It highlighted that the United Nations provided guidance across their official languages, suggesting that this could serve as a reference for future work. The Russian Federation supported further consideration of gender-neutral language in the ATS and stressed that any amendments to the ATCM Rules of Procedure and other documents could be adopted only by the ATCM, and that the Secretariat was not empowered to make any amendments to the Rules of Procedure, but could only review such documents and report back to the ATCM. The Russian Federation recommended that proponents prepare specific proposals to be considered by ATCM.

(204) Noting the recommendation that Observers and Experts use gender-neutral and inclusive language in their communications, COMNAP, CCAMLR and ASOC stated they had already incorporated gender-neutral language in their organisations. CCAMLR further offered to share its background analyses and the resultant changes it had made at a future meeting.

(205) The Meeting agreed to:

- encourage Parties, Observers and Experts to continue promoting inclusivity, equity and diversity in their national Antarctic programmes, relevant national authorities and other institutions responsible for Antarctic issues, particularly with respect to gender equality;
- together with the CEP, task the Secretariat to review, within existing resources, all relevant Antarctic Treaty documents pertaining to current and future cooperation, to provide options for potential adoption by the ATCM that would ensure gender-neutral language across these documents;
- task the Secretariat to ensure that personal information requested of ATCM participants and registration request forms use respectful, inclusive terms that embrace the diversity of participants, drawing on best practice; and
- recommend that Parties, Observers and Experts use gender-neutral and respectful inclusive language in spoken and written documentation, reporting and other forms of communication.

(206) SCAR referred to its IP 77 *The SCAR Equality, Diversity and Inclusion Action Group*, which described its Equality, Diversity and Inclusion Action Group established in 2021, that was involved in actively reviewing existing external diversity and inclusion resources, and working with other organisations to share experience and best practices.

(207) The United States introduced WP 55 *Reaffirmation of Commitment to Environmental Protocol Article 7*, prepared jointly with Argentina, Australia, Belgium, Bulgaria, Chile, Czechia, Finland, France, Germany, India, Italy, Japan, the Republic of Korea, the Netherlands, New Zealand, Norway, Peru, Poland, Spain, Sweden, Ukraine, the United

Kingdom and Uruguay. It proposed that a draft resolution be adopted to reaffirm the ATCM's ongoing commitment to the prohibition on Antarctic mineral resource activities, other than for scientific research. The United States recalled past reaffirmations of Parties' commitment to Article 7 of the Environment Protocol, including in the Santiago Declaration (2016), the Prague Declaration (2019) and the Paris Declaration (2021) as well as that numerous Parties had joined the Madrid Declaration (2021). It had nevertheless observed that there existed an erroneous belief in the public and among some experts that the Environment Protocol would expire in 2048 or that action by Parties would be necessary to maintain Article 7 in force beyond that date. In recognition of the 25th anniversary of the entry into force of the Environment Protocol, the co-authors proposed that a resolution be adopted to combat misinformation and reaffirm the ATCM's unchanging dedication to preserving Antarctica for peace and science and to protecting the Antarctic environment and dependent and associated ecosystems by reaffirming its collective commitment to Article 7. The United States highlighted that 24 out of 29 Consultative Parties were already co-authors to the paper and encouraged other Parties to join.

(208) The Meeting thanked the co-authors for their paper and reaffirmed the importance of Article 7 as a cornerstone of the Environment Protocol. Parties emphasised the importance of communicating clearly with the public regarding the status of the Environment Protocol. They stressed the need to further clarify the Protocol's legal framework, both to the general public and academics, and to dispel any rumours or misunderstanding, such as the notion that the Environment Protocol would expire in 2048.

(209) The Meeting agreed to adopt a Resolution to reaffirm the Parties' commitment to environmental protection for the Antarctic Treaty area embedded in the Environment Protocol, and confirm the Environment Protocol would not expire in 2048.

(210) The Meeting adopted Resolution 3 (2023) *Reaffirming ongoing commitment to the prohibition on Antarctic mineral resource activities, other than for scientific research.* The Meeting also agreed to make changes to the Secretariat website to ensure that the outward facing communication was clear on the meaning of Article 7 (see Appendix 1) and agreed to include this information and reaffirmation in the Host Country Communiqué (see Appendix 2).

(211) The Chair referred to SP 3 *List of Measures with status "not yet effective"* (Secretariat), which provided a list of Measures that, according to the information provided by the Depositary Government, were not yet effective. These included three Measures adopted at ATCM XXVII (Cape Town, 2004), ATCM XXVIII (Stockholm, 2005) and ATCM XXXII (Baltimore, 2009), respectively. It noted that Measure 4 (2004) *Tourism and Non-Governmental activities* had not yet been approved by Brazil, Bulgaria, China, Germany, India, Italy, Republic of Korea, Peru, Spain, Sweden or the United States. It also noted that Measure 1 (2005) *Annex VI Liability* had not yet been approved by Argentina, Belgium, Brazil, Bulgaria, China, India, Japan, Republic of Korea or the United States. It further noted that Measure 15 (2009) *Landing of Persons from Passenger vessels* had not yet been approved by Brazil, Bulgaria, Chile, China, Germany, India, Italy, Republic of Korea, Norway, Peru, Poland, South Africa, Spain, Sweden or the United States. Chile and Spain reported that they had approved the Measures listed as pending for both Consultative Parties in SP 3 and had informed the Depository Government.

(212) Some Parties reported on their progress in implementing and approving measures at a national level. The Meeting noted these developments, congratulated Parties on progress made and encouraged other Parties to continue with their efforts to ratify ATCM measures and implement them through their domestic legislation.

(213) The Meeting noted that two of these measures had existed for almost 20 years and that it was disappointing that they were not yet effective. Some Parties requested information and advice from Parties that had already completed the adoption of these measures. In response, some Parties that had approved the measures expressed their willingness to share their experiences in this regard. The Secretariat reminded Parties that information about domestic implementation of ATCM measures was available on the Secretariat website.

(214) The Russian Federation introduced WP 57 *Urgent Challenges for the Antarctic Treaty System*, which highlighted the dangers of the politicisation of the ATCM and its negative consequences to the Antarctic Treaty system and the traditions of the Antarctic community. The Russian Federation invited Parties to review the recent challenges of the ATCM and to exchange views as to whether politicisation was an indication of systemic changes or whether the Parties intended to make efforts to prevent its influence from affecting the future of the Antarctic Treaty system. The Russian Federation presented information about violations of the ATCM Rules of Procedure with respect to a discussion at ATCM XLIV relating to ATCM XLIV - IP 85 submitted by Ukraine, that included false statements, but did not contain any information on the scale of the national Antarctic programmes of Ukraine in previous years and did not allow any conclusion to be drawn regarding the extent of potential reduction in the programme of work and the reasons for it. WP 57 pointed out that appeals directed against one of the Consultative Parties were presented not only at the ATCM forum, but were also addressed by the head of the Ukrainian Antarctic station to a broad number of employees of the Antarctic stations of other States, including Russian Antarctic stations. The Russian Federation invited the ATCM to:

- note that politicisation threatened the integrity of the Antarctic Treaty system, and negatively affected its norms, in particular, the principle of international cooperation established by the Treaty;
- initiate an exchange of views on the enforcement of Rules 17-20 of the Rules of Procedure and on maintaining the established deadlines for translation; and
- initiate an exchange of views on whether there was a need to amend or reinforce these provisions.

(215) Ukraine stated that it was willing to engage in an exchange of views related to the politicisation of the Antarctic Treaty system. Ukraine stated that the Meeting was not being politicised by discussing and highlighting the many impacts of the Russian Federation's war of aggression on Ukraine's Antarctic activities. Ukraine emphasised that the Antarctic Treaty did not exist in isolation from the broader norms of the international legal system and forms part of a United Nations legal system. It stated that when one Consultative Party invaded another Consultative Party in violation of the United Nations Charter and the resolutions of the United Nations General Assembly, it impacted all of Ukraine's activities related to Antarctica. Ukraine cited the negative impacts on all of its Antarctic activities, including that bombs had destroyed its national Antarctic programme office. Ukraine also stated that many Antarctic scientists had to interrupt their research to fight and engage in the war as the military operations continued and that Ukrainian civilians had to hide in bomb shelters for safety from the shelling. Ukraine considered discussions on these issues appropriate for Antarctic Treaty system fora. Ukraine stated that, should the Russian Federation want to draw certain conclusions and lessons from the issue, it would be a very useful means to resume normal operations at the ATCM, but that it could only happen if the illegal attack on Ukraine stopped and if the Russian Federation observed the instruments of the United Nations.

(216) Most Parties condemned the Russian Federation's unlawful war of aggression on Ukraine and noted that the ATCM had the competency and responsibility to discuss the impacts of such events on national Antarctic programmes. These Parties noted that discussing these factual issues did not politicise the Antarctic Treaty system. Many Parties cited the bombing of the Ukrainian Antarctic programme's office in Kyiv as one of the examples of the impact of the unprovoked and unjustifiable attack on Ukraine's Antarctic operations and engagement. Many Parties also emphasised the broader impacts on the peaceful operation and engagement of Parties and the Antarctic Treaty system. Many Parties extended their sympathy and support to the people of Ukraine and the impacted members of the Ukrainian Antarctic programme.

(217) The Russian Federation called for a precautious approach and stated that the discussion on the situation in Ukraine could bring more negative than positive impacts.

(218) With respect to recommendation 1, many Parties expressed the view that it was not political to report upon and discuss one Consultative Party initiating a war against another and that the impacts on the Ukrainian Antarctic programme had been made clear. Regarding recommendation 2, many Parties agreed that the full-scale invasion by one Consultative Party of another Consultative Party indeed negatively affected the norms of the Antarctic Treaty system and noted that the impacts on ATCM XLIV (Berlin) and ATCM XLV (Helsinki) were factual events. Regarding recommendation 3, many Parties noted the skilled and fair handling by Host Countries Germany (ATCM XLIV) and Finland (ATCM XLV), as well as the extraordinary facilities Germany had provided to enable both virtual and in-person access to ATCM XLIV for all Parties. They noted it would be improper to relitigate any procedural issues raised at ATCM XLIV that, in the view of the Parties, had been appropriately decided by the Chair of ATCM XLIV according to the ATCM Rules of Procedure.

(219) Some other Parties expressed their continued concern about the ongoing war in Ukraine and condemned the threat to Ukraine's sovereignty and territorial integrity. These Parties noted that the war of aggression was against the principles of peace, collaboration, and cooperation embodied in the Antarctic Treaty. These Parties highlighted that they were not in favour of any politicisation of the Antarctic Treaty system. They recalled that, for the past 60 years, Parties had been overcoming their difficulties to ensure peace, collaboration, and cooperation in the Antarctic. These Parties expressed hope that the situation would soon change for the good of all the Parties.

(220) In response to the paper's claim that the ATCM should exercise oversight of the activities of SCAR and COMNAP, several Parties recalled the importance of SCAR and COMNAP to the work of the ATCM, and also emphasised their independence.

(221) COMNAP noted it was an independent, non-subsidiary, practical, technical and non-political association, as defined by its Constitution adopted in July 2008 during the COMNAP Annual General Meeting held in St Petersburg, Russia. It further highlighted that it had been formally recognised as such in Resolution 2 (2009).

(222) SCAR noted that, as a thematic organisation of the International Science Council, it was an apolitical scientific body and Observer to the ATCM. SCAR stated that it would continue providing the ATCM with independent advice based on best available science.

(223) The Russian Federation noted that during consideration of the request from Belarus to become a Consultative Party at the closed session of the Plenary Meeting one Party stated that under current political circumstances consensus on the issue could not be reached.

The Russian Federation reiterated that its paper was based on fact and contained its legal assessment on the departure from the Rules of Procedure at ATCM XLIV. The Russian Federation re-emphasised that it had endeavoured to prevent any attempt of politicising the Meeting.

(224) Ukraine responded to the Russian Federation's comments by stating that Ukraine was ready to reconsider the request from Belarus, if the latter wished to reapply for the Consultative Party status in the future, once it had stopped facilitating the war of aggression and complied with instruments of the United Nations, as it was one of the requirements applied to all Contracting Parties to the Antarctic Treaty. Ukraine thanked the Parties that had expressed support and solidarity during the continued Russian aggression. Ukraine stated that the spirit of cooperation noted by many Parties could only resume once the aggression on its territory ceased.

(225) Australia introduced IP 132 rev.1 *Strengthening Support for the Protocol on Environmental Protection to the Antarctic Treaty*, prepared jointly with France and Spain. Australia reported that, in the period from 2012 to 2019, Australia, France and Spain had coordinated four rounds of outreach by Consultative Parties to encourage States Party to the Antarctic Treaty, but not yet Party to the Environment Protocol, to accede to it. It noted that, since the commencement of these outreach efforts, there had been a further eight new Parties to the Environment Protocol. In the fifth round of outreach in 2023, 13 Contracting Parties to the Antarctic Treaty were encouraged to accede to the Environment Protocol. Two Parties indicated that they had initiated discussions regarding the possibility of accession, and a further two Parties would give further consideration to accession. Australia remarked that the co-authors were encouraged by the support expressed by a number of the States for the objectives and principles of the Environment Protocol and by the intention of some States to give further consideration to becoming Parties to the Environment Protocol. Australia and the co-authors stated their intention to continue these efforts following ATCM XLV and encouraged other Consultative Parties to do the same.

(226) The Meeting thanked the authors of IP 132 rev. 1 for their work strengthening support for the Protocol, and encouraged the outreach to continue.

(227) Australia noted that, as a further reflection of its commitment to the Environment Protocol, it had recently designated three arbitrators – Scientia Professor Rosemary Rayfuse, Professor Tim Stephens and Professor Bill Campbell – pursuant to the Schedule to the Environment Protocol.

(228) Ecuador presented IP 129 *XXXIII Reunión de Administradores de Programas Antárticos Latinoamericanos -RAPAL (Ecuador, 2022)*, and noted the 33rd meeting of Latin American Antarctic Managers of Antarctic Programmes (RAPAL), which was held in Quito. Ecuador noted the participation of Costa Rica, Colombia and Venezuela as Observers to the meeting, as well as simultaneous meetings on logistics, environmental, scientific and technical issues. The meeting also noted key information on the environment regarding the 2022/23 season.

(229) Colombia presented IP 128 *Foro Conmemorativo de la Firma del Tratado Antártico: El Decenio de las Ciencias Oceánicas en el Confín del mundo*, prepared jointly with Brazil, Chile, Ecuador, Peru, Uruguay, and Türkiye. It reported on the highlights of the latest Commemorative Forum of the signing of the Antarctic Treaty, which made it possible to facilitate the exchange of experiences and good practices among the RAPAL countries. Colombia noted that this event had included 250 people representing academic and public and private institutions.

(230) The Meeting thanked the authors for their papers and welcomed the progress made by the RAPAL countries. Türkiye thanked Ecuador for organising the forum and expressed its pleasure at having contributed a speech that had highlighted the UN Ocean Decade. Colombia thanked Ecuador and other RAPAL countries for creating this opportunity for the exchange of science as well as opportunities for the training of future scientists.

(231) The following paper was also submitted under this agenda item and taken as presented:

- IP 141 *National Measures on Antarctic Legislation* (India).

Item 7: Operation of the Antarctic Treaty System: Matters related to the Secretariat

(232) The Executive Secretary introduced SP 4 *Secretariat Report 2022/23*, which provided details on the Secretariat's activities in the Financial Year 2022/23 (1 April 2022 to 31 March 2023) including the organisation of the hybrid ATCM XLIV and CEP XXIV meeting in Germany and the preparation for ATCM XLV and CEP XXV in Finland. The Executive Secretary drew the Meeting's attention to the intersessional activities it had supported during this period including: the update of the Antarctic Treaty contacts database interface; EIES training and tutorials aimed to support the Parties use of the system; publications; coordination and contact including visits to the Secretariat; and the Secretariat Papers that were submitted to ATCM XLV and CEP XXV. The Executive Secretary reported that there had been no changes to the numbers of personnel. With regard to financial matters, the Executive Secretary provided an overview of contributions it had received, and presented its externally audited financial report for the financial year 2021/22. The Executive Secretary presented the provisional Financial Report 2022/23, remarking that appropriations were in line with the budget except for Financing which was affected by the strong devaluation against the US dollar, and Translation and Interpretation which included the cost of unforeseen requests for translation. The period ended with a provisional deficit for 2022/23 of USD 17 571 and the accumulated cash surplus in the General Fund amounted to USD 925 945.

(233) The Executive Secretary introduced SP 5 *Secretariat Programme 2023/2024*, which outlined the activities proposed for the Secretariat in the Financial Year 2023/24 (1 April 2023 to 31 March 2024). He summarised the Secretariat's regular activities such as the preparation of ATCM 46, the publication of reports, and other tasks assigned to the Secretariat under Measure 1 (2003). The Executive Secretary noted one personnel change due to retirement and no further personnel changes foreseen in the upcoming period. With regard to financial matters, the Executive Secretary drew the Meeting's attention to global inflation and the continued rising cost of living in Argentina, which was only partially compensated by the US Dollar's rise against the Argentine Peso. The Executive Secretary proposed to increase the Secretariat's salaries by 2.9%. The Executive Secretary reported that despite the impact of local and global inflation, a budget with only a minor deficit of USD 27 920 was attained and that the contributions for the financial year 2024/25 would not rise. In terms of intersessional activities, he announced continued work with several website and information system developments and improvements. The Secretariat noted that it would continue to offer continued EIES virtual training and discussion sessions, pending the outcomes of ongoing dialogues with the Parties around improvements.

(234) The Executive Secretary introduced SP 6 *Five Year Forward Budget Profile 2024/2025 – 2028/29*, which provided the Secretariat's budget profile for the period 2024-29. He

highlighted that travel costs had been adjusted to reflect estimated rising costs at the expected locations of the next ATCMs, in particular Japan in 2026 and the Republic of Korea in 2027. He noted that minor deficits might occur for the following fiscal years, but despite local and global inflation, the accumulated surplus in the General Fund allowed for a zero-nominal increase in contributions until 2028-29.

(235) While many Parties commended the management of the Secretariat budget, Germany suggested that a cautious approach should be taken for the sustainable use of the General Fund.

(236) Acknowledging the comments of Germany, the Secretariat recalled that contributions had remained fixed in nominal values since 2014 with no expected changes till 2028. The Secretariat noted this had not affected its services, despite rising costs and global inflation. The Executive Secretary explained that the surplus in the General Fund had been used recently to cover unexpected expenses authorised by the ATCM such as the organisation of the ATCM in Buenos Aires in 2018.

(237) The Executive Secretary presented SP 9 *Developments on the ATS website related to meeting paper preparation and submission*, which described new electronic tools and resources developed by the Secretariat aiming to assist delegations in the preparation and submission of papers to the ATCM and CEP.

(238) The Meeting expressed its gratitude to the Secretariat for the support it had provided and continued to provide the ATCM. It also commended the Executive Secretary for his leadership. The Meeting thanked the Secretariat for its maintenance of zero nominal growth, which allowed contributions to remain without change until 2028/29. Parties commended the Secretariat for the EIES training sessions and, reflecting on their positive experience, encouraged other Parties to utilise this opportunity. Several Parties noted that the training sessions and the opportunity to provide feedback to the Secretariat had been fruitful. Some Parties reported that their nationals had participated in internships at the Secretariat and expressed their gratitude for this opportunity. It was noted that it would be beneficial to develop established mechanisms for internships to allow for wider participation.

(239) The Executive Secretary informed the Meeting that he had been approached by a State that was not a Party to the Antarctic Treaty or Environment Protocol concerning the potential for that State to conduct activities in Antarctica. The Meeting requested that, in the event that a State that was not a Party to the Antarctic Treaty or Environment Protocol contacted the Secretariat to notify that they expected to conduct activities in Antarctica, the Secretariat inform Parties immediately.

(240) In response to a request that the Secretariat prepare updated documents concerning the selection procedure for a new Executive Secretary, which would take place at ATCM 47 in Italy, the Executive Secretary expressed the Secretariat's willingness to do this. He noted that these documents were routinely prepared in coordination with the Depositary Government and the Host Country Government and would be distributed to Parties by ATCM 46.

(241) Following further discussion, the Meeting adopted Decision 2 (2023) *Secretariat Report, Programme and Budget* and Decision 3 (2023) *Renewal of the contract of the Secretariat's external auditor.*

Item 8: Liability

(242) Australia introduced WP 30 rev. 2 *Proposal for an Informal Intersessional Process to Share Information on Domestic Implementation of Annex VI to the Protocol on*

Environmental Protection to the Antarctic Treaty, prepared jointly with Finland, France, Germany, the Netherlands, New Zealand, Norway, Spain, Sweden, the United Kingdom and Uruguay. The paper proposed an informal intersessional process to continue the ATCM's work on evaluating progress towards Annex VI becoming effective and to exchange information on the actions Parties could take to approve Measure 1 (2005). Australia highlighted that Annex VI was an important element in supporting the Environment Protocol's objective to comprehensively protect the Antarctic environment and dependent and associated ecosystems, and underlined that its entry into force would be a milestone for the Antarctic Treaty system. It also noted that the adoption of Annex VI into national legislation would not necessarily be a straightforward process, and that there was great value in sharing the experience and expertise between Parties that had implemented Annex VI and those that had not yet done so.

(243) The Meeting thanked the co-proponents of the paper and their work with facilitating adoption of Annex VI as a matter of priority. Many Parties that had ratified Annex VI noted their willingness to share, consult and collaborate with Parties that were interested in this kind of exchange of experiences. Some Parties expressed their hope that the initiative for increased information exchange on the actions that Parties that had ratified Annex VI had taken domestically, would lead to new ratifications and eventual adoption of Annex VI. The Meeting agreed to the proposed informal intersessional process, which would be convened by Australia and conducted via the ATCM Discussion Forum.

Item 9: Biological Prospecting in Antarctica

(244) While no Working Papers were submitted under this agenda item, the Meeting agreed to keep the subject on the Agenda for ATCM 46.

(245) The following paper was submitted under this agenda item:

- BP 28 *Russian Research in Bioprospecting* (Russian Federation).

Item 10: Exchange of Information

(246) The Secretariat presented SP 8 *Review of the utilisation of the EIES*, in response to a request made by ATCM XLIV. The paper highlighted the scarce or declining use of many sections of the EIES during the past decade. The percentage of annual reports submitted had fallen from 94% to 72% in previous years. The Secretariat proposed possible causes for this decline including that: the requested data were difficult to obtain; it may have been hard to understand exactly what was being requested; the information requested may have been perceived as being of limited use or not of interest; and national Antarctic programmes may have had difficulties in assigning and training people to use the EIES. The Secretariat suggested that a different approach may be needed, comprising a focused and comprehensive revision of the current number and type of information exchange requirements. It expressed its readiness to prepare additional material, or clarify any question, for Parties to make informed decisions on this issue.

(247) The Meeting thanked the Secretariat for its efforts and expressed appreciation for its important analysis. The Meeting recalled the obligation to exchange information and reaffirmed that information sharing and transparency were fundamental aspects of the Antarctic Treaty system. In this regard, it noted that the EIES was invaluable for the Parties to share information consistent with the requirements under the Antarctic Treaty system. The Meeting also considered improvements that could be made so that the EIES was more useful and could be better used by Parties.

(248) Some Parties stated their disappointment that the information in the EIES was incomplete, and that some Parties had not made sufficient efforts to improve the provision of information in the EIES. Some Parties requested that each Party register its activities to give other Parties notice in advance and appropriately, in accordance with the ATCM discussions. Parties encouraged others to actively pursue the Secretariat`s offer to train personnel and to assist with entering information into the EIES.

(249) The Meeting underlined the importance of using existing ways to exchange information, and developing proposals for improving the utilisation of the EIES as a next step. All Parties agreed that the simplification of the EIES and provision of information was important to the Antarctic Treaty.

(250) Spain introduced WP 16 *Report of the intersessional contact group to review the Scientific Information in the Electronic Information Exchange System.* Spain recalled that ATCM XLIV had agreed to establish an ICG to improve scientific information exchange within the EIES. It suggested three minor revisions to the consolidated information exchange requirements annexed to Decision 5 (2022) to achieve this. The ICG had also recommended that the Secretariat assess the viability of preparing an Excel file as a template to complete the fields of information to facilitate the uploading process by Parties.

(251) The Meeting thanked Spain for its paper and noted that greater provision of scientific information through the EIES would assist in promoting environmental protection, education and outreach, and scientific support in Antarctica.

(252) The Meeting agreed to the three minor revisions to the consolidated information exchange requirements annexed to Decision 5 (2022), and to request the Secretariat to assess the viability of preparing an Excel file as a template to complete the fields in the EIES. The Meeting adopted Decision 4 (2023) *Updated requirements for information exchange.*

(253) The Secretariat presented SP 11 *Report on records of non-compliance with the Treaty or Protocol*, which summarised the responses of ten Consultative Parties and one Non-Consultative Party to a questionnaire on collecting evidence of non-compliance with the Antarctic Treaty or Environment Protocol, circulated to all Parties as Circular 12/2022.

(254) The Meeting thanked the Secretariat for the paper. Some Parties stated that it would be useful to better understand the questionnaire responses, noting that there were often significant differences between the evidentiary requirements of Parties. The Meeting requested that the Secretariat prepare a set of best practice guidelines for reporting non-compliant activities that could be distributed to Antarctic operators and visitors, which would include a list of national competent authorities to whom evidence of non-compliance could be submitted, to be presented to ATCM 46.

Item 11: Education Issues

(255) Bulgaria introduced WP 25 *Fourth report of the Intersessional Contact Group on Education and Outreach*, prepared jointly with Belgium, Brazil, Chile, Czechia, Finland, India, Italy, the Republic of Korea, Malaysia, Poland, Portugal, Romania, South Africa, Spain, the United Kingdom, the United States, COMNAP, IAATO and SCAR. Bulgaria recalled that ATCM XLIV had supported the continuation of the ICG on Education and Outreach and reported on the ICG's work over the past year via the ATCM Discussion Forum. Bulgaria reported that the forum had attracted 26 posts and over 600 views from 20 Parties, Observers and Experts discussing education and outreach activities they had

carried out. These included examples of education concerning EDI as well as the future development of the ICG. Highlights of the reported activities included lectures and seminars, webinars, film festivals, art exhibitions, educational materials, symposia, publications and numerous social media campaigns. The co-proponents recommended that the ATCM recognise the usefulness of the Forum on Education and Outreach and support the work of the ICG during another intersessional period. They also proposed that the ATCM discuss the possibility of organising and planning for a second workshop on education and outreach.

(256) The Meeting thanked Bulgaria and the co-proponents for their report, and commended Bulgaria for its leadership in the ICG on Education and Outreach. Many Parties emphasised the importance of education and outreach activities as an essential element of cooperation enshrined in the Antarctic Treaty and the Environment Protocol. The Meeting agreed to support the recommendations, and several Parties welcomed, in particular, the ICG's active collaboration on EDI issues, as well as its plans for organising a second workshop on education and outreach in the coming years.

(257) The Meeting agreed to continue the ICG on Education and Outreach for another intersessional period with the aim of:

- Fostering collaboration at both the national and international level, on Education and Outreach;
- Identifying key international activities/events related to education and outreach for possible engagement by the Antarctic Treaty Parties;
- Sharing results of education and outreach initiatives that demonstrate the work of Antarctic Treaty Parties in managing the Antarctic Treaty area;
- Emphasising ongoing environmental protection initiatives that had been informed by scientific observations and results, in order to reinforce the importance of the Antarctic Treaty and its Protocol on Environmental Protection;
- Promoting related education and outreach activities by Experts and Observers, and encouraging cooperation with these groups;
- Sharing best practices and encouraging, enhancing and promoting diversity and inclusion across the global Antarctic community, including among scientists, logisticians, policy-makers and all others engaged in Antarctic matters, in order to lower any barrier to the engagement of all the talents needed to tackle the challenges of the future of Antarctica;
- Encouraging Parties to provide the Secretariat with link(s) to their web page(s) with educational and outreach resources (the Secretariat would include these links in its "Educational Resources" section of the Secretariat website); and
- Inviting Parties, Observers and Experts to review, during the intersessional period on the ATCM Education and Outreach Forum, the work carried out by the ICG, discussing its future development and the possibility to organise and plan for the second Workshop on Education and Outreach.

(258) It was further agreed that:

- Observers and Experts participating in the ATCM would be invited to provide input;
- The Executive Secretary would open the ATCM Forum for the ICG and provide assistance to the ICG; and

- Bulgaria would act as convener and report to the next ATCM on the progress made in the ICG.

(259) Portugal presented IP 34 *Topics and target audiences on education and outreach activities by* the *Antarctic Treaty Parties: a review*, prepared jointly with Belgium, Bulgaria, Chile, Spain, United Kingdom and WMO. It reviewed the key topics and target audiences mentioned in papers submitted to the ATCM between 1961 and 2022 relating to education and outreach. The review found that a total of 200 papers on education and outreach had been submitted to the ATCM, of which 110 had been submitted after 2015, as opposed to a total of 90 papers in all the preceding decades together. Portugal attributed this significant growth in activity to the workshop on education and outreach at ATCM XXXVIII in Bulgaria (2015) and the subsequent discussions at the ATCM (ATCM XXXVII - WP 9). The co-proponents jointly welcomed the activity of all Parties in the field of education and outreach, and encouraged continued efforts on the matter, including on new topics such as EDI education.

(260) Portugal presented IP 36 *Report of the activities of Polar Educators International (PEI): 2012-2022*, prepared jointly with India, Italy, Poland, SCAR, United Kingdom, United States and WMO. The paper reviewed the activities of Polar Educators International (PEI), a network established during the IPY Science Conference in 2012. Portugal highlighted PEI's role as an essential body of educators and researchers with a mission to connect polar education, research and the global community to provide a broad audience with a deeper understanding of polar sciences and the polar regions. Portugal informed the Meeting that PEI continued to work in close collaboration with SCAR and other international scientific bodies and that highlights of its recent work included a number of conferences and public outreach campaigns as well as ongoing participation in compiling an updated edition of the IPY Polar Resource Book.

(261) Portugal presented IP 37 *Association of Polar Early Career Scientists (APECS): An overview of the first 15 years*, prepared jointly with Australia, Belgium, Bulgaria, Canada, France, Germany, the Netherlands, Norway, SCAR, South Africa, Türkiye, United Kingdom and WMO. The paper summarised the achievements of the Association of Polar Early Career Scientists (APECS) since its foundation during the fourth IPY in 2007-08. Portugal reported that APECS' mission was to provide a platform for early career researchers to connect internationally, and to inspire and develop them as future leaders in polar science, as well as to promote education and outreach activities. It commended the association on its work to promote EDI, the regional representativeness of its membership, and the partnerships it had forged with many different organisations. Portugal highlighted that APECS was now recognised as a major voice for early-career scientists.

(262) The Meeting thanked the proponents for IP 34, IP 36 and IP 37 and Portugal for its leadership, together with Bulgaria, on cooperation in the field of education and outreach. Several Parties expressed their support for these ongoing and future education and outreach programmes and stressed the importance of encouraging early career researchers by safeguarding their opportunities throughout the Antarctic scientific community. Some Parties also highlighted their ongoing and planned initiatives relating to early career researchers including the provision of grants, scholarships and other targeted funding.

(263) IAATO presented IP 54 *IAATO Education, Outreach and Ambassadorship*, which gave an overview of IAATO's education and outreach efforts, including its Ambassadorship Challenge and Map, and well as the introduction of IAATO's Antarctic Ambassadorship Committee and the development of its Antarctic Ambassadorship Program.

(264) The following papers were also submitted under this agenda item and taken as presented:

- IP 44 *Indian Polar Education and Outreach Endeavours* (India).
- IP 68 *Live from Antarctica: The National Science Foundation's Education and Outreach Event* (United States).
- IP 108 *Polar STEAM: An Emerging National Science Foundation Education and Outreach Initiative* (United States).
- IP 148 *Ejecución de la Mesa Redonda "Influencia de la Academia en el Desarrollo de la Investigación Antártica Latinoamericana"* (Ecuador).

(265) The following papers were also submitted under this agenda item:

- BP 3 *Education & Outreach activities of Italy in 2021/2022* (Italy).
- BP 6 *Educación antártica en la pospandemia* (Chile).
- BP 14 *Uruguay's educational activities in 2022* (Uruguay).
- BP 32 *Education & Outreach Activities of Türkiye in 2022-2023* (Türkiye).
- BP 42 *Proyecto Colombiano de Arte en la Antártida. Una mirada artística al Continente Blanco 2022-2023* (Colombia).
- BP 48 *Programa de Difusión, Arte y Cultura en la Vigésimo Sexta (XXVI) Expedición Antártica Ecuatoriana* (Ecuador).
- BP 50 *Actividades de Difusión Exposición Fotográfica "El Perú en la Antártida"* (Peru).
- BP 55 *Romanian Antarctic Education and Outreach Activities 2022-2023 in Support of WP 25* (Romania).

Item 12a: Multi-year Strategic Work Plan: Policy, Legal and Institutional priorities

(266) The Meeting considered the Multi-year Strategic Work Plan adopted at ATCM XLIV (Decision 3 (2022)) relating to policy, legal and institutional priorities. It considered how to take each priority item forward in the coming years, and whether to delete current priorities and add new priorities.

(267) The Secretariat introduced SP 10 *A review of the use of the ATCM Multi-year Strategic Work Plan (MYSWP)*, which was prepared in response to a request made by the Meeting the previous year (ATCM XLIV Final Report para 182). The paper provided a summary of the usage of the MYSWP since its establishment under Decision 3 (2012) and Decision 5 (2013), focusing on the identified priority issues and the way in which priority issues had been introduced and presented. On the basis of its findings, the Secretariat made the following suggestions on issues that the ATCM could address to enhance its performance in the future:

- Establish a procedure for the discussion and adoption of the MYSWP, to ensure that enough time be devoted annually to analysing the MYSWP and proposing changes for the following year;
- Limit the number of priority issues per year to a certain maximum, in line with principle 3 of Decision 3 (2012) Annex 1 (the MYSWP has a "limited number of priority issues");

- Determine how many years the priority issues should cover (*ie*, minimum and maximum periods of validity for a given issue), to ensure the MYSWP was dynamic and flexible (principle 6 of Decision 3 (2012) Annex 1);
- Define criteria to propose candidates for new issues; and/or
- Standardise the way priority issues were written, in order to allow evaluation of the issue's effectiveness over time.

(268) Australia introduced WP 15 rev. 2 *Proposal for an Intersessional Process to Review the Use and Maintenance of the Multi-Year Strategic Work Plan* prepared jointly with Belgium, the Netherlands, New Zealand, Norway, Sweden and the United States. Recalling that the Meeting had previously reaffirmed the usefulness of the Multi-year Strategic Work Plan (ATCM XLIV Final Report para 181), Australia considered it timely for the ATCM to review its use and functions. To this end, Australia and the co-proponents proposed that the Meeting establish an ICG to further review and support the valuable findings made by the Secretariat in SP 10. They suggested that the ICG's work would consider the Secretariat's five key findings in SP 10 along with any other improvements that might be proposed by the Parties during the intersessional period.

(269) The Meeting thanked the Secretariat for SP 10 as well as the co-authors of WP 15 rev. 2. The Meeting agreed that the MYSWP had been a useful tool since its adoption under Decision 5 (2013). Many Parties highlighted the importance of the strategic outlook that it had provided, noting that it had facilitated the ATCM to act proactively to both current and new challenges. The Meeting noted that that there was, however, potential for improvements in the form, fit and function of the MYSWP.

(270) The Meeting agreed to establish an ICG on the Multi-year Strategic Work Plan with the aim of:

- Reviewing the use and functioning of the MYSWP to date, including with reference to the issues identified in SP 10, based on its findings; and
- Identifying and discussing opportunities for improvements to support the Meeting's work for the further consideration of ATCM 46.

(271) It was further agreed that:

- Observers and Experts participating in the ATCM would be invited to provide input;
- The Executive Secretary would open the ATCM forum for the ICG and provide assistance to the ICG; and
- Australia would act as convener and report on the discussion and findings of the review to ATCM 46.

Item 12b: Multi-year Strategic Work Plan: Science, Operations and Tourism priorities

(272) The Meeting considered the Multi-year Strategic Work Plan adopted at ATCM XLIV (Decision 3 (2022)) relating to science, operations and tourism priorities. It considered how to take each priority item forward in the coming years, and whether to delete current priorities and add new priorities.

(273) Following discussion, the Meeting agreed to remove Priority 8 ("Review and discuss

issues related to increased aviation activity in Antarctica, and assess the need for additional action") and updated the Multi-year Strategic Work Plan. It adopted Decision 5 (2023) *Multi-year Strategic Work Plan for the Antarctic Treaty Consultative Meeting.*

Item 13: Safety and Operations in Antarctica

Safety and Operations: Aviation

(274) Norway introduced WP 44 *Aviation in Antarctica: Communication mechanisms to increase safety and reduce risks*, prepared jointly with Belgium, Finland, Germany, Japan, the Netherlands and Sweden. It noted that increased levels of governmental and non-governmental activity in Antarctica would lead to an increase in aviation activity, including inter- and intra-continental flights, the use of drones, helicopters and weather balloons. It highlighted that the increase in aviation activity could lead to a higher risk of accidents, incidents and near misses. Norway drew the Meeting's attention to its experiences from the Dronning Maud Land Air Network Project (DROMLAN), which administered an updated communication list for all operators and stations – both governmental and non-governmental. Norway reported that this list, together with updated email lists for intercontinental and intracontinental flights, allowed for successful near real-time sharing of information on these activities. The co-sponsors suggested that the ATCM recommend that all Antarctic operators:

1. ensure that aircraft transponders were turned on at all times in line with point 6(b) in ATCM Resolution 3 (2022);
2. encourage the establishment of regional communication groups/networks for both national and non-governmental operators to provide information in real time on all types of aviation activity including flights, helicopters, drones, and balloons, for example through an updated email list; and
3. consider how to ensure that these email lists could be made available as appropriate so that new operators, or operators flying in other regions than they normally did, could easily access the correct email lists.

(275) The Meeting thanked Norway and the co-authors of the paper for their ongoing efforts to promote safe aviation operations in the region. Noting the increase in non-governmental activities in Antarctica, Parties highlighted the value of these recommendations on information sharing for improving safety of operations as well as minimising impacts on wildlife. The Meeting also expressed its appreciation to COMNAP and its Air Operations Expert Group for its extensive work on this topic, which had allowed for information sharing in a timely manner.

(276) The Meeting agreed that the establishment of regional communication groups or networks for both national and non-governmental operators to provide information in near real time on all types of aviation activity, including flights, helicopters, drones, and balloons, was important. In relation to the example used in WP 44, some Parties noted that information shared via email lists should not be relied on to avoid conflict between aviation activities, highlighting that applicable aviation safety activities, including controlled air space, air traffic control (ATC), and radio traffic information broadcasts by aircraft (TIBA) procedures, must be followed for all activities.

(277) COMNAP welcomed the paper, highlighting that it largely reflected the outcomes of the COMNAP Antarctic Aviation Workshop 2022 reported in ATCM XLIV - IP 6. COMNAP noted that, although its members had good relations with IAATO, not all non-governmental operators were IAATO members. For this reason, COMNAP reinforced the importance of focusing efforts to improve information sharing on new actors in Antarctica and operators that did not normally operate in a particular region. COMNAP

also noted that countries that were the key "air gateways" to Antarctica played a key role in information sharing and sharing flight plans.

(278) The co-proponents welcomed the discussion, and underlined that the use of email lists was intended to be in addition to applicable aviation safety activities, and noted that email lists had proven useful to ensure that other operators could be included in the DROMLAN flight information system. They further noted that it would be useful to hear from other Parties if they had experience with the use of tools other than email lists in this respect, and underscored the importance of developing real time systems and procedures for information sharing.

(279) The Meeting endorsed the three recommendations in WP 44, stressing the importance of ensuring transponders being turned on at all times. The Meeting noted that through the COMNAP Air Operations Expert Group the issues would continue to be discussed, with COMNAP bringing updates and advice to the ATCM when necessary.

(280) Chile presented IP 19 *Intervention on the runway of the "Teniente Marsh" airfield of the "Presidente Frei" Antarctic Air Base*, which reported on planned maintenance work on the Teniente Marsh airfield. Chile notified the Meeting that this work would lead to the airfield being temporarily closed for 10 to 20 days. The maintenance intervals would be confirmed in the next month to allow for those Parties that used this facility to plan accordingly.

(281) The United Kingdom highlighted the importance of information sharing via the Antarctic Flight Information Manual (AFIM) where all Parties could review and update the latest information on the facilities and services available from Antarctic airfields. The United Kingdom noted the closure of its own runway during January and February 2023-24. The Meeting highlighted the importance of keeping other Parties informed about ongoing work on Antarctic airstrips.

(282) The following paper was also submitted under this agenda item and taken as presented:

- IP 82 *Finalizing the construction of the gravel runway in the area of Mario Zucchelli Station, Terra Nova Bay, Victoria Land, Antarctica* (Italy).

(283) The following paper was also submitted under this agenda item:

- BP 25 *Renovation of the Airfield at Progress Station to Accommodate Heavy Aircrafts with Wheel Chassis* (Russian Federation).

Safety and Operations: Maritime

(284) Argentina introduced WP 56 *Proposal for the improvement of observations of sea ice and icebergs in polar and subpolar waters for the development of nautical safety products by Ice Services*. Argentina reported that its Naval Hydrography Service (NHS) was responsible for nautical safety in NAVAREA VI, a region that included the Antarctic Peninsula, and was active in preparing ice charts and generating models and forecasts of sea ice concentration and iceberg drift. Argentina noted that other countries also generated ice charts to aid navigation in the Antarctic region. It encouraged vessel operators, both national and non-governmental, that navigated in Antarctica, and used ice charting services, to collaborate by sending photographs and information in real-time on the ice state of the sea. This would allow services to adjust and improve both charts and models. To facilitate such an exchange, the NHS had developed an ice observer's manual, software for the simple recording and reporting of observations, and training for the role of ice observer through IOC-UNESCO's Ocean Teacher Global Academy (OTGA) virtual platform. Argentina recommended that Parties: routinely observe, record and report sea ice and iceberg observations with appropriate sea ice forecasting services in order to improve navigation safety in the Antarctic Treaty area; invite their non-

governmental ship and sailboat operators to take up this practice; and promote the training of ship personnel to carry out observations of sea ice and icebergs to ensure that these activities were performed properly and in accordance with international standards.

(285) The Meeting commended Argentina for its work, noting that WP 56 promoted the Parties' common goal to improve vessel safety and reporting on ice observations in the Antarctic Treaty Area. Several Parties noted that many different organisations and services collected information on sea ice and iceberg conditions. While supporting Argentina's proposal to enhance ice observation and reporting, they emphasised the importance of avoiding the duplication of efforts or receiving contradictory information from different service providers. Some Parties also noted that a common challenge for data collection was the lack of a standard format for observations.

(286) Echoing Parties' views and experiences, IAATO reported that its operators had been asked to submit data by multiple services, which often led to diminished returns. It highlighted that a standardised format for the submission of sea ice and iceberg observations would be useful for tour operators to provide better data to ice forecasting services.

(287) Some Parties reported their participation in the International Ice Charting Working Group (IICWG), and suggested that IICWG might be an appropriate forum for sharing ice observation data among multiple programmes. COMNAP informed the Meeting that it attended annual IICWG meetings and that, this year, together with the IAATO and CCAMLR secretariats, it had provided data to IICWG on its members' vessel operation patterns.

(288) The Meeting welcomed efforts to improve the collection and coordination of real-time sea ice and iceberg data in the Antarctic Treaty Area, and encouraged Parties to continue providing this information through appropriate organisations and services. The Meeting highlighted the value in the development of a common format to provide information to ice forecasting services and a mechanism to better engage with ice forecasting services, and noted the key role COMNAP played in sharing best practice relating to this work.

(289) The United States presented IP 21 rev. 1 *Report on the Deaths of Four U.S. Citizen Tourists in Three Incidents*, prepared jointly with the Netherlands, Norway and Portugal. It reported on the death of four United States citizens in three separate incidents on tour expeditions authorised by the United States, the Netherlands and Norway during the 2022/23 season. The United States expressed its appreciation for support it had received during the ongoing investigations and thanked tour operators and IAATO for their timely notification of the incidents. The United States further emphasised the importance that tour operators should place on safety. It noted that this was the first time an American tourist had died undertaking a tourism activity in Antarctica and sincerely hoped it would be the last.

(290) In response to IP 21 rev. 1, Portugal recalled that its competent authority, the Maritime Accident Investigation and Aeronautical Meteorology Authority office, had produced a safety investigation report regarding the November 25 incident. A safety recommendation was issued to *World Explorer* Company to assess the advantages of prioritising the operational safety of the zodiacs with guests onboard, by having two crew members on board with specific functions: one skipper and one look-out. The proposed safety recommendation was accepted by the recipient. Furthermore, other actions were also taken by the passenger vessel company and by the charter on improved reaction time to similar incidents, such as having tenders ready at the embarkation deck station and providing information in a more effective manner.

(291) IAATO thanked the Antarctic community for its concern. IAATO noted that it would continue to collaborate with various governmental agencies through these ongoing

investigations, and that it was committed to sharing information amongst all stakeholders that would help increase safety in Antarctica.

(292) The Meeting extended condolences for the deaths, and agreed that Parties should encourage tour operators to make clear to their crew, staff, and passengers that undertaking any activity was inherently risky due to the climate and distance from medical assistance. The Meeting noted its interest in the results of the ongoing investigations so as to better prevent future incidents and increase human safety.

(293) Argentina presented IP 80 *MSI broadcasting of NAVAREA VI through the World Wide Navigational Warning System (WWNWS)*, which reported on the broadcasting of the NAVAREA VI National Warning. Argentina advised Parties to inform mariners and tourist operators that organise cruises to Antarctica about the availability of forms to report news affecting safety of navigation in NAVAREA VI. It also requested that mariners inform the NAVAREA VI Coordinator about anomalies and failures of warning signals or any other information they considered relevant to the broadcasting of a NAVAREA Warning.

(294) Argentina presented IP 81 *AIS AtoN installation in the Antarctic by the Argentine Republic (2011-2023 Programme)*. Argentina invited Parties to note the development of the Automatic Identification System (AIS) aid to navigation (AtoN), which had been deployed in eight Argentinian Antarctic stations for the purpose of safeguarding human life at sea and the protection of the marine environment. It also requested Parties inform mariners and tourist operators about the availability of AIS AtoN and for those operators to inform the NAVAREA VI Coordinator about any operational failures of AIS AToN, or share any other information relevant to service improvement.

(295) Chile presented IP 83 *Report on the 25th edition of the Joint Antarctic Naval Patrol between Chile and Argentina - 2022/2023*, prepared jointly with Argentina. It provided information on the activities carried out during the 25th edition of the Joint Antarctic Naval Patrol in the 2022/23 Antarctic season. The paper reported on search and rescue, salvaging, pollution monitoring, and remediation activities carried out to safeguard navigation and human life at sea, and to keep waters pollution free. Chile noted that the proponents would continue the joint patrols in the future.

(296) Bulgaria presented IP 147 *The First Operational Year of the New Bulgarian Research Vessel Sv. Sv. Kiril i Metodii (RSV 421)*, which reported on the acquisition of the first Bulgarian Antarctic research and survey vessel. Bulgaria outlined the activities conducted in the vessel's first operational year, noting that it had provided more flexibility to the Bulgarian Antarctic programme. Bulgaria reported that the vessel would sail to the South Shetland Islands again the following year and was available to assist with scientific research and logistical support. It expressed gratitude to Parties that had supported Bulgaria in its Antarctic research and logistics in the previous years.

(297) The Meeting congratulated Argentina and Chile for their continued efforts to keep this activity in place for 25 years in the Peninsula Area region, and Bulgaria, on the acquisition of its Antarctic research and survey vessel and emphasised the valuable addition it would bring to its Antarctic scientific research, operations and logistics.

(298) The IHO presented IP 15 *Report by the International Hydrographic Organization (IHO)*, which described the activities the IHO carried out in the context of Antarctica, including those related to the Hydrographic Commission of Antarctica (HCA) and the updates of its statutes to align its activities with the objectives of the ATCM. It also informed the Meeting of developments in the compilation of the second version of the International Bathymetric Chart of the Southern Ocean (IBCSO) data set. The IHO underlined that harmonised standards were of high importance. It noted that, due to climate change, unchartered areas in the polar regions caused challenges for the IHO to provide sufficient

updated maps for safe passage. It thanked IAATO for facilitating information regarding new shipping routes and encouraged Parties to share all available data. The IHO informed the Meeting about the accession of Poland, the Netherlands and Türkiye as member states, and welcomed further participants. It also reported on the proposal for a new IHO Resolution on the recognition of the existence and the limits of the Southern Ocean around Antarctica, which had been submitted by the HCA Chair. The IHO noted that it contained a cartographic report and that national positions and comments would be included in the resolution. The IHO invited Parties to participate in the next Conference of the HCA to be held in Italy in 2024.

(299) The Meeting thanked the IHO for its report, noting that the IHO's work was essential to ensuring safe navigation in Antarctica. It underlined the importance of a broad information exchange between all Parties, organisations and operators to produce high-accuracy maps of Antarctic waters.

(300) Argentina informed that in the IHO meeting it had expressed the following reservation to the IHO Resolution on the Recognition of the Southern Ocean: "Argentina considers that there are no technical grounds to support a separate reference for the area referred to as "Southern Ocean", which corresponds to the southern zones of the Indian, South Atlantic and South Pacific Oceans. Furthermore, considering the technical and consultative character of the IHO, the present resolution is not intended to provide legal advice on which any individual, Member State of the IHO or any entity may rely upon for political or legal purposes, and should not be considered as such. The statement is offered without prejudice to or limitation of the views of the IHO or any IHO Member State regarding any subject or matter."

(301) The following paper was submitted and taken as presented under this agenda item:

- IP 86 *COMNAP Search and Rescue (SAR) Workshop 5 (2023)* (COMNAP).

(302) The following papers were also submitted under this agenda item:

- BP 20 *Report on the hydrographic and beaconing works in the Antarctic* (Argentina).
- BP 23 *Fire Incident on the Research Vessel Akademik Fedorov and the Conclusions Drawn* (Russian Federation).
- BP 29 *New Research Vessel for the Russian Antarctic Expedition* (Russian Federation).
- BP 37 *The Seventh Turkish Antarctic Expedition (TAE-VII)* (Türkiye).
- BP 54 *41st Antarctic Operation (XLI OPERANTAR)* (Brazil).

Safety and Operations: Stations

(303) Norway presented IP 20 *Renewal of the Norwegian Troll Research Station, Dronning Maud Land*, which updated Parties on the future development of the Norwegian Troll Research Station. It reported that the Norwegian Government had decided to plan for a complete renewal of the station in April 2023. Norway stated that the construction would be ongoing for several seasons and the new Troll Research Station would be operational in 2030 at the earliest. Norway also stated that it would provide further information in later ATCMs and would complete a comprehensive evaluation of the construction process with a plan to submit to CEP 28 and ATCM 48.

(304) Noting the importance of the topic of the modernisation of stations in the Multi-year Strategic Work Plan, the Meeting requested that the Secretariat provide a summary of documents submitted on the modernisation of Antarctic stations from 2016 to 2023.

(305) Poland presented IP 146 *Revitalization of the A. B. Dobrowolski Polish Antarctic Station (Bunger Hills, East Antarctica)*. It detailed the inspection of the infrastructure of the Dobrowolski Station after 42 years of non-use as part of a joint visit by four Polish scientists and the 67th Russian Antarctic Expedition which started in November 2021. Poland stated that after all necessary works were completed the station would be ready to serve as a summer station for future expeditions. Poland noted that future plans for the station included installing an automatic and autonomic magnetometer and seismometer to minimise human presence in the area.

(306) The Meeting thanked Poland for its paper. Several Parties noted that, should Poland install these proposed automatic stations, it would be advisable to include them in the EIES.

(307) The United States presented IP 123 *Improving Tools for Preventing and Responding to Sexual Assault and Sexual Harassment in the U.S. Antarctic Program*, which reported on a recent assessment that concluded that sexual assault, sexual harassment, and stalking were ongoing problems for their deployers. The United States described a broad strategic effort to strengthen prevention and response tools, not only for the United States Antarctic Program, but for all research locations where work was funded by the National Science Foundation. The United States noted that it was open to engaging with other Parties on this important topic.

(308) In response to a question about whether the discussion on gender equality should be addressed under the diversity issues in Agenda Item 15 or Item 6e (General Matters), the United States confirmed that the submission of its paper to the agenda item on safety and operations was deliberate. It stressed that sexual assault and harassment related to the safety of all people working on Antarctica, and added that Parties could decide when the issue would be discussed.

(309) The Meeting thanked the United States for its paper and for drawing attention to the significant safety issue that sexual assault and harassment represented. While recognising its relevance to discussions on safety and operations, the Meeting noted that more substantive discussion would be held on this topic under Item 15.

(310) The following papers were submitted under this agenda item and taken as presented:

- IP 30 *Report on the Replacement of the Cape Shirreff Field Camp, Livingston Island, Antarctica* (United States).
- IP 125 *The Antarctic Infrastructure Recapitalization (AIR) Program: An Enduring Approach to Maintaining and Modernizing Antarctic Stations* (United States).

(311) The following papers were also submitted under this agenda item:

- BP 12 *Update of Information on the Progress of the Renovation of the Henryk Arctowski Polish Antarctic Station on King George Island, South Shetland Islands* (Poland).
- BP 13 *Campaña Antártica de Verano 2022-2023 Estación T/N Ruperto Elichiribehety (ECARE)* (Uruguay).
- BP 18 *Closing of the Arctowski Polish Antarctic Station for tourist traffic* (Poland).
- BP 26 *Use of GSM Communication Equipment to Improve the Safety of the Russian Antarctic Expedition Activities* (Russian Federation).
- BP 27 *New Building Assembly Continues at Vostok Station in the Austral Summer of 2022/2023* (Russian Federation).
- BP 44 *Equipamiento de la Sala de Mando y Control de la Estación Antártica Ecuatoriana "Pedro Vicente Maldonado" y su Utilidad* (Ecuador).

- BP 45 rev.1 *Ejecución de la XXVI Expedición Antártica Ecuatoriana (2022-2023)* (Ecuador).
- BP 47 *Remodelación de Módulo II de Servicios y Habitabilidad Durante la XXVI Expedición Antártica Ecuatoriana* (Ecuador).
- BP 52 *Removal of the Antarctic Emergency Modules (MAE)* (Brazil).
- BP 53 *Brazilian automated scientific modules in the Antarctica ice sheet CRIOSFERA 1 e 2* (Brazil).

Issues related to management of the spread of infectious diseases

(312) The United States introduced WP 3 *Surveillance and coordination for the prevention and detection of Highly Pathogenic Avian Influenza in Antarctica*, which highlighted the largest worldwide outbreak of Highly Pathogenic Avian Influenza (HPAI) and its potential introduction to Antarctica. The United States noted that it had developed and implemented procedures to detect and prevent the introduction or spread of HPAI between seabird and marine mammal colonies. It encouraged Parties to develop and implement their own procedures for preventing the introduction or spread of HPAI by their national Antarctic programmes and to share information on HPAI detections in Antarctica. It also requested that SCAR provide the CEP and ATCM with updates on the potential impacts of HPAI to native birds and mammals in Antarctica.

(313) The Meeting thanked the United States for its paper and expressed support for its recommendations. It encouraged Parties to develop and implement procedures for preventing the introduction or spread of HPAI by their national Antarctic programmes. It also encouraged Parties to share information on HPAI detections in Antarctica, including the location of the outbreak, the species, and approximate number of individuals affected, and the symptoms observed. Some Parties suggested that competent authorities could engage in further discussions via the forum on Communications among national competent authorities, located on the Secretariat website, to develop a common approach.

(314) Some Parties reported on their efforts to detect and prevent the transmission of the virus to and within Antarctica, including introducing HPAI-related measures into their Antarctic programmes and national permitting requirements. The United Kingdom referred to its IP 39, and Chile referred to its IP 122, which provided information on their procedures to prevent the introduction or spread of HPAI in Antarctica. The Republic of Korea referred to its IP 23 rev.1, which called for proactive monitoring and rapid diagnosis to detect HPAI in accordance with established protocols by WHO and the World Organisation for Animal Health (WOAH).

(315) SCAR highlighted its work with COMNAP and IAATO to continue developing practical advice to identify suspected cases of HPAI and to eliminate risk associated with direct transfer of the virus from human activity (IP 101). It reported that its Antarctic Wildlife Health Working group would continue developing practical advice on this issue and that further advice would be circulated in 2024.

(316) COMNAP and IAATO expressed their willingness to continue collaboration with SCAR's Antarctic Wildlife Health Working Group. COMNAP emphasised that HPAI was a globally reportable disease and that countries had the responsibility to report the disease if it appeared in their countries. It also noted that the disease was not identified in Antarctic species to date but that there was a high risk of introduction through natural migration of species. IAATO reported that it had developed new HPAI-related biosecurity measures in addition to its existing biosecurity procedures, and made reference to IP 51 and 52.

(317) The Meeting welcomed these updates and requested that SCAR provide CEP 26 and ATCM 46 with an update on the potential impacts of HPAI to native birds and mammals in Antarctica.

(318) The following papers were submitted under this agenda item and taken as presented:

- IP 18 *Presence of SARS-CoV-2 in waste water in Antarctica and risk assessment* (Chile).
- IP 23 rev.1 *Need for Rapid Detection of Avian Influenza Virus in Antarctic Wildlife* (Republic of Korea).
- IP 24 *Scientific and Science-related Cooperation with the Antarctic Community and Responses to COVID-19* (Republic of Korea).
- IP 39 *United Kingdom procedures for preventing the introduction or spread of Highly Pathogenic Avian Influenza in Antarctica* (United Kingdom).
- IP 101 *Heightened Risk of Avian Influenza in the Antarctic Treaty Area* (SCAR, IAATO and COMNAP).
- IP 122 *Implementation for Behavioral Protocol in Antarctica and Monitoring for the Highly Pathogenic Avian Influenza (HPAI) Virus in the Magallanes Region* (Chile).

Issues related to management of natural hazards

(319) SCAR presented IP 96 *Seismic activity and associated risk in Antarctica.* In response to the invitation by the Meeting (Resolution 7 (2021)) to present a report on seismic activity in Antarctica, the paper provided information on the causes and locations of seismic activity in Antarctica as well as associated seismic hazards. It also included an inventory of stations monitoring seismic activity and recommended ongoing support for seismic monitoring and research. SCAR informed the Meeting that it continued to work with COMNAP towards enhanced assessments of seismic risks near Antarctic research facilities, and recommended the prioritisation of a number of regions with identified seismic clusters.

(320) COMNAP presented IP 85 *Natural Hazards Awareness in Antarctica: An update on the COMNAP project,* and noted that it was an update to ATCM XLIV - WP 18. COMNAP reported that, during the intersessional period, it had invited national Antarctic programmes to include experts in a technical collaboration group to review current seismic monitoring stations, identify knowledge gaps and enhance the exchange of relevant information. COMNAP noted that it had also continued its collaboration with SCAR in identifying seismic activity and related risk in Antarctica.

(321) Spain presented IP 99 *Renovation of the Deception Island Volcanic Surveillance Network*, which highlighted Spain's activities to update and complete its volcanic surveillance network deployed in Deception Island. Noting that it had monitored seismic activities in Deception Island since 1986, Spain reported that its network of monitoring stations had now been linked so that its findings were accessible in real time from Madrid. Spain also underlined that it conducted its seismic monitoring in close collaboration with Argentina and that their relevant authorities were preparing an agreement of collaboration which would enable further sharing of seismic information and cooperation. Spain invited all Parties to share similar information and to continue to jointly establish regional surveillance networks.

(322) Argentina presented IP 130 rev. 1 *Deployment of the first permanent Argentine Volcano Monitoring Network in Deception Island*, which summarised Argentina's efforts to install its first permanent volcanic monitoring network on Deception Island. Argentina

highlighted its collaboration with Spain to jointly create a regional monitoring network, coordinate management activities, and identify and manage seismic risks on the island. Argentina also acknowledged the ongoing process of signing a MoU on the collaboration and noted that the joint monitoring activity was not only useful in terms of science and management of seismic risk in facilities, but it was also beneficial to air and naval traffic and contributed to the protection of the specially protected area in the region.

(323) The Meeting thanked the proponents for their papers and welcomed the fruitful and sustained collaboration for improving safety at Deception Island and elsewhere. It encouraged all Parties to continue discussing the management of seismic risks in Antarctic facilities. The Meeting also encouraged sharing information on their seismic monitoring activities through the EIES.

Item 14: Inspections under the Antarctic Treaty and the Environment Protocol

(324) The United Kingdom presented IP 46 *Report of Informal UK Government Inspection of Base A, Port Lockroy*, which reported on an informal United Kingdom government inspection of Base A, Port Lockroy, undertaken in February 2023. The United Kingdom noted that it periodically inspected operations that it permitted and considered that this report may be of interest to other Parties.

Item 15: Science issues, future science challenges, scientific cooperation and facilitation

Science issues and future science challenges

(325) The United States introduced WP 9 *The United States Recognizes the Emperor Penguin as a Threatened Species and Provides Additional Protection for Emperor Penguins*, which provided information about the November 2022 designation and protection of the emperor penguin as a threatened species by the United States under its Endangered Species Act. The United States highlighted that the designation was based on the best scientific, technical, and commercial information available, which included an estimate that, by 2050, the global population size would decrease by 26 to 47 percent, and that the impact of climate change on sea ice, which provided breeding habitat for the species, was the primary threat to the penguin. It pointed out that the designation provided the emperor penguin with protections in addition to those in the United States' Antarctic Conservation Act. The United States recommended that the ATCM encourage Parties to:

- note that Parties' domestic legislation may contribute to the protection of Antarctic species under threat;
- implement the draft Antarctic Specially Protected Species Action Plan for the emperor penguin, attached to ATCM XLIV-WP 34; and
- report recent research results on the status of the emperor penguin to ATCM 46 to reconsider recommending the designation of the emperor penguin as a Specially Protected Species under Annex II to the Protocol.

(326) Many Parties expressed regret that ATCM XLIV did not designate the emperor penguin as an Antarctic Specially Protected Species. Some Parties noted that they were seeking to apply protected species status to the emperor penguin in their national legislation and were using the draft Action Plan from ATCM XLIV - WP 34 as guidance to support their actions. Several Parties emphasised that the protection of the emperor penguin was a responsibility for the ATCM as a whole. Several Parties reaffirmed their view that the scientific evidence regarding the impacts of climate change on the penguins provided by

Parties, the CEP and SCAR was of a threshold high enough to designate the emperor penguin as an Antarctic Specially Protected Species at this meeting.

(327) IAATO noted that a recent routine review of its Operational Procedures for Visiting Emperor Penguin Colonies, attached to IP 51, was informed by the draft Antarctic Specially Protected Species Action Plan. It also reminded the Meeting that it had procedures in place to avoid vessel transit through fast ice in near coastal and ice shelf environments unless for safety or under appropriate permission from a national competent authority.

(328) China thanked the United States for its paper and drew attention to the scientific conclusion of the draft Antarctic Specially Protected Species Action Plan as attached to ATCM XLIV - WP 34 that, except for the projected reduction of sea ice due to climate change, other known and emerging terrestrial and marine threats affecting the emperor penguin were considered relatively small if not negligible, and that further scientific research and monitoring was needed to inform the CEP and ATCM in deciding what steps should be taken in terms of the status of the emperor penguin. China noted that Annex II of the Environment Protocol already protected the emperor penguin and that it was too early to designate the emperor penguin as an Antarctic Specially Protected Species.

(329) The Meeting expressed broad support for the recommendation that Parties note that their domestic legislation may contribute to protecting Antarctic species under threat. It also encouraged Parties to report recent research results on the status of the emperor penguin to CEP 27. Noting the recommendation to implement the draft Antarctic Specially Protected Species Action Plan for the emperor penguin, attached to ATCM XLIV - WP 34, many Parties expressed support and indicated that they would continue to take actions consistent with the draft Plan.

(330) Germany presented IP 59 *International Science & Infrastructure for Synchronous Observation (Antarctica InSync)*, prepared jointly with Australia, France, Italy, Norway, the United Kingdom and the United States. It presented a proposal for a synchronous scientific observation mission (*Antarctica InSync*) to assess the connections between ice, ocean, climate, environment and life, including human pressures. Germany explained that the preparatory phase for *Antarctica InSync* would start in 2024 with a series of workshops to identify and coordinate the activities and pan-Antarctic field missions to be carried out in the implementation phase (2027-2029). The results of *Antarctica InSync* would be reported in 2030 at the end of the international Ocean Decade, which would also contribute to the preparations of the 5th International Polar Year 2032-33. The intention was to seek the logistical contributions of all national Antarctic programmes via COMNAP. It also pointed out that the mission was planned in close collaboration with SCAR and would be registered as a thematic programme with regional focus under the UN Decade for Ocean Science for Sustainable Development, with SCAR, acting as a UN Decade Collaborative Centre (DCC) for the Southern Ocean. Germany underscored that simultaneous research, carried out by all disciplines around Antarctica with similar approaches, common methods and shared goals, had not been carried out in this region at the level proposed.

(331) The Meeting commended Germany and the co-authors for this proposal. Many Parties expressed their interest in supporting and participating in *Antarctica InSync*, noting its scale and significance, and that it promoted international cooperation and had the potential to produce an incredible set of data. The Meeting also noted that participation in the project was not restricted to nations with their own infrastructure but was open to all Parties and that higher levels of participation would lead to better results.

(332) France presented IP 74 *The Ice Memory Programme*, prepared jointly with Italy, which

provided an update on the Ice Memory Programme and addressed questions raised by Parties during CEP XXIV. It noted that the first phase of the Programme was currently underway, and involved collecting ice cores from the deep layers of key endangered glaciers before they lost their ability to preserve environmental history in optimal conditions. The second phase of the Programme would develop the long-term storage of these ice cores for future generations of scientists at Concordia Station. France emphasised that operational procedures would include safeguards to prevent any risk of non-native species contamination. Further storage at negative temperature would provide the best guarantee of preventing any release of microbial content from within the ice cores into the surrounding environment. France explained that these conditions were naturally met on the Antarctic Plateau, where Concordia Station was located, and where ambient temperature never rose above 0°C. It further noted that the carbon footprint created from storing the ice cores in Antarctica would be one third of that created by storing them in Europe.

(333) The Meeting thanked France and Italy for their paper and their responses to questions raised at ATCM XLIV. Many Parties expressed interest in supporting the project. While commending the co-authors on their visionary project, the United States noted that it could not participate due to its commitment to its own ice core storage programme to allow for accessibility to its research community.

(334) In response to concerns raised regarding the risks of non-native species introduction and logistical costs, France noted it would address those issues with any concerned Parties directly.

(335) Italy presented IP 84 *Progress of the activities of the Beyond EPICA Oldest Ice project*, prepared jointly with France, Germany, the Netherlands, Norway, Sweden and the United Kingdom. The paper provided a synthesis of ongoing activity in the Beyond EPICA project, which had several parts in common with the Ice Memory Programme (IP 74). Italy explained that the objective of the Beyond EPICA project was to extract a continuous ice core to Antarctic bedrock to obtain the longest known climate record of the planet, potentially yielding 1.5 million years' worth of greenhouse gas and climate feedback data. The project was funded by the EU Horizon 2020 framework and involved 16 scientific institutions from ten countries from within and beyond Europe. So far, the project had conducted three field campaigns and its international team had reached the depth of 800 metres, obtaining climate information from as far back as 50 000 years ago. Italy reported that part of this ice core had been processed at Concordia Station, while another part was being transferred to Europe for further analysis.

(336) The Meeting congratulated Italy and the co-proponents on the continuing success of the Beyond EPICA project and welcomed the update with enthusiasm. It noted the project's scientific importance, and that gaining access to the past record of climate conditions and climate change would provide invaluable information for ongoing efforts to model future conditions. This would provide the basis for communicating the urgency and reality of climate change to decision-makers and the general public alike.

(337) Many Parties noted their long-term support for the project and applauded the positive cooperation they had observed among the project's researchers. The paper's co-proponents also reaffirmed their commitment to continue as project participants.

(338) The following papers were submitted under this agenda item and taken as presented:

- IP 49 *SCAR Lecture: "Satellite-based science and the changing nature of what it means to "explore" Antarctica"* (SCAR).

(339) The following papers were also submitted under this agenda item:

- BP 30 *"LOSUMEA": Local Surface Energy Balance Measurements in East Antarctica* (Switzerland).

- BP 31 *Can Snow Change the Fate of Antarctic Sea Ice?* (Switzerland).

Scientific cooperation and facilitation

(340) SCAR presented IP 50 *Plans for a fifth International Polar Year 2032/33,* and reported that, since 2021, an interim planning group had been engaging in early discussions to plan for a fifth IPY in 2032-33. SCAR noted that, in addition to the International Arctic Science Committee (IASC) and SCAR, initial planning efforts were being supported by WMO, the International Science Council (ISC), the University of the Arctic, the International Arctic Social Sciences Association (IASSA), the Association of Polar Early Career Scientists (APECS) and other partners worldwide representing both poles.

(341) WMO presented IP 28 *Further Plans of the Year of Polar Prediction in the Southern Hemisphere (YOPP-SH) and Completion of the Polar Prediction Project.* It summarised recent activities undertaken in the Antarctic region as part of the WMO World Weather Research Programme's (WWRP) Polar Prediction Project (PPP), which had formally concluded in 2022 but whose activities would continue through 2023. WMO noted that the WWRP had a follow-on project approved, known as the Polar Coupled Analysis and Prediction for Services, which was expected to commence in 2024. The new project would continue research efforts in both the Arctic and Antarctic regions, with a focus on both physical and social science. WMO also noted that it had appointed a new Secretary-General, Celeste Saulo of Argentina, who was the first female in the position.

(342) The Meeting thanked SCAR and WMO for their papers and for their work preparing for a fifth IPY.

(343) Portugal presented IP 33 *Scientific use of Remotely Piloted Aircraft Systems (RPAS) in Antarctica: a review,* prepared jointly with Germany and the United Kingdom. It presented a summary of a recent comprehensive review concerning the use of RPAS for scientific activities in Antarctica. The co-sponsors noted the predicted increase in the use of RPAS for Antarctic research and encouraged: more collaborative RPAS research; continued efforts to minimise associated environmental impacts; the sharing of research data; and the regular review and update of existing policy documents and guidelines, as necessary. Portugal thanked its co-sponsors and called for enhanced international cooperation on the use of RPAS.

(344) The Republic of Korea presented IP 29 *The 4th Basic Plan for the Promotion of Research Activities in Antarctica of the Republic of Korea (2022-2026).* The Republic of Korea highlighted that the aim of the Plan was to promote research activities in the Antarctic and the Southern Ocean to contribute to the development of science and technology that would help the understanding of earth systems. It stressed that this work would reinforce its role as a Consultative Party and reiterated its work on climate change.

(345) The Republic of Korea presented IP 87 *The First Basic Plan for the Promotion of Polar Activities of the Republic of Korea (2023-2027),* which presented a five-year action plan outlining the Korean government's vision and strategy to foster research activities in Antarctica as well as the Arctic, including setting goals for scientific research, contributing to environmental protection, and nurturing experts in Polar research. The Republic of Korea stated that it planned to expand its polar programme and reiterated its commitment to being a reliable partner.

(346) Australia presented IP 88 *Update on the Australian Antarctic Strategy and 20 Year Action Plan and major initiatives,* and reported that its updated Strategy and Action Plan identified a number of activities to further strengthen opportunities for Antarctic science. Australia noted its enhanced focus on ice sheet science, global impacts of climate change

and Antarctica and the Southern Ocean's role in the global climate system. The paper highlighted new measures and reported on the progress of major initiatives including the state-of-the-art icebreaker, RSV *Nuyina*, Australia's traverse capability to support drilling for a million-year ice core, development of new marine science in the Southern Ocean and a krill research facility in Hobart. The paper additionally highlighted Australia's greater focus on environmental management in Antarctica and support for Hobart as an Antarctic gateway. Australia stated that it looked forward to discussing its new strategy and action plan with interested parties.

(347) Türkiye presented IP 136 *Ecuadorian Projects completed within the Seventh Turkish Antarctic Expedition and signing of a Memorandum of Understanding between the Scientific and Technological Research Council of Türkiye (TÜBİTAK) Marmara Research Center (MAM) Polar Research Institut (PRI) and the Oceanographic and Antarctic Institute of the Navy (INOCAR) Ecuador on Scientific Cooperation in Antarctic Research.* It described cooperation between Ecuador and Türkiye in 2022, including the signing of a MoU between its national agencies with a focus on scientific cooperation in Antarctic research. Türkiye noted that scientific and logistic collaboration enhanced the states' international cooperation and reduced their carbon footprint in Antarctica.

(348) Türkiye presented IP 142 *A Memorandum of Understanding between the Ministry of Science, Technology and Innovation of the Federative Republic of Brazil and the Scientific and Technological Research Council of Türkiye.* It provided information about the signing of a MoU between Brazil's Ministry of Science, Technology and Innovation, and Türkiye's Scientific and Technological Research Council (TÜBİTAK) to promote cooperation on polar research. Türkiye acknowledged the countries' common interest in exploring shared opportunities to address global issues for the benefit of humanity.

(349) Brazil thanked Türkiye for its paper and reaffirmed its commitment to strengthening cooperation between the two countries.

(350) Türkiye presented IP 137 *Signing of a Memorandum of Understanding and Scientific Cooperation between the Republic of Chile and Türkiye,* which provided information about the signing of a MoU between Chile and Türkiye on cooperation in polar research, and reported on Chile's scientific and educational support of a Turkish researcher to carry out field research and high-school students for education and outreach purposes in the 2022/23 season.

(351) Chile thanked Türkiye for its paper and reiterated its support for their joint scientific activities on Antarctica.

(352) The Meeting encouraged Parties to continue updating the EIES with new formal Antarctic cooperation agreements.

(353) The following papers were submitted under this agenda item and taken as presented:

- IP 47 *Summary of SCAR's Strategic Plan 2023-2028* (SCAR).
- IP 104 *Update on the Southern Ocean contribution to the United Nations Decade of Ocean Science for Sustainable Development* (SCAR), prepared jointly with Belgium, the Netherlands and WMO.
- IP 147 *The First Operational Year of the New Bulgarian Research Vessel Sv. Sv. Kiril i Metodii (RSV 421)* (Bulgaria).

(354) The following papers were also submitted under this agenda item:

- BP 1 rev. 3 *Antarctic research accomplishments acquired under cooperation between Romania and Republic of Korea 2015-2020* (Romania).
- BP 21 *The 20th Council of Managers of National Antarctic Programs (COMNAP) Symposium (2023)* (COMNAP).

- BP 33 *Scientific Cooperation between Belarus and Türkiye in Antarctica* (Türkiye).
- BP 34 *Colombian Project Completed within the Seventh Turkish Antarctic Expedition* (Colombia, Türkiye).
- BP 35 *Czechia-Türkiye Scientific and Logistical Collaboration in Antarctica* (Czechia, Türkiye).
- BP 36 *Spain-Türkiye Scientific Collaboration in Antarctica* (Spain, Türkiye).
- BP 46 *Nuevos Ejes de Investigación Antártica Implementados Desde el 2022* (Ecuador).
- BP 53 *Brazilian automated scientific modules in the Antarctica ice sheet CRIOSFERA 1 e 2* (Brazil).

Diversity issues in Antarctic science

(355) The United Kingdom introduced WP 10 *Promoting Diversity and Inclusion among Antarctic operators and expeditions*. Recalling the successful pilot of a Code of Conduct to encourage all British Antarctic operators and expeditions during the 2022/23 season to make a voluntary commitment to promote equity, diversity and inclusion (EDI) issues, the United Kingdom proposed that the ATCM consider further ways to operationalise the desire that everyone working on Antarctic matters felt safe, welcomed, respected and free from discrimination. In addition to encouraging Parties, Observers and Experts to continue to share experiences and best practices on relevant activities and initiatives regarding equity, diversity, and inclusion, the United Kingdom recommended that Parties consider developing EDI implementation plans. The United Kingdom also proposed that the ATCM's commitment to promoting EDI be reflected on the Secretariat website. It suggested that this could be achieved by including a new topic under 'About' on 'Equity, Diversity and Inclusion'. Once established, this page could be regularly updated as the ATCM continued to discuss these important issues, as well as provide links to the work of SCAR, COMNAP and others in this field.

(356) The Meeting thanked the United Kingdom for its paper and highlighted the importance of addressing and promoting EDI in Antarctica. The Meeting emphasised the need to enhance collective and national efforts to ensure that everyone working on Antarctic matters was safe, welcomed, respected and free from discrimination. Many Parties expressed broad support for the paper's recommendations.

(357) Several Parties and Observers shared their experiences in promoting and implementing EDI in their national programmes including by: working to achieve and promote gender parity; creating national institutions with a focus on gender and inclusion; recruiting women in key Antarctic management roles; drafting protocols and procedures that promote safe and equitable work environments; promoting EDI-related education and outreach; and developing EDI codes of conduct and best practices with their national programmes. Chile referred to its IP 17 on the actions implemented by the Chilean Antarctic Institute (INACH) to advance gender parity among its Antarctic staff and to offer them safe spaces, free of violence and discrimination.

(358) SCAR and COMNAP expressed their willingness to share information and best practices on EDI activities and to provide relevant links to their Secretariat websites as requested.

(359) While many Parties expressed support for the recommendation to include a new topic on EDI on the Secretariat website, the Russian Federation noted that the ATCM had not yet determined definitions or best available practices in relation to EDI. Until addition work was carried out on this matter, the Russian Federation considered it premature to include a

new topic related to EDI on the Secretariat website. In response to a suggestion that wording agreed at previous ATCMs could be used on the website instead, the Russian Federation stated that the existing system of Antarctic operations assumed safe and non-discriminatory conditions for all Antarctic researchers and that it was inappropriate to question this.

(360) Some Parties stated that, given the many ATCM papers submitted on EDI, as well as existing evidence and work undertaken by COMNAP and SCAR, it was not possible to conclude that there were no existing issues related to EDI in Antarctica.

(361) The Meeting concluded by agreeing on the recommendation to encourage Parties, Observers and Experts to continue sharing experiences and best practices on relevant EDI activities and initiatives, and consider developing EDI implementation plans. The Meeting did not reach consensus regarding the recommendation to reflect the ATCM's commitment to promoting EDI on the Secretariat website.

(362) Spain introduced WP 33 *The awareness-raising strategy on equality, diversity and inclusion addressed to the personnel participating in the Antarctic campaigns*, and noted that it had developed many legislative measures in recent years to promote EDI. In the Antarctic context, Spain had introduced an EDI training course into its mandatory training for participants of Spanish Antarctic activities. The training aimed to consolidate basic concepts related to equality, recognise and consider diversity, guarantee equal rights, responsibilities and opportunities, and facilitate the move from a legitimised inequality to a fundamental right that must be effectively guaranteed. Spain recommended that Parties incorporate similar objectives in their training courses for their Antarctic staff.

(363) The Meeting congratulated Spain for its leading example in taking action to promote EDI in its Antarctic research and operations. Many Parties echoed Spain's sentiments, and reported on their efforts to develop similar EDI policies and training programmes. The Meeting reaffirmed that tackling discrimination and related misconduct in Antarctica constituted an ongoing challenge which required sustained cooperation and action from all Parties.

(364) The Meeting supported Spain's recommendations that Parties incorporate EDI objectives in their training courses for their Antarctic staff.

(365) Ecuador presented IP 131 *Vinculación de la mujer en el Programa Técnico, Científico y Ambiental de la XXVI Expedición Antártica Ecuatoriana*. Ecuador reported that, within the review and selection process phases, the parameter relating to gender parity had been included in the selection of research projects. This allowed a broad participation from women in the Ecuadorian Antarctic campaign. Protocols of the Ecuadorian navy were also applied in cases of discrimination and harassment against women. It had resulted in a wide female participation and gender parity in the expedition.

(366) Türkiye presented IP 126 *Gender equality action plan & practices of TÜBİTAK MAM Polar Research Institute*, which reported on the gender equality action plan developed by Türkiye's scientific and Technological Research Council (TÜBİTAK). Türkiye highlighted its mandatory pre-expedition trainings, which covered gender-based violence, sexual harassment and assault, and the established procedures for reporting gender-based violence or harassment during national Antarctic expeditions.

(367) Australia presented IP 144 *Diversity and inclusion in the Australian Antarctic program*, which provided an update on ongoing work to improve diversity and inclusion in the Australian Antarctic Program. Australia's highlights from the previous year included: a new Respect and Equality Reform Council; reinforcing the obligation to prevent unacceptable behaviour and workplace harm; creating a safe reporting culture that

ensured support and no adverse consequences; facilities to support "Independent Safe Space"; additional resources to provide advice, support and incident response; raising awareness of the nature and impacts of bullying, harassment and discrimination; training for all staff in unconscious bias and bystander obligations; training for all leaders to address unacceptable behaviour and provide support; breaking down barriers to progression based on gender or background; Antarctic workplace facilities and equipment designed for safety, inclusion and respect; and international collaboration to prevent workplace harm in Antarctica.

(368) The Meeting thanked the proponents for their papers on EDI, and encouraged Parties to present their EDI plans and programmes to the next ATCM, particularly those that had not yet done so.

(369) The following papers were also submitted under this agenda item and taken as presented:

- IP 17 *Gender Perspective and Actions in the Antarctic Scientific Expedition of the Chilean Antarctic Institute* (Chile).
- IP 77 *The SCAR Equality, Diversity and Inclusion Action Group* (SCAR).
- IP 107 *Initiatives to Increase Accessibility and Inclusion in Antarctic Research* (United States).

National Programmes' main scientific activities and results

(370) The Republic of Korea presented IP 24 *Scientific and Science-related Cooperation with the Antarctic Community and Responses to COVID-19.* It reported that King Sejong Station had welcomed 120 Korean and international visitors from 31 research and expert groups during the 2022/23 summer season, and that ecosystem science was the focus of research in areas near the station. Jang Bogo Station hosted seventy scientists and experts from multiple disciplines conducting scientific research in the Ross Sea and the Northern Victoria Land. It also outlined its COVID-19 management measures, which had included vaccination, testing and quarantining prior to entering the station or into Antarctica, as well as strict managed isolation with medical care and treatment. The Republic of Korea also noted its close cooperation with many national Antarctic programmes, especially with that of New Zealand, Chile, Italy and the United States, and affirmed its interest to deepen collaboration with Parties in the Antarctic.

(371) The United States presented IP 31 rev. 1 *ASPAs 152/153: Western Bransfield Strait and Dallmann Bay: Highlights of Scientific Research Results*, which highlighted research on the unique fish populations in ASPA 152 (Western Bransfield Strait) and ASPA 153 (Dallmann Bay). Recognised as an important habitat and probable spawning grounds for several fish species, these ASPAs were established in 1991 as Sites of Special Scientific Interest to protect the dynamic fish and benthic communities there. The United States encouraged Parties to collaborate in conducting scientific activities in the region.

(372) Australia presented IP 71 *Australian Antarctic Science Program Highlights 2022-23*, which provided information on the main activities and results of Australia's Antarctic science programme in 2022-23. Australia collaborated with 23 countries during the season. Research highlights included: the retrieval of the first test ice cores from the site of the Million Year Ice Core Project; participation in the International Year of Polar Prediction in the Southern Hemisphere; the establishment of a field camp in the Bunger Hills to support the upcoming Denman Terrestrial Campaign; and fieldwork at Australia's three continental stations to support ongoing climate science, wildlife monitoring, and environmental protection and management. Development of the Australian Decadal Plan for Science and the new initiatives, East Antarctic Monitoring and Integrated Digital East Antarctica, would mean that Australia was well placed to capitalise on science enabled by the new ice-breaker RSV *Nuyina.*

(373) Japan presented IP 133 *Progress of glaciological research activities at the Dome Fuji II Camp*, which described recent field research and associated activities in the Dome Fuji area. The Japanese Antarctic Research Expedition (JARE), in collaboration with international partners had conducted field studies to locate a new drilling site for the oldest ice core in the Dome Fuji II Camp. The project was intended to directly contribute to the IPICS Oldest Ice Core Project, which stated the need for multiple ice cores, sharing the same purpose with France, Italy and Australia.

(374) Japan presented IP 134 *Japan's Antarctic Research Highlights 2022 – 23*, which outlined the various research activities carried out by Japan last year around the Syowa Station area, with particular emphasis on three major topics: the Year of Polar Prediction in the Southern Hemisphere; the Reconstruction of East Antarctic ice sheet fluctuations and rapid ice sheet melting mechanisms; and the elucidation of the mechanisms of sea ice fluctuations in the ice edge, the pack ice zone, and the fast ice.

(375) Ecuador presented IP 138 *Programa Técnico, Científico y Ambiental y la Cooperación Científica en la XXVI Expedición Antártica Ecuatoriana*, which reported on the research activities carried out by Ecuador last year around the Pedro Maldonado Station area and other Antarctic stations. Ecuador noted that such projects focused on areas of Antarctic science related to climate risks, ocean acidification, oceanographic, geological and biological characterisation, microplastics, heavy metal analysis and psychological adaptation.

(376) Ecuador presented IP 139 *Cuantificación de la Contaminación por Macro y Microplásticos en el Área de Influencia de la Estación Científica Pedro Vicente Maldonado-Isla Greenwich (2023-2025)*, which summarised a project to evaluate and quantify plastic waste in the area around Pedro Maldonado station.

(377) Ecuador presented IP 140 *Informe sobre la Modelización de Ecosistemas Antárticos con Técnicas de Machine-Learning y sus Perspectivas Futuras*. It outlined a project which applied mathematical modelling and machine-learning techniques to study the dynamics of Antarctic ecosystems near Türkiye's Scientific Research Camp on Horseshoe Island.

(378) Ecuador presented IP 143 *Exploración de Factores Bióticos y Abióticos en el Efecto de la Acidificación Oceánica sobre Calcificadores Antárticos*, which reported on a project to determine the species and ecosystem response to the natural or induced variability of physical-chemical parameters associated with ocean acidification.

(379) Canada presented IP 12 *Update on Canada's Engagement in the Antarctic*, and recalled that it had been involved in scientific research in the Antarctic for over 100 years, and that Canadian researchers had authored approximately 1500 science journal articles on Antarctic and Southern Ocean science. It highlighted four high-level themes of Canada's Antarctic Research Program Framework: State and fate of the Antarctic Ice Sheet and global sea-level rise; Antarctica in the global climate system; Antarctica as a platform for observing space weather and the universe; and anthropogenic effects on the Antarctic environment and mitigation by conservation, cold-regions technology and green infrastructure solutions. Canada recognised the need to increase scientific collaboration to address shared challenges in the Antarctic and noted that it would continue to increase its engagement with international partners and stakeholders.

(380) Canada presented IP 112 *Advancing Antarctic Research with Canadian Space Science and Technology*, which stated important contributions of the Canadian space programme that had enabled Antarctic research across a variety of priority science research areas. The paper discussed how open and available Canadian satellite data contributed to international collaboration and coordination on Antarctic research, including

environmental monitoring and climate change. It pointed out that, during Canada's 28 years of RADARSAT I and II operations, a unique set of data had been collected. It also outlined additional activities by the Canadian space programme and its potential impact on future Antarctic studies and research.

(381) Switzerland presented IP 110 *DEAIS: Changes in the Drainage Pattern of the East Antarctic Ice Sheet through Time,* which outlined the research activities of scientists from the University of Bern's Glacial Geology Research Group at the Belgian Polar Station Princess Elisabeth Antarctica. Scientists focused on the changes in the drainage of the East Antarctic Ice Sheet as a response to climate forcing and associated ice surface lowering through time. Switzerland reported that preliminary results showed that the ice masses on the high-elevated plateau and the lower elevated foreland started to separate between three and one million years ago, which suggested that, since then, the ice on the plateau and the foreland had responded differently and independently to climate changes. Switzerland thanked Belgium and Türkiye for their cooperation on this project.

(382) The following paper was submitted under this agenda item and taken as presented:

- IP 26 *First inventory of unintentional persistent organic pollutants emission in Antarctica* (Belarus).

(383) The following papers were also submitted under this agenda item:

- BP 2 *Overview of Dutch research into Antarctic tourism* (Netherlands).
- BP 4 *Resumen de la Campaña Antártica de Verano 2022-2023 del Programa Nacional Antártico de Uruguay* (Uruguay).
- BP 5 *Nuevas publicaciones del Instituto Antártico Chileno* (Chile).
- BP 10 *Malaysia's activities and achievements in Antarctic research and diplomacy* (Malaysia).
- BP 19 *Finland's research activities in the Antarctic* (Finland).
- BP 37 *The Seventh Turkish Antarctic Expedition (TAE-VII)* (Türkiye).
- BP 38 *Turkish Polar Science Workshop (2022/2023 Update)* (Türkiye).
- BP 39 *Scientific Contributions of Türkiye to Antarctic Research (2022/2023 Update)* (Türkiye).
- BP 40 *Avances del proyecto de investigación "Efecto del estrés térmico agudo sobre la diversidad y las características Funcionales de la microbiota asociada a Microspio moorei (Polychaeta; Spionidae) de la Isla Rey Jorge, Península Antártica"* (Colombia).
- BP 41 *IX Expedición* Antártica *de Colombia – IX EAC* (Colombia).
- BP 43 *Ejecución de la Mesa Redonda "Influencia de la Academia en el Desarrollo de la Investigación Antártica Latinoamericana"* (Ecuador).
- BP 49 *Implementación de Comité Científico Ecuatoriano de la Comisión para la Conservación de los Recursos Vivos Marinos Antárticos (CCE-CCVRMA)* (Ecuador).
- BP 51 *Vigésimo Novena Expedición Científica del Perú a la Antártida – ANTAR XXIX* (Peru).
- BP 54 *41st Antarctic Operation (XLI OPERANTAR)* (Brazil).

Item 16: Implications of Climate Change for Management of the Antarctic Treaty Area

(384) Papers relating to climate change were considered under agenda item 6c. Consequently, no papers were considered under this agenda item.

Item 17: Tourism and Non-Governmental Activities in the Antarctic Treaty Area, including Competent Authorities Issues

Policy and Management

(385) The Netherlands introduced WP 13 *Dedicated process for the development of a comprehensive and consistent framework for Antarctic tourism and other non-governmental activities,* prepared jointly with Belgium, Finland, France, Germany, India, New Zealand, Norway, Poland, Spain, Türkiye and the United Kingdom. It drew attention to an informal meeting of Parties and Experts, held on 8-10 March 2023 in Paris, France, on a strategic vision and policy programme for Antarctic tourism (IP 11), following the previous informal meeting held in Rotterdam in 2019. The Netherlands stated that the concerns associated with the growth, diversification and compliance in relation to Antarctic tourism and other non-governmental activities could not all be solved by industry and national competent authorities. The proponents indicated that a dedicated negotiation process was required to move away from the current piecemeal approach and move towards a more comprehensive and consistent framework for the management of tourism at the international level that was in line with the values and principles of the Antarctic Treaty system. The proponents suggested that a series of Antarctic Treaty Special Consultative Meetings be held to develop a comprehensive and consistent framework for the management of tourism and other non-governmental activities in Antarctica.

(386) The Meeting thanked the proponents for the paper. Participants expressed gratitude to France and the Netherlands for organising the informal workshop and noted the broad participation it had attracted.

(387) The Meeting noted the resumption of rapid growth in visitor numbers following the global pandemic, the continued diversification of tourism activities, and spatial expansion. In light of these trends, many Parties raised concerns over the possibility that cumulative impacts overall could be more than minor or transitory, noted that ensuring safety was critical, and encouraged urgency in acting on these issues. It was also noted that it was important for Parties who had not yet ratified Measure 4 (2004) and Measure 15 (2009) to do so as soon as possible so that they could come into effect.

(388) While acknowledging the suite of existing agreements, measures, resolutions, and guidelines applicable to tourism and non-governmental activities, including the Environment Protocol, Measure 4 (2004), Measure 15 (2009) and Resolution 7 (2009), and that this had allowed mitigation of the impacts of tourism, many Parties noted the lack of a holistic approach to tourism management and regulation, and expressed concern that a piecemeal approach to managing tourism issues was no longer sufficient. Many Parties noted the benefits of a coordinated and strategic approach to building a framework, and supported the recommendations of the Working Paper. Parties noted that the proposed process would provide the opportunity to consider the full suite of issues and challenges in a holistic way. Some Parties noted that discussions should be underpinned by information, and a pragmatic and precautionary approach.

(389) Several Parties suggested that the five building blocks mentioned in WP 13 – namely managing growth and diversification, monitoring, compliance and enforcement, and

overall governance – could be used to guide further discussions. Parties also highlighted: the need for more data related to the trends in tourism; a need for better cooperation between national and non-governmental activities; the challenges associated with relying heavily on self-regulation by the tourism industry; issues arising from specific activities including air supported land-based tourism; the need to consider trends in relation to other human activities in Antarctica, including those of national Antarctic programmes; and the benefits arising from Antarctic tourism, including the education of visitors, and the creation of ambassadors for Antarctica. ASOC and IUCN thanked the co-sponsors of WP 13 and supported the development of a framework for the management of tourism to ensure that it was consistent with Antarctic values, now and in the long term.

(390) A number of delegations noted the benefits of organising the proposed focused discussions in the framework of the regular ATCM, including to help ensure equity of participation, as well as participation by the ATCM's Observer and Expert organisations.

(391) Suggestions were made for informal virtual or hybrid intersessional workshops, which may be organised by Parties in advance to support the preparation of the proposed first meeting, and for Consultative Parties to develop and exchange proposals in advance. Some concerns were raised relating to the format of intersessional workshops, arising from differences in time zones and limited staffing, which could affect how a hybrid or virtual workshop would work.

(392) The Meeting agreed to organise an intensive dedicated process to discuss the development of a comprehensive and consistent framework for the regulation of tourism and other non-governmental activities in Antarctica, and decided to convene a special working group of the ATCM that would have its first meeting of two days at ATCM 46. The Meeting observed that ideally the special working group should not conflict with other sessions of the ATCM and CEP. The Meeting agreed that the special working group would be temporary, and its work might take a number of years in light of its aim to develop a comprehensive and consistent framework for the regulation of tourism and other non-governmental activities in Antarctica. The Meeting encouraged Parties to take into account the great difficulties posed by the limited capacity and different time zones of Parties before they proposed to organise a workshop or other preparatory events.

(393) The Meeting adopted Decision 6 (2023) *Dedicated process for the development of a comprehensive and consistent framework for Antarctic tourism and other non-governmental activities.*

(394) The Netherlands introduced WP 4 *Infrastructure supporting tourism and other non-governmental activities in Antarctica.* It recalled that ATCM XLIV had agreed to continue the ICG on permanent facilities for tourism and other non-governmental activities in Antarctica. The Netherlands, as Convener, reported that the ICG had developed an inventory of existing permanent and semi-permanent infrastructure currently used or co-used for tourism and other non-governmental activities, and had exchanged views on possible concerns relating to such facilities, including: cumulative impacts on ecosystems and wilderness values; a lack of spatial planning to prevent expansion of infrastructure; risks of negative effects on scientific research and scientific values of Antarctica; the potential assertion of property rights and related concepts; the complexity of ownership structures and related questions, for instance in relation to liability; increasing air traffic and related emissions; and concerns about search and rescue responses.

(395) The Netherlands proposed that the ATCM update the Multi-Year Strategic Work Plan with a number of related priority issues, and adopt a Resolution on infrastructure for tourism and other non-governmental activities in Antarctica. The proposed Resolution would establish, through information exchanged by the Parties using the EIES, a

repository of information about infrastructure supporting tourism and other non-governmental activities in Antarctica, with a publicly available summarised report. The Resolution would also recommend that Parties make every effort to prevent, and not authorise, permit or approve for the expansion of tourism and other non-governmental activities:

- new situations in which research stations allow co-use for tourism and other non-governmental activities;
- increase in size or capacity of existing permanent infrastructure for tourism or other non-governmental activities;
- the establishment of new semi-permanent and temporary infrastructure for tourism or other non-governmental activities.

(396) In addition, the Resolution would recommend that Parties, for existing permanent infrastructure, consider setting a maximum ratio of national Antarctic programme staff to tourists, and not allow further expansion of co-use for tourism and other non-governmental activities; and that Parties, when establishing or authorising new facilities for logistical scientific support, would clearly indicate as early as possible in the process whether co-use for tourism and/or other non-governmental activities was considered appropriate and, if applicable, to identify a limit to the level of such co-use.

(397) The Meeting thanked the Netherlands for its paper and for convening the ICG discussions. Many Parties expressed the desirability of addressing issues related to infrastructure supporting tourism and other non-governmental activities in Antarctica. Several Parties highlighted that the proposed recommendations could promote transparency related to tourist activities and infrastructure, noted that they were consistent with the objective of preventing tourism from having more than a minor or transitory impact, and emphasised the importance of following a precautionary approach. Although some Parties agreed with the idea to work on an inventory, they did not agree with the rest of the proposal.

(398) The Meeting discussed the proposal to include several items as priorities in the Multi-Year Strategic Work Plan, but did not decide to do so at this point. In relation to one item, it was suggested that Resolution 3 (2022) *Air Safety in Antarctica* had been adopted following complex discussions, and that it was not timely to reopen debates related to air traffic. Work already underway or planned, including COMNAP's upcoming fifth workshop on search and rescue, was also noted.

(399) The Meeting supported the use of information exchange to share information related to infrastructure used for tourism and non-governmental purposes in Antarctica, but a number of issues were raised concerning how this could be done in a simple and clear manner, and without creating burdensome reporting requirements. Suggestions were made about further defining types and characteristics of infrastructure, including capacity and dimensions. Some Parties also noted that the use of the EIES was decreasing, and reminded Parties of their responsibility to submit and update information to the EIES.

(400) There was a suggestion that inspections under the Antarctic Treaty and Environment Protocol could also provide relevant information on infrastructure used for these purposes, noting Resolution 3 (2010) which supported Parties in conducting inspections by providing checklists. Some Parties referred to the role of environmental impact assessment processes conducted under Annex I of the Protocol as the specific tools to address infrastructure in Antarctica.

(401) It was noted that it would be undesirable to duplicate the efforts of COMNAP with regard to collating and presenting information about Antarctic facilities. Some Parties also suggested that more discussion was needed to understand the intent of establishing ratios of national Antarctic programme staff to tourists. It was also suggested that because

Resolution 5 (2022) dealt with issues relating to permanent infrastructure used exclusively for tourism purposes, that it would not be advisable to return to these discussions at this stage.

(402) Some Parties noted that some infrastructure use for tourism and non-governmental purposes, for example station visits, contributed to education and understanding among visitors. Some Parties also noted that it would be undesirable to prevent investment in facilities with lower environmental impacts, such as temporary facilities, by unduly constraining such infrastructure, as this might result in activities with more significant impacts being pursued.

(403) IAATO reaffirmed that its members were not interested in promoting or constructing permanent infrastructures in Antarctica. It noted that the establishment of permanent facilities in Antarctica would conflict with IAATO's by-laws and would threaten the wilderness and aesthetic values that motivated many tourists to visit Antarctica.

(404) ASOC welcomed the proposal in WP 4 as a first step, noting that a common approach to the infrastructure issue across Parties was critical, and encouraged further discussion on semi-permanent infrastructure, and the use of research stations for tourism and non-governmental purposes.

(405) The Netherlands expressed its respect for the position of every Party. It also expressed disappointment that substantial decision-making had not been possible through the adoption of the proposed Resolution. The Netherlands reiterated its view that tourism was an urgent issue, and noted that it looked forward to further cooperation on the matter.

(406) Many Parties expressed disappointment that consensus on the draft Resolution could not be reached. Recalling Resolution 7 (2009), Parties highlighted that tourism should not be allowed to contribute to long-term degradation of the Antarctic environment. They noted the importance of developing a comprehensive and consistent framework, whilst at the same time ensuring the adoption of Measures on the basis of a precautionary approach, as appropriate, as well as utilising all means and instruments available in the Protocol and the Antarctic Treaty system. They also highlighted that all appropriate tools should be used for effective management of Antarctic tourism.

(407) The Meeting agreed to keep these issues under consideration, and encouraged interested Parties to work together and bring forward proposals at a future meeting as relevant.

(408) France introduced WP 19 *Urgent measures to be taken with respect to certain tourist and non-governmental activities*, and referred to IP 11 *Workshop "The future of Antarctic tourism: towards a strategic vision and policy program", 8-10 March 2023, Paris – Chair's report*, both of which were prepared jointly with the Netherlands. In light of rapid change in Antarctica and in Antarctic tourism activities France emphasised the need to act quickly to address urgent issues associated with tourism in Antarctica, such as those related to specific tourism activities. France noted that the proposal was parallel to the proposal in WP 13, and that the intention was to take urgent action on these issues in the short term, while longer term discussions were underway. The paper proposed a Resolution to recommend that Parties require operators to refrain from activities of four types: overnight camping in the 20 most visited sites; any off-ship activities from vessels carrying more than 500 passengers; using helicopters or motorised land vehicles (except for emergencies or enhancing human safety); and landing at sites not covered by ATCM or IAATO site specific guidelines and visits to sites that have never been visited by tourism or non-governmental activities.

(409) France stated that the Resolution would make it easier to ensure compliance with Antarctic Treaty System rules, provide homogeneity across competent authorities in how they deal with such activities as well as provide them with guidance and support in the

conduct of their national processes under Annex 1 of the Environment Protocol, and address impacts of human activities for areas under other pressures such as loss of sea ice. France also stated that in its view, the Resolution should not impact the activities of responsible operators, but simply prevent certain potentially undesirable trends.

(410) The Netherlands, as co-sponsor of the paper, emphasised that the aim of the proposal was to take concrete steps and respond to the sense of urgency shared by all. While noting that tourism could be good for creating awareness of the values of Antarctica, the Netherlands highlighted that Parties should ensure that it had no more than a minor or transitory impact on the Antarctic environment. It pointed out that helicopter flights had impacts including noise and emissions including black carbon, and were allowing operators to access remote areas, making them more accessible and posing new challenges.

(411) The Meeting thanked France and the Netherlands for their paper. Several Parties expressed support for the proposed Resolution and underlined the need to take immediate action and a precautionary approach. Some Parties particularly welcomed the proposal to restrict helicopters and motorised vehicles for recreational purposes.

(412) Several Parties suggested that some issues in the proposal required further discussion. Some Parties noted that EIAs were particularly important in relation to authorising tourist activities and should be conducted in a rigorous manner. In relation to overnight camping, it was noted that some of the twenty most visited sites were regarded as suitable for short overnight stay activities, as reflected in their site guidelines, and that encouraging such activities to occur elsewhere may have undesirable effects. Some Parties regarded overnight camping as adequately addressed by existing guidelines and EIA processes, with a site-by-site approach being preferable. In reference to discouraging use of motorised vehicles, it was noted that this might encourage use of aircraft as an alternative, which might have a greater impact.

(413) Referring to its IP 145, the United States noted that it was aware of interest in activities that would circumvent the prohibition on landing of passengers from vessels carrying more than 500 passengers contained in Measure 15 (2009), and supported the adoption of a Resolution that would reinforce the intent of Measure 15 (2009) to ensure such vessels conducted cruise-only activities.

(414) The Meeting adopted Resolution 4 (2023) *Urgent measures to be taken with respect to certain tourist and non-governmental activities.*

(415) The Co-Chair of Working Group 2, Dr Phillip Tracey (Australia), presented IP 91 *Competent authorities discussion forum on tourism regulatory activities: report by the convener*, recalling that ATCM XLII established a permanent web-based forum for national competent authorities to discuss tourism regulatory activities and exchange knowledge and experience. It reported on discussions during the intersessional period. Australia encouraged Parties to invite their competent authorities to participate in the forum.

(416) The United States presented IP 145 *Preventing a Potential Circumvention of Measure 15 (2009).* It noted that an operator had sought guidance on potential activities that appeared to be designed to circumvent the restrictions contained in Measure 15 (2009), which prohibited tour operators from making landings in Antarctica from vessels carrying more than 500 passengers. Advice had been sought on a proposal to transfer passengers to a smaller vessel not subject to that restriction, or other similar options. The United States noted that it strongly discouraged this potential circumvention, and encouraged Parties to consider the possibility of circumvention when reviewing operators' proposed expeditions to the Treaty Area and to act to support the provisions and intent of Measure 15 (2009).

(417) The Meeting thanked the United States for the information provided in its paper.

(418) Highlighting the importance of complying with Measure 15 (2009), IAATO remarked that it would raise the issue of this potential interest in circumventing aspects of Measure 15 (2009) with its members.

(419) ASOC presented IP 116 *Slow Antarctic Tourism* which, building on its comments at ATCM XLIV, introduced the term and concept of 'slow tourism' and discussed how it could be applied to Antarctica. ASOC stated that Antarctic tourism needed to slow down to remain viable and that such a slowdown could be achieved without adversely impacting the tourism industry. The paper presented potential ways forward that resonated with current policy discussions around new paradigms and a comprehensive framework for Antarctic tourism, and ASOC underlined that slow tourism comprised one component of the latter. It noted that this would be in addition to further components that should be considered in the planned focused discussion of a consistent and comprehensive framework, including encouraging low-impact modalities of tourism, ensuring consistent assessment of tourism activities, developing dedicated programmes for monitoring of tourism impacts, expanding area protection under Annex V, and evaluating the effectiveness of existing tourism regulation.

(420) Several participants thanked ASOC, and it was noted that the concept of slow tourism had been raised in the Paris informal tourism workshop in March 2023 and had inspired some of the discussions (reported in IP 11).

Information, activities and trends

(421) Norway introduced WP 34 *More data needed to manage air-supported land-based tourism*. Norway noted that the focus of ATCM discussions on tourism management had predominantly, and understandably, focused on cruise tourism. Norway highlighted that, because air-supported land-based activities seemed to be increasing, information was also required for Parties to assess and understand trends and changes in air-supported land-based tourism. Underscoring that a lack of information impaired the ability to consider management needs, Norway proposed that the ATCM agree to develop mechanisms for standardised post-visit reporting for air-supported land-based tourism and non-governmental activities, using information exchange and post visit reports. Norway noted that IAATO was engaged in developing post visit reports for these activities for its member deep field operators, and noted the value of engagement with IAATO in advancing this work.

(422) Some Parties noted that some land-based tourism operations contributed to support of National Antarctic Programme activities, and, in addition to having their own contingency plans and SAR capabilities, contributed to broader SAR resilience. The diversity of such activities was recognised, including established operators through to smaller independent expeditions. Additional sources of information on these activities were noted, including information derived from EIA processes, and information from aviation authorities. The value of collecting information of this type for understanding greenhouse gas emissions was also raised.

(423) The Meeting welcomed WP 34, and noting the specific challenges and characteristics of these activities, thanked Norway for focusing attention on the need for improved information collection and exchange. The Meeting noted the importance of carefully identifying and specifying information exchange requirements, with clear formats for data entry into the EIES. The Meeting agreed with Norway's recommendations to move toward standardised information exchange for air-supported land-based tourism, and welcomed Norway's offer to work intersessionally with interested Parties and IAATO, and in coordination with the Secretariat, on a standardised post visit report and additions

to the information exchange requirements, and to bring a proposal to a future meeting. Several Parties expressed their interest to engage in intersessional discussions.

(424) IAATO indicated its willingness to contribute to discussions and help inform Parties about IAATO deep field and air operator activities. IAATO noted that it had developed a separate deep field section of the IAATO database, and that this project had included a new specific post visit report which could be shared with Parties. It noted that it would be possible to arrange for data on its member activities to be exported in a format that would assist operators and Parties in providing information to the EIES, as was the case for information on vessel-based activities.

(425) ASOC thanked Norway and, noting that there were some gaps in knowledge about these activities which could be a potential source of impacts, welcomed the progress on this issue.

(426) The United Kingdom introduced WP 41 *Monitoring the impacts of human activity in Antarctica*, which summarised some of the programmes the United Kingdom had undertaken or supported that provided data relevant to the monitoring of human impacts. The United Kingdom described the result of a project to test the utility of satellite imagery for monitoring human impacts at some of the most visited tourist sites. It stated that satellite imagery had so far only been partially successful in monitoring human impacts. It further noted that it was considering continuing projects to assess the use of RPAS imagery to monitor human impacts at highly-visited tourist sites.

(427) The Meeting thanked the United Kingdom and expressed its support for the recommendations set out in the paper, and some Parties noted their own positive experiences with use of RPAS for similar monitoring work. It noted the value of monitoring efforts by Parties and other bodies, and highlighted the utility of data on human impacts for improved tourism management. The Meeting also noted the value of new technologies that could improve the understanding of human impacts associated with tourist activities and the value of complementing the use of remote monitoring techniques with those that were applied in the field. It was noted that some potential impacts, for example on soil microbiology, or compaction impacts, were important, and required additional techniques. The Meeting encouraged Parties to continue to provide information about work relevant to monitoring human impacts.

(428) IAATO noted that its members had supported several of the monitoring programmes the United Kingdom had undertaken, either by carrying researchers in the field for data collection or by providing logistical assistance.

(429) ASOC welcomed the paper and supported the recommendations, noting the importance of monitoring and that the identification of information gaps would be important in future discussions. ASOC encouraged monitoring specifically for tourism impacts, including cumulative impacts.

(430) The United Kingdom presented IP 40 *Data Collection and Reporting on Yachting Activity in Antarctica in 2022-23*, prepared jointly with Argentina, Chile, the United States and IAATO. The paper presented consolidated information relating to yachts sighted in Antarctica, or that indicated an intention to travel to Antarctica during the 2022/23 season. The United Kingdom noted that it had been presenting this paper annually for several years, in part because the information had not been collected through the EIES. It called attention in particular to Table 3 in the paper, which listed eight yachts that appeared to have visited Antarctica without authorisation from a Treaty Party. Noting that this number of unauthorised yacht visits had been fairly consistent across several years, the United Kingdom urged the ATCM to consider the matter of unauthorised yachts.

(431) The Meeting thanked the proponents for their paper and for highlighting the specific issue of unauthorised yachts. Noting that this was an ongoing issue, the Meeting acknowledged that it could be valuable to consider how to pursue this concern in future meetings. Some Parties further indicated that they would discuss specific yachting activities reported in the paper with the paper's proponents.

(432) IAATO noted that it continued to see several unauthorised vessels on the Antarctic Peninsula, including those that had already been identified by competent authorities as bad actors, some of which were having more than a minor or transitory impact on the environment. It expressed that it understood that competent authorities encountered difficulties in penalising these vessels, but highlighted that the presence of these vessels undermined Antarctic Treaty processes and intentions and set a poor example for responsible operators who complied with authorisation requirements. IAATO affirmed that it remained committed to reporting on yacht activity, and that it would continue to share ATCM and IAATO guidelines with non-IAATO yachts.

(433) IAATO presented IP 56 *IAATO Vessel Overview of Antarctic Tourism: The 2021-22 Season, and Preliminary Estimates for 2022-23*. In addition to historical data around visitors and activities, IAATO provided data compiled from Post Visit Reports for the 2022/23 season and noted that the numbers reflected only those travelling with IAATO operator companies. IAATO reported that the overall number of visitors in 2022/23 was 104,076, which reflected a return to pre-pandemic levels, though it noted that this was partly a result of operators fulfilling previously-made contracts that had been postponed by the pandemic. IAATO's estimates for 2023/24 indicated that passenger numbers would rise to approximately 78,232 passengers making landings, and that there would be 39,140 passengers travelling on cruise-only vessels. IAATO emphasised that all IAATO member and operator activities were planned to have no more than a minor or transitory impact on the Antarctic environment.

(434) IAATO presented IP 57 *IAATO Deep Field and Air Overview of Antarctic Tourism: 2022-23 Season and Preliminary Estimates for 2023-24 Season*. In addition to historical data around visitors and activities, IAATO provided data compiled from post visit reports for the 2022/23 season for those travelling with IAATO Operator companies, comprising four deep field and air operators, and one air-cruise operator also offering short expeditions in the South Shetland Islands. Activities by these operators generally had a high guide to client ratio. IAATO reported that the overall number of visitors in 2022/23 was 821. IAATO's estimates for 2023/24 indicated that passenger numbers would be approximately 717. IAATO noted that the information in IP 57 was intended to support discussion of air-supported land-based tourism activities, and growth and diversification. IAATO noted that all deep field and air-borne operators had received authorisation from their national competent authorities and followed relevant ATCM, COMNAP and IAATO guidelines. Activities were planned to have a no more than minor or transitory impact, and had contingency plans in place consistent with Measure 4 (2004). IAATO highlighted that like ship-based tourism, there had been a resumption of standard levels of activity in the 2022/23 season. IAATO reiterated its commitment to continue providing information on deep field and air activities.

(435) IAATO presented IP 51 *IAATO Operational Procedures for responsible wildlife watching – An update*, which provided information about recent updates to its operational procedures for responsible wildlife watching in Antarctica. These were reviewed routinely by relevant committees and working groups within IAATO in consultation with outside experts and some national competent authorities. IAATO also noted that overarching obligations for responsible wildlife watching, derived from ATCM and IAATO requirements, had been created for IAATO Operators. IAATO welcomed input from Parties and national competent authorities. These procedures were available in

IAATO's field operations manual, which was available to national competent authorities on request.

(436) IAATO presented IP 52 *IAATO Deep Field and Air Operations Biosecurity Procedures – An update*. It reported that IAATO deep field operators had implemented procedures tailored to their activities, following tools provided by COMNAP and SCAR for many years. Existing practices had been collated into a single procedural document specific to IAATO deep field and air operations to ensure consistent application. This document had been formally adopted by IAATO, having been trialled successfully during the 2022/23 season. Referring to its IP 101, IAATO expressed gratitude for having been involved in discussions on highly pathogenic avian influenza (HPAI) and noted that air and deep field post visit reports would be supplemented to appropriately account for the threat of HPAI.

(437) The Meeting thanked IAATO for its valuable papers and acknowledged the importance of receiving updates on activities and forecasts from the tourism industry. The Meeting also noted that the information provided was useful to both the CEP and the ATCM.

(438) Germany presented IP 62 *Tourism monitoring in Antarctica – Report on the progress in developing a concept for the analysis of the impacts of tourism on the assets to be protected in the Antarctic*. Since not enough was known about the long-term and cumulative impacts of tourism, and little was known of the effectiveness of current tourism management, Germany had initiated this research project in 2021 and provided an update on it to develop a comprehensive monitoring concept to investigate and monitor the environmental impacts of tourism in Antarctica. Germany noted that the draft monitoring concept would be further discussed at a workshop in October 2023, the outputs of which would include the development of criteria for prioritising the impacts that should be monitored. Germany welcomed all Parties, stakeholders and other interested groups to participate in the project.

(439) France presented IP 105 *Feedback on the monitoring on board tourist vessels conducted during the 2022 / 2023 season,* prepared jointly with New Zealand and IAATO. The paper provided information on a joint monitoring carried out by France and IAATO, on board *Le Commandant Charcot*, from the company Ponant. The observer was from France's national competent authority and conducted the monitoring in accordance with Resolution 9 (2021), and also carried out an observation under IAATO's mandatory observation scheme. France and New Zealand cooperated on a separate joint monitoring exercise, on a voyage of *Le Commandant Charcot*, in which a New Zealand-appointed observer conducted monitoring in accordance with Resolution 9 (2021) and reported to both France and New Zealand. France reported that these activities resulted in the identification of a range of benefits and challenges, including in implementing Resolution 9 (2021) at the international level, and called on Parties to join this international effort.

(440) New Zealand noted that it had welcomed the opportunity to collaborate with France under the terms of Resolution 9 (2021), and that the activity, part of New Zealand's long-standing Antarctic observer programme, had been a mutually beneficial collaboration.

(441) IAATO welcomed its collaboration with France, which had resulted in a valuable exchange of lessons which would contribute to the robustness of its observer scheme. IAATO noted that 25 dockside and onboard inspections had been conducted under its mandatory scheme in 2022/23, and that 32 were planned for 2023/24. Each inspection required considerable advance planning between the IAATO Secretariat, the vessel and the observer. IAATO noted a number of successful dual observations, where a national competent authority observer also conducted an IAATO observation.

(442) Germany referred to IAATO's observer scheme, and thanked IAATO for its assistance

in coordination of German participation in dual observations of German permitted vessels. Germany noted the additional importance of observations occurring in the language spoken onboard the vessel.

(443) Argentina introduced IP 106 *Report on Antarctic tourist flows and cruise ships operating in Ushuaia during the 2022/2023 Austral summer season*, which provided information on flows of passengers and vessels visiting Antarctica through the port of Ushuaia in 2022/23. The paper updated information provided by Argentina since 2009, in support of discussions of Antarctic tourism in the ATCM. Argentina highlighted that the information included number of voyages, passengers, areas visited, and registry of vessels, and drew attention to the increases in these metrics following compared with pre-COVID figures, noting that the total number of passengers that had visited Antarctica via the port of Ushuaia had increased by 40 % and that the voyages through this port had increased by 29 %.

(444) Argentina presented IP 109 *Antarctic tourism through Ushuaia: Comparative data from fifteen seasons*. Argentina provided an analysis of trends in Antarctic tourism use of the port of Ushuaia over a 15-year period (2009-23). Variations in total numbers of passengers and voyages, visitors, number of vessels and length of the Antarctic visit season were analysed.

(445) Parties welcomed the provision of information by Argentina on this topic over fifteen years, which contributed valuable data to inform discussions in the ATCM.

(446) IAATO thanked Argentina for the paper, and noted that it welcomed the close collaboration between IAATO, Ushuaia and all Antarctic gateway cities, and extended its willingness to communicate and cooperate with all Antarctic gateways.

(447) Spain introduced IP 135 *Monitorización de embarcaciones turísticas y no gubernamentales en el entorno de la Isla Decepción*. The paper presented the results of a study of movements of tourism vessels in Deception Island in 2018/19 and 2019/20, drawing on both land-based records and satellite information. Spain noted that Automatic Identification Systems (AIS) offered the opportunity to identify vessels. For tourism vessels the information provided in the EIES was found to be adequate, but for yachts there were discrepancies. Spain suggested the appropriateness of establishing a network of receiving stations of Class A AIS in the Peninsula region to contribute to a better understanding of the spatial and temporal patterns of tourism and non-governmental vessel activities, and planned to bring a proposal forward to ATCM 46. Spain invited interested Parties to join in these efforts.

(448) IAATO noted that issues with AIS use by some yachts were a concern for IAATO members, and that its yacht committee had provided advice on AIS use. It noted that many yachts use AIS type B which was low powered, could be blocked by terrain and did not operate over long distances. Further, some flag states only required AIS that received a signal, without transmitting. These issues were of interest to IMO and to flag states, in addition to the ATCM and IAATO.

(449) The Secretariat presented SP 12 *Summary of non-IAATO vessel activities during 2021-22*. Following a request of ATCM XLIV, the report was prepared summarising information on activities carried out by non-IAATO vessels as reported by Parties in the EIES, as part of their Annual Report 2021/22 on Non-Governmental Expeditions: Vessel-Based Operations. The summary noted that: of the 56 vessels reported, 34% were operated by non-IAATO members; Parties reported 225 voyages of non-governmental vessels in the 2021/22 season, 13% of which corresponded to non-IAATO operators; and that of the 21,761 passengers transported by non-governmental operators, eight vessels operated by non-IAATO members transported 170 passengers. The paper noted that 11 of the 15 vessels without passenger information were reported to be non-IAATO

members and that there were possible inaccuracies in the data reported, which resulted from the Parties' different levels of reporting to the EIES. The Secretariat thanked IAATO for some of the information provided to prepare this summary.

(450) The Meeting thanked the Secretariat for its comprehensive summary report on non-governmental activities, noting a suggestion that the Secretariat might consider providing an updated report in the future.

(451) In response to a question about the reliability of the data presented due to potential incomplete information-sharing by Parties through the EIES, the Secretariat noted that, while the information could not be considered an exact reflection of what happened on the ground, due to the above-mentioned discrepancies, the content presented in the document could provide a reasonable explanation of activities.

(452) ASOC noted that some of the vessels, although non-governmental, were not engaged in tourism and their operators would have no reason to become members of IAATO. ASOC considered that linking all operators together obscured the picture of tourism activity in Antarctica and suggested identifying, whenever possible, whether the vessels engaged in commercial tourism activity or not.

(453) The following papers were submitted under this agenda item and taken as presented:

- IP 53 *A Five-Year Overview and 2022-23 Season Report on IAATO Operator Use of Antarctic Peninsula Landing Sites and ATCM Visitor Site Guidelines* (IAATO).
- IP 55 *Report of the International Association of Antarctica Tour Operators 2022-23* (IAATO).
- IP 58 *Implementation of the IMO Polar Code: A practical perspective* (IAATO).

(454) The following papers were also submitted under this agenda item:

- BP 2 *Overview of Dutch research into Antarctic tourism* (Netherlands).
- BP 18 *Closing of the Arctowski Polish Antarctic Station for tourist traffic* (Poland).
- BP 22 *National Inspection of the Russian Operator Activities in Antarctica in 2022* (Russian Federation).

Item 18: Preparation of the 46th Meeting

a. Date and place

(455) The Meeting welcomed the kind invitation of the Government of India to host ATCM 46 and CEP 26 in Kochi, from 20 to 30 May 2024.

(456) For future planning, the Meeting took note of the following likely timetable of upcoming ATCMs:

- 2025 Italy
- 2026 Japan

(457) The following paper was submitted under this agenda item:

- IP 43 *Hosting of the 46th Antarctic Treaty Consultative Meeting (ATCM) at Kochi, India, 2024* (India).

b. Invitation of International and Non-governmental Organisations

(458) In accordance with established practice, the Meeting agreed that the following organisations having scientific or technical interest in Antarctica should be invited to send experts to

attend ATCM 46: the ACAP Secretariat, ASOC, IAATO, the International Civil Aviation Organization (ICAO), IHO, IMO, IOC, IOPC Funds, IPCC, the International Union for Conservation of Nature (IUCN), UNEP, UNFCCC, WMO and the World Tourism Organization (WTO).

c. Preparation of the Agenda for ATCM 46

(459) The Meeting approved the Preliminary Agenda for ATCM 46 (see Appendix 3).

d. Organisation of ATCM 46

(460) In accordance with Rule 11 of the Rules of Procedure, the Meeting decided to propose the following Working Groups for ATCM 46. WG 1 would deal with policy, legal and institutional issues and WG2 would have responsibility for operations, science and tourism. In addition, the Meeting agreed to establish a Special Working Group (WG 3) which would deal with the Development of a Tourism Framework.

(461) According to the Rules of Procedure, Chairs for these groups should be appointed before the close of the Meeting and, in the absence of any nomination, Chairs would be appointed at the start of the next ATCM. The Meeting agreed to appoint Mr Theodore Kill from the United States as Chair of WG 1 in 2024. The Meeting agreed to appoint Ms Sonia Ramos Garcia from Spain and Dr Phillip Tracey from Australia as Co-Chairs of WG 2 in 2024. The Meeting agreed to appoint the Chair of WG 3 at the start of the next ATCM in 2024.

e. The SCAR Lecture

(462) Taking into account the valuable series of lectures given by SCAR at a number of ATCMs, the Meeting decided to invite SCAR to give another lecture on scientific issues relevant to ATCM 46.

Item 19: Any Other Business

(463) The Russian Federation stated that there was a discrepancy in the position of a number of Consultative Parties on the most important issues discussed at this meeting. The Russian Federation considered this to be a matter of principle. It does not join the consensus on the whole of the Final Report. If a vote were to take place, the Russian Federation would oppose the inclusion of paragraphs 11, 15-18 and 224 into the body of the report.

(464) Most Parties were of the view that the paragraphs of the draft Report had been adopted by consensus.

(465) The Meeting congratulated Finland on the adoption of the Helsinki Declaration, and commended the Chair for her wonderful work to steer the Meeting towards consensus.

(466) Many Parties noted that the Helsinki Declaration was based in a broader set of documents that Parties had adopted together over the past two years, particularly Resolution 4 (2022) and Resolution 8 (2021). They also noted that the research recommendations appropriately focused on changes in the region that had significant implications for the Earth System and for society, and on the expected impacts of climate change on the region's biodiversity. These Parties also highlighted their shared commitments to seek to avoid or mitigate additional identified non-climatic stresses to the Antarctic terrestrial and marine environment, including its biodiversity and ecosystems, in order to increase resilience to climate change effects. These Parties expressed their view that these

decisions reflected the ATCM's shared concern about the interconnectedness of the climate change crisis and the biodiversity crisis, both globally and in Antarctica, and its dedication to appropriate action on these crises at all levels. These Parties further underscored that the ATCM had the competence, means and tools to take appropriate action in the context of Antarctica, and that the Parties had the mandate and had been tasked to discuss climate change in the context of the Antarctic Treaty system.

(467) Many Parties also highlighted the quality research and advice of SCAR, and the importance of taking actions based on the best available science.

(468) Several Parties noted that they considered the Helsinki Declaration was a balanced text, reflecting Parties' different positions. Those Parties noted that they were pleased to see the UNFCCC principles reflected in the Declaration, as these were the cornerstone of the international climate regime. These Parties also noted the reference to the Paris Agreement adopted under the UNFCCC. Although these Parties noted with regret that the specific mention of "common but differentiated responsibilities", and "means of implementation", two very important tools in tackling climate change, were not mentioned, they expressed their view that their meaning was reflected in the text of the Helsinki Declaration.

(469) China noted that it was glad that the mention in the Helsinki Declaration of increasing knowledge was stated in broad, rather than specific terms, which would serve to combat climate change and other environment and dependent and associated ecosystem challenges that served the interests of human beings the most.

(470) SCAR noted that it looked forward to continuing to provide objective advice based on the best available scientific evidence.

(471) ASOC noted that it found the discussions on biodiversity and climate concerning. It noted that everywhere else in the world, the climate and biodiversity crises were linked, and there was already evidence of this in Antarctica. ASOC stated that an ATCM that could make timely management decisions was a necessary component of the global response to climate change and biodiversity loss.

(472) Japan expressed the view that it did not support parts of the Helsinki Declaration that mentioned the UNFCCC. Japan noted its position that the UNFCCC and Paris Agreement were two different documents. In the spirit of compromise, Japan stated that it respected the leadership of the Chair and did not block consensus.

(473) The United States gave an Explanation of Policy to the Helsinki Declaration, particularly regarding the reference to the principles of the UNFCCC and importance of addressing greenhouse gas emissions.

(474) Several Parties supported Japan and the United States.

(475) Belarus informed the ATCM that it wished to be considered to be a Consultative Party at ATCM 46 in India.

(476) Canada thanked the Host Country and the Secretariat and looked forward to intersessional discussion on its request for Consultative Party status and looked forward to consideration at ATCM 46.

Item 20: Adoption of the Final Report

(477) The Meeting adopted the Final Report of the 45th Antarctic Treaty Consultative Meeting. The Russian Federation noted after adoption of paragraphs 11, 15-18 and 224 that it opposed these paragraphs. The Chair of the Meeting, Ms Päivi Kaukoranta, made closing remarks.

Item 21: Close of the Meeting

(478) The Meeting was closed on Thursday, 8 June at 18:51.

2. CEP XXV Report

Report of the Twenty-fifth Meeting of the Committee for Environmental Protection (CEP XXV)

Helsinki, Finland, May 28 – 1 June, 2023

(1) Pursuant to Article 11 of the Protocol on Environmental Protection to the Antarctic Treaty, Representatives from 39 of the 42 Parties to the Protocol (Argentina, Australia, Belarus, Belgium, Brazil, Bulgaria, Canada, Chile, China, Colombia, Czechia, Ecuador, Finland, France, Germany, India, Italy, Japan, Malaysia, Monaco, the Netherlands, New Zealand, Norway, Peru, Poland, Portugal, Republic of Korea, Romania, the Russian Federation, South Africa, Spain, Sweden, Switzerland, Türkiye, Ukraine, the United Kingdom, the United States, Uruguay, and Venezuela) met in Helsinki, Finland, from 28 May to 1 June 2023, for the purpose of providing advice and formulating recommendations to the Parties in connection with the implementation of the Protocol.

(2) In accordance with Rule 4 of the CEP Rules of Procedure, the meeting was also attended by representatives of the following Observers:

- the Scientific Committee on Antarctic Research (SCAR), the Scientific Committee for the Conservation of Antarctic Marine Living Resources (SC-CAMLR), and the Council of Managers of National Antarctic Programs (COMNAP); and
- scientific, environmental and technical organisations: the Antarctic and Southern Ocean Coalition (ASOC), the International Association of Antarctica Tour Operators (IAATO), the International Union for the Conservation of Nature (IUCN), United Nations Environmental Program (UNEP) and the World Meteorological Organization (WMO).

Item 1: Opening of the Meeting

(3) The CEP Chair, Ms Birgit Njåstad (Norway), opened the meeting on Sunday 28 May 2023 and thanked Finland for arranging and hosting the meeting.

(4) The Chair summarised the work undertaken during the intersessional period, noting that many of the actions arising from CEP XXIV with outcomes anticipated for CEP XXV had been addressed (IP 79).

Item 2: Adoption of the Agenda

(5) The Committee adopted the following agenda and confirmed the allocation of 44 Working Papers (WP), 69 Information Papers (IP), 5 Secretariat Papers (SP) and 6 Background Papers (BP) to the agenda items:

1. Opening of the Meeting
2. Adoption of the Agenda
3. Strategic Discussions on the Future Work of the CEP
4. Operation of the CEP
5. Cooperation with other Organisations
6. Repair and Remediation of Environment Damage
7. Climate Change Implications for the Environment
    a. Strategic Approach
    b. Implementation and Review of the Climate Change Response Work Programme
8. Environmental Impact Assessment (EIA)

a. Draft Comprehensive Environmental Evaluations

b. Other EIA Matters

9. Area Protection and Management Plans

a. Management Plans

b. Historic Sites and Monuments

c. Site Guidelines

d. Marine Spatial Protection and Management

e. Other Annex V Matters

10. Conservation of Antarctic Flora and Fauna

a. Quarantine and Non-native Species

b. Specially Protected Species

c. Other Annex II Matters

11. Environmental Monitoring and Reporting

12. Inspection Reports

13. General Matters

14. Election of Officers

15. Preparation for the Next Meeting

16. Adoption of the Report

17. Closing of the Meeting

Item 3: Strategic Discussions on the Future Work of the CEP

CEP Five-year Work Plan

(6) The CEP Chair introduced WP 62 *CEP strategic priorities and the 5-year work plan: Outcomes and recommendations from the intersessional discussions and workshop,* and referred to IP 150 *Informal CEP Workshop on strategic priorities and 5-year work plan – convener's preliminary report.* These papers presented an overview of the outcomes of informal intersessional discussions and an informal workshop held to consider the CEP strategic priorities and the Five-year Work Plan. The Chair reported that three fruitful rounds of discussions had taken place on the CEP Discussion Forum and that Members and Observers had provided useful inputs on issues that contributed to shape the background material for an informal CEP Workshop held in Helsinki prior to the meeting. WP 62 recommended that the CEP:

- exchange views and reflections on the outcomes of the informal CEP workshop;
- establish an ICG to further develop a final draft revised Five-year Work Plan for discussion and adoption at CEP 26 and further develop a draft checklist to guide the CEP in its efforts in initiating, pursuing, and monitoring progress on actions under the Five-year Work Plan; and
- encourage Members, on the basis of the outcomes of the informal CEP workshop, to continue developing a framework that could guide the CEP in its efforts to frame and monitor knowledge needs in the future.

(7) The Committee commended the Chair and Vice-Chairs for leading these intersessional discussions and convening the informal workshop, noting the value of the Five-year Work Plan as a central tool for framing the work of the CEP. Many Members highlighted that the discussions on CEP strategic priorities had been important and constructive, resulting

in relevant reflections and exchanges on how to promote the effectiveness and enhance the work of the Committee. Members noted that, although much had been accomplished in the past 25 years, significant work remained ahead to reach the objectives of the Environment Protocol.

(8) Members highlighted some of the priority issues that had been discussed, such as the importance of improving the EIA process, managing growing tourism, responding to climate change and protecting biodiversity in Antarctica. Members commented on the valuable exchanges that had taken place and ideas that had been discussed on potential new mechanisms and tools for progressing work-plan actions and on engaging a broader participation both within the Committee and with the wider body of expertise. SCAR noted appreciation for the discussions that had taken place on further development and improved understanding of the Committee's science needs. Members expressed high interest in being involved in further intersessional discussion. Members also expressed gratitude to Finland for hosting the informal workshop, which had provided an excellent arena for stimulating discussions and exchanges on important matters relating to the Committee's work.

(9) The Committee endorsed the recommendations in WP 62 and agreed to establish an ICG to further develop a final draft revised Five-year Work Plan for discussion and adoption at CEP 26.

CEP advice to the ATCM on the development of a revised Five-year Work Plan

(10) The Committee agreed to advise the ATCM that it had established an ICG on the development of a revised Five-year Work Plan with the following Terms of Reference (ToR):

- Develop a draft revised five-year prioritised work plan for consideration at CEP 26;
- Prepare advice on practical measures that the CEP might consider in initiating, pursuing and monitoring progress on work plan actions; and
- Report back to CEP 26.

(11) The Committee welcomed the offer from Norway to act as ICG convener.

---

(12) The Committee considered the Five-year Work Plan adopted at CEP XXIV (SP 2) and, in keeping with its agreement at CEP XV (2012), briefly considered the work plan at the end of each agenda item.

(13) The Committee revised and updated its Five-year Work Plan (Appendix 1).

Item 4: Operation of the CEP

(14) Norway introduced WP 21 rev. 1 *Update to the Procedure for CEP consideration of draft CEEs*, prepared jointly with Germany and India. It contained a revised version of the procedure for intersessional CEP consideration of draft CEEs, as adopted in Appendix 3 of the CEP XX Report (2017). Based on the past five years of experience in the processing of draft CEEs in the Committee, Norway highlighted three proposed changes to the procedure relating to timely notification of planned submission, communication procedures in the submission process and enabling timely availability of translated documents.

(15) The Committee thanked the co-authors for their paper, welcoming their proposal as a positive step towards making the procedure relating to the review of draft CEEs as clear

and efficient as possible. The Committee also noted the paper's importance in the context of the CEP's revision of the Five-year Work Plan. After incorporating minor amendments proposed by Members, the Committee agreed to update its procedure for consideration of draft CEEs. The Committee noted that the revised procedure did not alter the mandatory requirements for circulation of draft CEEs under Annex I.

CEP advice to the ATCM on the update to the procedure for CEP consideration of draft CEEs

(16) The Committee agreed to advise the ATCM that it had updated its *Procedure for CEP consideration of draft CEEs* (Appendix 2). The Committee also agreed to draw the ATCM's attention to the provisions reflecting the Secretariat's role to facilitate the handling and translation of draft CEEs.

---

(17) Norway introduced WP 22 *Nomination and election procedures – CEP Chair*. Observing that the current CEP Rules of Procedure gave little guidance on the nomination and election process of the CEP Chair, Norway proposed the CEP agree to a procedure for nominating a CEP Chair, and suggested that the CEP Rules of Procedure be updated to reflect this nomination procedure, as well as the earlier agreed-upon procedure for election (CEP XVII Report paragraph 275). Norway also proposed revising the term of Chairs and Vice-Chairs from two years to two meetings, to account for possible interruptions in the regular annual cycle of meetings.

(18) The Committee thanked Norway for its proposal and expressed general support for the need to clarify procedures and further formalise the process of electing the CEP Chair. Noting the utility of having similar procedures for the Vice-Chair positions, and ensuring flexibility in case nominations were not received within the recommended timeframe or there were no candidates, the Committee agreed to update its Rules of Procedure. The Committee noted a comment that it could be valuable to, at a future stage, consider allowing a CEP Chair and Vice-Chairs from all Members, not just from Consultative Parties.

(19) The Committee also noted several gendered references in the CEP Rules of Procedure and agreed to update those references to gender-inclusive language.

CEP advice to the ATCM on the update of CEP Rules of Procedure on elections and nominations

(20) The Committee agreed to advise the ATCM that it had endorsed modifications to the CEP Rules of Procedure to incorporate procedures for nominating and electing the CEP Chair and Vice-Chairs, and gender inclusivity, and forwarded a revised version to the ATCM for approval through a Decision.

Item 5: Cooperation with other Organisations

(21) SC-CAMLR presented IP 6 *Report by the SC-CAMLR Observer to the CEP*, which reported on its activities relevant to the CEP conducted during the 2022/23 intersessional period. SC-CAMLR noted that it had extended seven scientific scholarships and created two new internships, and reported on the development of its new five-year strategic plan. It highlighted six issues of common interest to the CEP and SC-CAMLR, including one on the reporting of marine debris. It also stated that ongoing work on these issues

included a hybrid workshop on climate change and the Antarctic marine environment planned for September 2023. SC-CAMLR reported that no agreements on MPA proposals had been reached at CCAMLR-41 and that an extraordinary meeting to develop a roadmap to support discussions on MPA design, designation, implementation and the establishment of research and monitoring plans would be held in Santiago, Chile in June 2023. It noted that CCAMLR-41 had not reached consensus on the merging of management plans for ASPA 152 and ASPA 153, but that the proposed revisions to the management plan for ASPA 145 had been endorsed.

(22) SCAR presented IP 10 rev. 1 *The Scientific Committee on Antarctic Research Annual Report 2023 to the XLV Antarctic Treaty Consultative Meeting*. SCAR reported on the launching of its new five-year strategic plan for 2023-2028 titled "Urgent Messages from the South: Antarctic and Southern Ocean Science and Policy". It highlighted its work on the initial planning for a fifth International Polar Year in 2032-33 (IP 50). It also announced that it had awarded five early career scholarships. SCAR noted the Humanities and Social Sciences conference to be held in Lisbon on 22-24 June 2023, the SCAR Biology Symposium to be held in Christchurch on 31 July – 4 August 2023, the inaugural Southern Ocean Observing System (SOOS) Symposium to be held in Hobart on 14-18 August 2023, and the SCAR INSTANT Conference to be held in Trieste on 11-14 September 2023. It also reported on recent activities relevant to the work of the CEP including:

- its three Scientific Research Programmes providing outputs supporting the CEP's objectives;
- its 10th Open Science Conference held online in August 2022, hosted by India's National Centre for Polar and Ocean Research;
- advice to CCAMLR-41 with a focus on climate change in the Southern Ocean;
- work by the Plastic in Polar Environments group (Plastic-AG) to create a repository summarising national and international projects focused on plastic pollution in the Antarctic and Sub-Antarctic regions; and
- the SCAR Krill Group (SKEG), which was granted Expert Group status in September 2022.

(23) COMNAP presented IP 7 *Council of Managers of National Antarctic Programs (COMNAP) Annual Report 2022/23*. The 2022 COMNAP Annual General Meeting had discussed issues such as modernisation of aging infrastructure to improve environmental performance and enabling of science, vulnerability related to a changing Antarctica, and new vessels that incorporated noise reduction, efficiencies and improved safety responses into their design and use. COMNAP reported on its continued work on COVID-19 preparedness and response included the sharing of technical information related to the prevention of reverse zoonosis from direct human contact to Antarctic species. Recognising the heightened risk of Highly Pathogenic Avian Influenza (HPAI) presenting in Antarctic wildlife through natural migration of species, COMNAP noted that it was collaborating with SCAR and IAATO on the topic. It also highlighted the upcoming 20th COMNAP Symposium which would showcase the multifaceted work of national Antarctic programmes as they facilitated Antarctic research and implemented environmental protection mechanisms.

(24) WMO presented IP 16 *Annual Report of the World Meteorological Organization (WMO)*, which outlined its recent activities in Antarctic observations, infrastructure, and science, with the latter conducted through its co-sponsored World Climate Research Programme (WCRP) and World Weather Research Programme. The highlights included the Global Cryosphere Watch, the Antarctic Regional Climate Centre Network, the

Climate and Cryosphere Core Project, Antarctic CORDEX, Antarctica 2300 Projections, and the Year of Polar Prediction final summit and next steps. WMO also noted its newest high-level publications of interest, which were available in the public domain.

(25) IAATO presented IP 55 *Report of the International Association of Antarctica Tour Operators 2022-23*, which reported on its activities during the previous year. IAATO noted that its membership comprised 109 Operators and Associates. IAATO reported that tourist numbers were increasing again after the COVID-19 pandemic with a total of 104 897 visitors in the 2022/23 season. There had been three tourism incidents during the season resulting in the death of four individuals travelling with IAATO operators. During its annual meeting in Hamburg, IAATO members agreed on a five-year strategy, *Embracing Our Role as Stewards of Antarctica* as well as additional measures, such as evolving operational procedures for wildlife viewing, an increase to the whale slow-down geo-fenced areas, and further investment in the 2022 Climate Pledge. IAATO noted that through work with other stakeholders and feedback from its operators, it was developing effective tools and measures which supported IAATO's mission of safe and environmentally responsible travel to Antarctica. It concluded that collaborations like those would be crucial as IAATO implemented its strategy.

(26) ASOC presented IP 115 *ASOC Report to the ATCM*, which summarised ASOC's intersessional activities and support for policy-relevant science and science communications over the previous year. ASOC had contributed to intersessional discussions on the CEP Discussion Forum and participated in SCAR's Integrated Science to Inform Antarctic and Southern Ocean Conservation (AntICON) programme and in tourism research projects. It had also attended meetings relevant to the work of the CEP including the UNFCCC COP 27. ASOC also noted its appreciation for the opportunities to collaborate with CEP Members and Observers throughout the intersessional period.

(27) The Committee thanked the Observers for their contributions and work. It noted the spirit of cooperation and community that had been expressed and developed in recent years among Observers.

(28) The Committee noted the following Information Paper submitted under this agenda item:

- IP 1 *Report by the CEP Observer to the XXXVII SCAR Delegates' Meeting* (France).

Item 6: Repair and Remediation of Environment Damage

(29) The Republic of Korea presented IP 66 *Antarctic Ecosystem Recovery: Recolonization of Adélie Penguins at Cape Hallett (ASPA No. 106), Ross Sea*, prepared jointly with New Zealand and the United States. The Republic of Korea reported that Adélie penguins had recolonised Cape Hallett 46 years after Cape Hallett Station had been decommissioned in 1973. It highlighted a study illustrating the importance of clean-up efforts that had taken place from 2000 to 2007 and the enhancement of habitats in restoring penguin colonies affected by human-induced disturbances. It also drew attention to the importance of environmental planning, long-term monitoring, and EIA in the Antarctic regions.

(30) The Secretariat presented a Map of Past Activities, which had been created based on the requirements of Annex III, Article 8, paragraph 3 of the Environment Protocol. The Secretariat emphasised that because the map reflected information submitted through the EIES, the map would only be as good as the information provided by Parties. It noted that Parties had used varying criteria to report either on sites of past activities or on clean-up operations, limiting the map's utility. The Secretariat noted that it would welcome feedback to inform further development of the map for Members' use.

(31) The Committee noted the following Background Paper submitted under this agenda item:

- BP 7 *Optimización y mantenimiento de las plantas de tratamiento de aguas - servidas de la Base Aérea Antártica "Presidente Frei" Año 2023* (Chile).

Item 7: Climate Change Implications for the Environment

7a) Strategic Approach

(32) SCAR introduced WP 42 rev. 1 *SCAR updates on Antarctic Climate Change and the Environment*, which summarised the 18 recommendations and priority actions arising from the 2022 ACCE Decadal Synopsis. SCAR highlighted the need for immediate implementation of collaborative international responses to address critical research needs. This was especially important in light of new data suggesting a record sea-ice minimum, projections for changes to Antarctic Bottom Water, changing terrestrial and marine ecosystems, and the likelihood that the global average surface temperature would rise above 1.5°C over preindustrial levels in the next five years. SCAR reiterated its commitment to provide regular advice to the CEP and ATCM on the best available science representing current understanding of, and projections for, climate change and its impacts on Antarctica and the earth system. SCAR encouraged Members to: continue their efforts to implement the 2022 ACCE Decadal Synopsis recommendations with urgency; continue to engage with the research community to deepen understanding of the key messages emerging from research as well as to determine what science and types of information would best support the development of robust policies and actions; and consider how to provide regular assessments of progress against the recommendations and priority actions.

(33) The Committee thanked SCAR for its report on the ACCE Decadal Synopsis and commended it on its continued commitment to provide updates based on the best available science. The Committee further noted that science information from SCAR was fundamental in its work to understand and address environmental management in Antarctica in the light of climate change, and provided even greater impetus to efforts to implement the CCRWP as a matter of priority. The Committee also commended recent efforts that Members had taken to fulfil the need for multinational, large-scale, well-resourced and coordinated research efforts, such as the International Science and Infrastructure for Synchronous Observation (Antarctica InSync). It expressed its support for all the recommendations in WP 42 rev. 1, underscoring in particular the need to:

- continue efforts to implement the 2022 ACCE Decadal Synopsis recommendations with urgency;
- determine what science and what types of information would best support the development of robust policies and actions, and note ongoing work by the Committee in considering the framing of its science needs; and
- consider how to provide regular assessments of progress against the recommendations and priority actions identified by the 2022 ACCE Decadal Synopsis in the context of the CCRWP and the Five-year Work Plan.

(34) Members made additional observations, for example: the importance of following up recommendations from other complementary sources and processes such as the joint 2016 CEP/SC-CAMLR workshop on climate change and monitoring; the interconnectedness of the global climate and the Antarctic environment and biodiversity;

the use of projections and scenarios to better predict which areas were likely to be vulnerable or resilient to climate change; the need to improve knowledge of Antarctic biodiversity and address non-native species risks; the utility of developing tools that could translate science into rapid management actions; the need to take bold research efforts; and, included in this, the connection between Antarctica and other related ecosystems.

(35) SCAR thanked Members for their comments and their positive response to the paper. It appreciated the exchange on the updates to the emerging science and associated recommendations. SCAR acknowledged the complexity associated with climate change and noted that the language that was used in the ACCE Decadal Synopsis reflected this.

(36) COMNAP introduced WP 29 *Implementation of ACCE Imperatives: A COMNAP perspective*. It noted that national Antarctic programmes had been the first-hand witnesses to a changing Antarctic region, had facilitated the science that had provided the evidence of a changing Antarctica, and were developing and delivering large-scale integrated research projects. It pointed out that national Antarctic programmes were facing new challenges and working to understand how sea-level changes and sea-ice conditions would affect critical Antarctic infrastructure and the delivery of science. It outlined some initiatives it had taken to address these challenges. These included infrastructure vulnerability assessments, work on energy efficiency practices and new technology to reduce the relatively low level of carbon emissions from national Antarctic programmes, without compromising the safety of human life in Antarctica or impacting science. COMNAP recognised that current biosecurity guidance may not be sufficient to protect Antarctica and the surrounding marine environment in the context of climate change. COMNAP recommended that the Committee:

- encourage Members to continue supporting national Antarctic programmes to engage in internationally collaborative research;
- fill knowledge gaps and reduce uncertainty in relation to the changing Antarctic region;
- develop, with the ATCM, key messages for the global community about the significance and impact of a changing Antarctica, as well as ways to stop or mitigate changes through global actions;
- encourage Members to continue supporting national Antarctic programmes' efforts to decarbonise or reduce fossil fuel use;
- review and update the Non-native Species Manual and improve biofouling and ballast water management to better respond to marine non-native species introduction in a changing ocean; and
- review the CEP Clean-up Manual to consider areas that may be affected by changing environmental conditions near sites of past activity.

(37) The Committee thanked COMNAP for its report and its work in mitigating and addressing climate change. It expressed its support for all COMNAP's recommendations noting the important role of national Antarctic programmes in managing the implications of climate change for human activities and the environment in Antarctica. The Committee especially noted the alignment of COMNAP's proposals to review the Non-native Species Manual and CEP Clean-up Manual with ongoing work initiated within the framework of the CCRWP, and the importance of long-term monitoring, highlighting the value of outreach and communication and noting ongoing initiatives in national Antarctic programmes.

(38) Finland introduced WP 43 *The Recommendations of SCAR on Climate Action in the*

Antarctic: The Finnish Perspective. Referring to SCAR's ACCE Decadal Synopsis, Finland noted that Antarctic climate change had major global consequences and stressed that the impacts could be mitigated only through global collective climate action. In support of SCAR's recommendations in WP 42 rev. 1, Finland highlighted the importance of: constant cooperation and exchange of information between the UNFCCC and the ATCM as well as between IPCC and SCAR; enhanced scientific cooperation between both polar regions in terms of scientific advances and policy advice; assessment of the carbon footprints of scientific operations in the Antarctic and the designing of low-emission research programmes; and an operative and holistic approach. Finland also emphasised how international collaboration and coordination were important in reducing emissions and other environmental impacts of research programmes, and urged Parties to increase their climate action by revisiting their Nationally Determined Contributions (NDCs) under the Paris Agreement.

(39) The Committee thanked Finland for its reflections, and noted the paper would be considered during the upcoming joint session of the CEP and the ATCM on climate change. Members supported Finland in highlighting several aspects of the paper, including the importance of national measures for the mitigation of carbon footprints, the promotion of holistic approaches in climate action, and the communication of scientific information between SCAR and the IPCC. They called upon scientific operations to also assess their environmental footprint more generally.

(40) Finland introduced WP 38 rev. 1 *Helsinki Declaration on Climate Change and the Antarctic*. It recalled that the ATCM had agreed to hold a full-day joint session of the CEP and the ATCM to consider the implementation of the recommendations in SCAR's ACCE Decadal Synopsis. Finland informed the Committee that it had led fruitful intersessional discussions on the ATCM discussion forum to formulate a Joint Declaration emphasising the need for urgent climate action in Antarctica, which would be discussed at the upcoming joint session of the CEP and the ATCM on climate change. Finland thanked all those who had actively participated in the discussion. Furthermore, Finland suggested that the CEP considered suggesting to the ATCM an operative paragraph that could be included in the Declaration, reflecting the CEP's commitment to climate change work.

(41) The Committee commended Finland for its work in the preparation of the Helsinki Declaration, noting the importance of calling for action on the implications of climate change in Antarctica. The Committee welcomed Finland's invitation to draft its own paragraph for the ATCM's consideration, which would enable the Committee to underline its commitment to the goals of the Declaration.

CEP advice to the ATCM on the Helsinki Declaration

(42) The Committee agreed to advise the ATCM of an operative paragraph to be provided at an appropriate place in the Helsinki Declaration on Climate Change and the Antarctic, reflecting the CEP's commitment to climate change work:

> *Reaffirm the importance of the ongoing work of the Committee on Environmental Protection to support efforts within the Antarctic Treaty system to mitigate, prepare for, and build resilience to, the environmental impacts of a changing climate, and commit as a matter of priority to continue the implementation and regular review of the Climate Change Response Work Programme.*

---

(43) Australia presented IP 45 *Managing threats to Antarctic terrestrial biodiversity*, prepared jointly with Belgium, France, Japan, New Zealand, Norway, Spain, United Kingdom, United States, SCAR, ASOC and IAATO. The paper highlighted recent

research which found that an estimated 65% of terrestrial species groups and land-associated seabirds were likely to decline by the year 2100 under existing management mechanisms and current trajectories of global climate change. In assessing the benefits of several possible threat management strategies, the research had found that influencing global policy to effectively mitigate climate change would deliver the greatest benefits, while a range of actions to minimise threats from activities within the Antarctic region would also be highly beneficial. The study had concluded that the best way to protect Antarctica's terrestrial biodiversity would be to simultaneously pursue global and regional efforts. The co-authors highlighted the relevance of these findings for the Committee's work to implement the CEP Five-year Work Plan and CCRWP, and the upcoming joint CEP/ATCM session on informing and supporting global action to address climate change.

(44) WMO presented IP 93 *Antarctica 2300 (ISMIP6) Projection*s and explained that the Ice Sheet Model Intercomparison Project (ISMIP) was a crucial element in the effort to provide reliable projections of global sea-level rise for the IPCC reports used globally by decision makers. WMO noted that the upcoming seventh cycle of the Project would extend ice-sheet projections from the year 2100 to 2300, in order to better account for potential tipping points beyond the 21st century. Such events could potentially lead to a much larger and longer-lasting contribution of Antarctic sea-level rise with consequences on multigenerational time scales. The paper invited ice-flow modellers, physical oceanographers, atmospheric scientists, climate modellers, and data scientists, as well as other interested groups worldwide, to join the initiative.

(45) WMO presented IP 94 *The Climate and Cryosphere (CliC) Project of the World Climate Research Programme (WCRP),* which reported on the World Climate Research Programme's Climate and Cryosphere project (CliC). WMO explained that, according to the Programme's findings: the west Antarctic ice sheet continued to diminish at an accelerating rate; Antarctic summer sea ice was at a record low extent, with the ice shelves thinning and in some cases collapsing catastrophically; the permafrost was thawing; the Southern Ocean was warming and freshening with global consequences; and Antarctica was experiencing extreme weather events such as heat waves and atmospheric rivers. WMO recalled that its activities involved strong and long-standing partnerships with SCAR, commended SCAR's work in the 2022 ACCE Decadal Synopsis, and fully supported its recommendations.

(46) WMO presented IP 97 *Policy-relevant science highlights from the Antarctic CORDEX project.* It provided background information and recent science highlights from the Antarctic Coordinated Regional Downscaling Experiment (CORDEX) activity. CORDEX aimed to better understand the influence of climate processes on Antarctica's sea ice, ice shelves and the ice sheet at the regional scale. WMO noted that new findings had been made in understanding the vulnerabilities and temperature thresholds of ice shelves, as well as on the importance of near-surface warming in the melting of ice shelves. It invited all Members to consider supporting targeted observational campaigns focussed on poorly understood or observed areas to help further improve the model estimates of Antarctic Surface Mass Balance.

(47) Acknowledging WMO for its international research efforts addressing the recommendations of the SCAR Decadal Synopsis, SCAR referred to IP 95 *Understanding Future Sea-level Change Around Antarctica*, jointly prepared with COMNAP. SCAR noted that the paper outlined the risks for operations, research, tourism, and specially protected and managed areas arising from sea-level changes, and noted that ongoing work led by SCAR's INSTANT programme would help Members and national Antarctic programmes to better predict sea-level changes and manage the risks through effective adaptation.

(48) COMNAP acknowledged the national Antarctic programmes that had facilitated the science informing sea-level models and expressed its intention to work with contributors to understand sea-level projections given its potential to impact operations, infrastructure, and science activities in coastal areas.

(49) The Committee thanked WMO for its papers and for the sobering information contained in them. The Committee also commended SCAR and COMNAP for IP 95, and noted the Antarctic coastline was not immune to the consequences of sea-level changes. Noting the number of papers and interventions referring to new findings on the consequences of Antarctic ice sheets and cryospheric changes on coastal sea-level changes in Antarctica, some Members suggested that it might be appropriate to include issues relating to coastal sea-level changes in the Five-year Work Plan and CCRWP.

(50) ASOC presented IP 117 *Irreversible near-term consequences of Southern Ocean acidification with current CO2 emissions pathways*. It highlighted research indicating that, unless the world pursued a path of significant emissions reductions, there would be widespread shell damage due to ocean acidification throughout the Southern Ocean within the next few decades.

(51) ASOC presented IP 120 *Increasing evidence of critical sea-level rise with emissions above 1.5°C Paris agreement limit*. It emphasised that recent research on projected Antarctic ice-sheet loss pointed to thresholds of irreversible sea-level rise at lower temperatures and emissions pathways than previously considered, even within the upper 2°C Paris Agreement limit. ASOC encouraged the CEP to take note of these trends in ocean acidification and sea-level rise, as they would result in dramatic effects on Antarctica and its marine species and ecosystems.

(52) ASOC presented IP 121 rev. 2 *Carbon Footprints of Antarctic Activities,* which proposed to produce an analysis and estimate of the emissions generated by activities in the Antarctic. It suggested that a better understanding of the total carbon footprint of Antarctic activities would be a useful foundation for developing future ATCM instruments designed to reduce the environmental impact of those activities.

(53) The Committee noted the following Information Papers submitted under this agenda item:

- IP 25 *Logistical Challenges due to Changing Environmental Conditions: Experiences from the Korean Antarctic Program 2022-23* (Republic of Korea).
- IP 64 *Decarbonizing Antarctic Operations: best practices for renewable energy deployment at Antarctic research stations* (ASOC, Uruguay).
- IP 98 *Marine Ecosystem Assessment for the Southern Ocean (MEASO) - Key Findings and Recommendations* (SCAR).

7b) Implementation and Review of the Climate Change Response Work Programme

(54) The convenor of the SGCCR, Dr Heike Herata (Germany), introduced WP 48 *Report of the CEP Subsidiary Group on Climate Change Response (SGCCR) 2022-2023*, which outlined the work and outputs of the SGCCR during the intersessional period. Dr Herata reported that the Group's focus was to prioritise activities already described in the CCRWP to advance its implementation. Accordingly, the SGCCR had identified six activities from the CCRWP to be advanced during the next intersessional period. Dr Herata noted that the SGCCR had held an informal meeting prior to CEP XXV and had discussed upcoming tasks and exchanged information on relevant activities related to the priority actions.

(55) The Committee thanked Dr Herata for leading the work of the SGCCR. Noting the CEP's

responsibility in taking action, it expressed support for the SGCCR's useful work of identifying the priority activities of the CCRWP and encouraged further Members to take actions to advance them. SGCCR members also called for broader participation in the SGCCR to contribute to its important work on the implementation of the CCRWP. Members also raised several points for further consideration, including: the relevance of enhancing cooperation with SC-CAMLR; the possibility of further promoting research on vulnerable species, including the status, trends, vulnerability and distribution of the species as reflected in the science needs of the Five-year Work Plan; the relevance of including sea-level impacts in climate change response work; and the importance of assessing full-scale and cumulative impacts.

CEP advice to the ATCM on the implementation and review of the Climate Change Response Work Programme (CCRWP)

(56) The Committee agreed to advise the ATCM that it continued work to implement the CCRWP (2016). The Committee discussed the following actions that had been delivered or concerned ongoing research that was regularly provided to the Committee:

- Action 1b. Review of IMO biofouling guidelines to check adequacy for the Southern Ocean and vessels moving from region to region. See WP 14 *Review of International Maritime Organization (IMO) and Antarctic Treaty system (ATS) guidelines and agreements concerning ship biofouling and ballast water management* (Australia, New Zealand, United Kingdom).
- Action 2a. Support and undertake research to improve understanding of current and future change and to inform response. For example, see IP 45 *Managing threats to Antarctic terrestrial biodiversity* (Australia, Belgium, France, Japan, New Zealand, Norway, Spain, United Kingdom, United States, SCAR, ASOC, IAATO).
- Actions 2b./3b. Support and undertake long-term monitoring of change, including collaborative efforts. See for example WP 49 rev. 1 *Antarctic Near-shore and Terrestrial Observing System (ANTOS)* (SCAR, New Zealand, Australia, Italy, Republic of Korea, United States).
- Action 2e. Review and revise where necessary existing management tools to consider if they afford the best practical adaptation measure to areas at risk from climate change. For example, see WP 47 *Subsidiary Group on Management Plans Report of activities during the intersessional period 2022-2023* (India) which described an ongoing process of prioritising and reviewing protected area management tools in the context of climate change.
- Action 3e. Maintain regular dialogue (or sharing of information) with SC-CAMLR on Climate Change and the Southern Ocean, in particular on actions being taken. See for example IP 6 *Report by the SC-CAMLR Observer to the CEP* (SC-CAMLR) and WP 12 *Preparation of the next Joint CEP/SC-CAMLR Workshop* (France).
- Action 5b. Assess risk of changes in climate to HSM/heritage ASPA. See IP 102 *Assessing the risk of climate change impacts on Antarctic heritage values: an update on progress* (Argentina, Australia, New Zealand, Norway, United Kingdom, SCAR).
- Action 6a. Encourage research by national programmes on marine and terrestrial species at risk due to climate change. For example, see WP 52 *A five-year assessment of the impacts on emperor penguins of low sea-ice extent* (United Kingdom, France, Germany, United States).

(57) The Committee agreed to support the SGCCR's recommendation that the Members continue to work actively to implement the CCRWP. It also endorsed the following six

priority activities to be advanced by the SGCCR in the next intersessional period:

- Supporting work to assess the status of climate-vulnerable Antarctic species (Action 6c);
- Developing guidance on climate change considerations in documents for establishing and managing protected areas (Action 2e);
- Keeping the Non-native Species Manual updated with current developments (Action 1a);
- Intensifying coordination on climate change response in the marine realm with SC-CAMLR (Action 3e);
- De-contamination of past sites of activities in the Antarctic area (Action 5f); and
- Assessing the risk of climate change for Antarctic existing and projected infrastructure and associated environmental consequences and considering the impacts of climate change linked with the EIA guidelines, *eg*, ensuring proposed long-term facilities are suitably resilient to climate change (Action 5a and 5d).

---

(58) France introduced WP 12 *Preparation of the next Joint CEP/SC-CAMLR Workshop*, which proposed draft Terms of Reference and several modalities for organising the next Joint CEP/SC-CAMLR Workshop. France highlighted that the workshop's ToR should take full account of the review presented in CEP XXIV - WP 16, the ongoing work of the SGCCR, the Terms of Reference of the SC-CAMLR Climate Change Workshop planned for September 2023, and any guidance arising from the ATCM/CEP joint session on Climate Change. France proposed that the workshop be held in 2024 at a date that would ensure broad participation. It invited Members to consider whether the workshop could be held back-to-back with CEP 26 or SC-CAMLR-43, and whether a hybrid or virtual workshop would be most appropriate. It also suggested that Members could consider adopting a similar approach to the planned 2023 SC-CAMLR Climate Change Workshop, which would consist of regional hubs to facilitate broad participation, if this proved to be an efficient approach.

(59) In response to a question by China regarding the use of "impact" versus "effects" in the draft Terms of Reference, WMO clarified that according to the IPCC "Impacts generally refer to effects on lives; livelihoods; health and well-being; ecosystems and species; economic, social and cultural assets; services (including ecosystem services); and infrastructure. Impacts may be referred to as consequences or outcomes, and can be adverse or beneficial."

(60) The Committee thanked France for its work and fully supported the proposal for a joint CEP/SC-CAMLR workshop in 2024 or 2025 focusing on climate change and its impacts in Antarctica. Members highlighted the importance of enhancing collective efforts, welcomed the positive response by SC-CAMLR to identify a co-convenor, and supported the establishment of a Steering Committee with participation of both bodies to finalise practical arrangements. It further agreed to hold informal discussions, if necessary, on the CEP Forum in order to facilitate the planning of the joint workshop.

CEP advice to the ATCM on the preparation of the next joint CEP/SC-CAMLR workshop

(61) The Committee agreed to report to the ATCM that it had adopted the following Terms of Reference for the next joint CEP/SC-CAMLR workshop:

- Examine how to progress on matters of mutual interest in the marine realm in the context of climate change (including the five joint priority areas identified in the

2009 joint workshop);

- Identify common research needs;
- Examine the need to enhance existing monitoring programmes to assess and integrate the impacts[1] of climate change; and
- Propose improvements to strengthen cooperation and coordination between the CEP and SC-CAMLR.

(62) It further agreed to request support from the Secretariat and that Parties consider funding options for the workshop, recalling also that at ATCM XLI the Meeting had expressed its willingness to consider future proposals for funding to assist the CEP to undertake priority work, on a case-by-case basis.

Item 8: Environmental Impact Assessment (EIA)

8a) Draft Comprehensive Environmental Evaluations

(63) Argentina introduced WP 61 rev. 1 *Draft Comprehensive Environmental Evaluation (CEE) for the renovation of Petrel Base, Dundee Island, Antarctica*, which reported on its plans to renew Petrel Base while continuing scientific and operational activities at the station, both on-site and in the facilities supported by the station. Argentina noted that the CEE had been prepared following the requirements of Annex I to the Environment Protocol, the *Guidelines for Environmental Impact Assessment in Antarctica*, and relevant Argentine legislation. Argentina noted that a series of changes in the status of Petrel Base over several decades, as well as deterioration over time, resulted in a need for large-scale upgrades. Argentina highlighted that the draft CEE was intended as a comprehensive evaluation of a project that was broad in scope, which consisted of renovation and use of the station's facilities, construction and use of a new runway for aircraft, construction of a photovoltaic power plant, and improvements in the use and consumption of water supply lakes. It further noted that the project would address both the need for upgrades at Petrel Base and some logistical challenges experienced at Marambio Base. After a comprehensive evaluation of the proposed activities and associated mitigation measures, Argentina concluded that the proposed activities were likely to have a more than minor or transitory impact on the Antarctic environment. Argentina had concluded that the proposed activities could proceed, on the basis that the positive impacts in terms of improvements to safety, environmental protection and capacity to support science outweighed the negative impacts associated with proposed activities. Argentina further highlighted that this was its first experience in submitting a draft CEE, and expressed its appreciation for the feedback of Members on improving the draft.

(64) New Zealand introduced WP 32 *Report of the intersessional open-ended contact group (ICG) to Review the Draft Comprehensive Environmental Evaluation prepared by Argentina for the 'Redevelopment of Petrel Station, Dundee Island, Antarctica'*. On behalf of the ICG participants, New Zealand commended Argentina on several aspects of the draft CEE. The ICG had considered that the draft CEE was generally clear, well-structured and largely conformed to the requirements of Article 3 of Annex I to the

---

[1] According to the IPCC's Glossary "Impacts generally refer to effects on lives; livelihoods; health and well-being; ecosystems and species; economic, social and cultural assets; services (including ecosystem services); and infrastructure. Impacts may be referred to as consequences or outcomes, and can be adverse or beneficial." https://www.ipcc.ch/sr15/chapter/glossary/

Environment Protocol. Due to the scale and complexity of the proposed project, ICG participants had considered that the proposed activities were likely to have more than a minor or transitory impact on the environment and that a CEE was the appropriate level of EIA for the proposed activity.

(65) New Zealand noted that the ICG participants considered that the supporting description of the proposed activity in the main body of the CEE was lacking information, making it difficult to assess whether all the environmental impacts of the proposed activities had been identified and whether the suggested mitigation measures were appropriate. Participants in the ICG had identified a number of aspects of the draft CEE for which additional information or clarification would be useful to include in the final CEE if Argentina decided to proceed with the proposed activity, including further details on:

- the description of the proposed activity particularly including more detail of both construction and operational activities of the future station;
- alternatives to the proposed activity;
- the initial environmental reference state;
- the methodology used to forecast impacts of the proposed activity including how impact significance ratings were determined given the scale and complexity of the proposed activity;
- a more comprehensive assessment of cumulative impacts that might arise with the proposed activities, existing activities, and other known planned activities in the area;
- a more comprehensive assessment and description of mitigation measures;
- the environmental monitoring programme before, during and after construction activities; and
- gaps in knowledge relevant to the proposed activities.

(66) Argentina presented IP 114 *Preliminary responses to comments on the draft Comprehensive Environmental Evaluation (CEE) for the renovation of Petrel Base, Dundee Island, Antarctica.* It thanked ICG convener Ceisha Poirot (New Zealand), as well as the Members who had participated in the ICG. It noted the value it had found in looking to previous CEEs by other national Antarctic programmes, which had served as reference points for Argentina's draft CEE, and welcomed Members' valuable comments and suggestions to improve the structure and clarity of the document. Argentina highlighted, in particular, its intention to: improve the identification of impacts based on best available science; include a clearer, more comprehensive presentation of mitigation measures; incorporate a better analysis of alternatives; and improve the document's overall structure and clarity. Emphasising that the draft CEE was not a finalised document, but rather part of an ongoing process, Argentina noted that specific answers to each comment resulting from work of the ICG would be reflected in the final CEE.

(67) The Committee congratulated Argentina on its effort to prepare the draft CEE, noting the robustness of the document and that it was part of an ongoing process in the context of a large-scale project. It also expressed appreciation to the ICG participants for their work and commended Ceisha Poirot for her excellent work in convening and coordinating the discussions. It further thanked Argentina for its preliminary responses to the work of the ICG (IP 114), welcoming Argentina's commitment to continue research activities during the proposed activities with the least possible environmental impact. Several Members also raised specific issues, including questions about the intended use of the station and proposed runway, especially for tourist and non-

governmental activities, as well as how the facilities would be made available for international scientific cooperation. The Committee also emphasised that the discussion demonstrated the overall effectiveness of CEP procedures for considering draft CEEs.

(68) Argentina provided preliminary responses to the issues raised by Members. It highlighted that its priority in renovating Petrel Base was to support its scientific plans, noting that it did not intend to use the base for tourism purposes beyond the ways in which existing bases currently received visitors, and stated that the runway was not intended for commercial use. Recalling its long history of collaboration with other Parties, Argentina noted its intention to clarify how the base could be used to improve international engagement. Argentina emphasised its intention to follow up on all comments and questions raised both by the ICG and by Members during the meeting.

(69) Members noted that the process was still ongoing and welcomed Argentina's willingness to address all comments.

CEP advice to the ATCM on the draft Comprehensive Environmental Evaluation for the renovation of Petrel Base, Dundee Island, Antarctica

(70) The Committee agreed to advise the ATCM that it had discussed in detail the draft CEE prepared by Argentina for the renovation of Petrel Base, Dundee Island, Antarctica (WP 61 rev. 1). The Committee discussed the report by New Zealand of the ICG established to consider the draft CEE in accordance with the Procedures for Intersessional CEP Consideration of Draft CEEs (WP 32), and information provided by Argentina in an initial response to the ICG comments (IP 114). The Committee also discussed additional information provided by Argentina in response to issues raised during the meeting.

(71) The Committee also agreed to advise the ATCM that:

1) The draft CEE largely conformed to the requirements of Article 3 of Annex I to the Protocol on Environmental Protection to the Antarctic Treaty, although there was a need to address some elements of Article 3 in greater detail.
2) Argentina should consider the issues raised during the ICG and, if it decided to proceed with the proposed activity, there were several aspects for which additional information or clarification should be provided in the required final CEE. These matters had been outlined in detail in the submissions made by participants, and had been summarised in the ICG report. In particular, the Committee suggested that further details should be provided regarding:
    - the description of the proposed activity, particularly including more detail of both construction and operational activities, including for touristic and non-governmental purposes, if applicable, of the future station;
    - alternatives to the proposed activity;
    - the initial environmental reference state;
    - the methodology used to forecast the impacts of the proposed activity including how impact significance ratings were determined given the scale and complexity of the proposed activity;
    - a more comprehensive assessment of cumulative impacts that might arise with the proposed activities, existing activities, and other known planned activities in the area;
    - a more comprehensive assessment and description of the mitigation measures;
    - the environmental monitoring programme before, during and after construction activities; and
    - gaps in knowledge relevant to the proposed activities.
3) Due to their scale and complexity, the proposed activities outlined in the CEE for

the Redevelopment of Petrel Station were likely to have more than a minor or transitory impact on the environment, and a CEE was the appropriate level of environmental impact assessment for the proposed activity. The conclusion of the draft CEE did not align with the environmental impact assessment and identified mitigation measures and it was suggested that a review of the environmental impact assessment and a more thorough description and consideration of mitigation measures would be needed to support the conclusion of the CEE.

4) The draft CEE was generally clear, well-structured, and well-presented although due to the scale and complexity of the proposed activities, suggestions had been made to enhance the presentation and clarity of the document.

---

(72) Members observed that there was not yet a standard method for addressing and incorporating comments into a final CEE in accordance with Article 3(6) of Annex I to the Environment Protocol. The Committee therefore agreed to request the Secretariat to review how comments and responses had been reflected in final CEEs in the past, as a basis for future CEP discussion.

8b) Other EIA Matters

(73) The United Kingdom introduced WP 40 *Improving the Effectiveness of Antarctic Environmental Impact Assessment*, which presented a summary of informal intersessional discussions on improving the effectiveness of the EIA system. The United Kingdom noted that it had convened these discussions following CEP XXIV, at which the Committee had agreed to review and progress some of the recommendations outlined in CEP XXIV - WP 33. Based on the intersessional discussions, the United Kingdom recommended that the Committee: continue to share information on EIA processes; recommend the ATCM draft a Resolution on the requirement to include mitigation measures in preliminary and IEE stage assessments; request the Secretariat provide a summary of previous CEP discussions on assessing cumulative impacts, and include a programme of work on improving the effectiveness of the Antarctic EIA system in the CEP Five-year Work Plan.

(74) The Committee thanked the United Kingdom for the comprehensive intersessional work and for its recommendations. The Committee underlined the importance of improving EIA processes as a fundamental component of the Environment Protocol and crucial for environmental protection. Many Members fully supported the recommendations and the draft Resolution, and stressed the importance of assessing cumulative impacts. Some Members highlighted challenges relating to the interpretation of mitigation at the preliminary assessment stage, and differing approaches to preliminary as well as IEE assessments in various domestic legislation and processes. Members noted that flexibility regarding preliminary evaluations was needed.

(75) Noting the increase in human activities and their footprint, ASOC stressed the need to improve and refine EIA processes in the context of improved data availability and collection methods.

(76) After having addressed concerns raised by Members, the Committee agreed to a draft Resolution on Improving the Effectiveness of Antarctic Environmental Impact Assessment.

(77) The Committee welcomed the proposal to schedule further work on improving the effectiveness of the Antarctic EIA system, particularly regarding consistency, cumulative impact assessments, monitoring, and thresholds for when EIA documents should be amended or a new EIA conducted when an activity changes.

(78) The Committee also encouraged Members to share - via Information Papers, templates, guidance and other documents - information associated with the operation of their EIA processes for the benefit of Members.

CEP advice to the ATCM on Improving the Effectiveness of Antarctic Environmental Impact Assessment

(79) The Committee advised the ATCM that, to contribute to the process of improving the effectiveness of the Antarctic EIA system, it had agreed to:

- forward a draft Resolution on Improving the Effectiveness of Antarctic Environmental Impact Assessment to the ATCM for approval;
- request the Secretariat to prepare a comprehensive summary of previous CEP discussions on assessing cumulative impacts as a first step for progressing work on improving the assessment of cumulative impacts; and
- update the CEP Five-year Work Plan to implement a programme of work for taking action to improve the effectiveness of the Antarctic EIA system.

---

(80) Belarus presented IP 27 *The retrospective modeling as an approach to cumulative impacts assessment due to operation of scientific stations in the Antarctic*, which drew attention to the need for methodological progress in assessing the cumulative impacts of ongoing and planned activities on the Antarctic environment. Belarus proposed that the approach used in a recent scientific paper could be valuable in assessing environmental impacts related to atmospheric emissions throughout the region.

(81) Italy presented IP 82 *Finalizing the construction of the gravel runway in the area of Mario Zucchelli Station, Terra Nova Bay, Victoria Land, Antarctica*, which reported on recent developments in the construction of the runway in the area of Mario Zucchelli Station. The paper described technical work, the runway's first aircraft landing, the implementation of an environmental monitoring plan, and the next steps to finalise the runway.

(82) The Committee noted the following Information Papers and Secretariat Paper submitted under this agenda item:

- IP 30 *Report on the Replacement of the Cape Shirreff Field Camp, Livingston Island, Antarctica* (United States).
- IP 133 *Progress of glaciological research activities at the Dome Fuji II Camp* (Japan).
- SP 7 *Annual list of Initial Environmental Evaluations (IEE) and Comprehensive Environmental Evaluations (CEE) prepared between 1 April 2022 and 31 March 2023* (Secretariat).

(83) The Committee noted that the following Background Paper had been submitted under this agenda item:

- BP 24 *Permit for the Russian Antarctic Expedition Activities in 2023-2027* (Russian Federation).

Item 9: Area Protection and Management Plans

9a) Management Plans

i) Draft Management Plans which have been reviewed by the Subsidiary Group on Management Plans

(84) The convener of the Subsidiary Group on Management Plans (SGMP), Anoop Kumar Tiwari (India), introduced WP 47 *Subsidiary Group on Management Plans Report of activities during the intersessional period 2022-2023*, on behalf of the SGMP. In accordance with Terms of Reference #1 to #3, the convenor of the SGMP noted that the Group had been referred one draft revised ASPA management plan and one management plan for a proposed new ASPA for intersessional review in the past intersessional period. The convener of the SGMP thanked Polly Penhale (USA) for moderating the pre-meeting review of management plans which were not submitted to the SGMP review process, Martín Díaz (Argentina) for coordinating the review of the management plan for the merger of ASPAs 152 and 153 submitted by the United States, and Astrid Høgestøl (Norway) for coordinating the review of a new ASPA management plan submitted by Belgium for parts of the Western Sør Rondane Mountains, Dronning Maud Land, East Antarctica. The SGMP convenor also thanked all active participants in the SGMP for their work and reminded the Committee that all Members were welcome to join the SGMP.

(85) Regarding the revised management plan for the merger of ASPAs 152 and 153 proposed by the United States, the SGMP advised the Committee that the revised management plan was well-written, of high quality and consistent with relevant CEP guidelines, and adequately addressed the key points raised in its advice to the proponent. Accordingly, the SGMP recommended that the Committee approve the revised management plan for the ASPA.

(86) As provided for in Decision 9 (2005), the United States noted that the revised management plan had been submitted to CCAMLR for consideration to determine if the plan's provisions might prevent or restrict CCAMLR-related activities. The United States reported that as CCAMLR had not reached consensus on approving the revised management plan, should the ATCM adopt the proposed management plan, the plan would need to be reconsidered by CCAMLR.

(87) The Committee thanked the United States for its comprehensive work on the merger of ASPAs 152 and 152. Following minor revisions, the Committee agreed the merger of ASPAs 152 and 153 and, in accordance with Decision 9 (2005), noted the United States would re-submit the revised Management Plan to SC-CAMLR for approval, with the intent to forward it to ATCM 46 for adoption.

(88) Regarding the proposal for a new ASPA in parts of the Western Sør Rondane Mountains, Dronning Maud Land, East Antarctica (Belgium), the SGMP advised the Committee that the management plan was well-written, of high quality, and consistent with relevant CEP guidelines, and adequately addressed the key points raised in its advice to the proponent. Accordingly, the SGMP recommended that the Committee approve the management plan for the new ASPA.

(89) Belgium expressed its gratitude to the convener of the SGMP, the Members who had participated in the SGMP, Norway for providing one of the included maps, and the coordinator appointed by the SGMP for the review of the draft Management Plan. Belgium listed the main changes it had made during the intersessional period in response to the SGMP advice, namely: the improvement of the maps; the introduction of buffer zones; the expansion of site F to include the catchment area of the lakes in this site and the inclusion of an appendix containing photographs in order to demonstrate the aesthetic values. Belgium also referred the Members to its IP 103 *Data from the molecular diversity studies in the proposed ASPA in parts of Western Sør Rondane Mountains,*

Dronning Maud Land, East Antarctica for more information about the microbial diversity of the different sites and the scientific research that had been done with regard to these sites. Belgium welcomed the advice of the SGMP and expressed its hope that the Committee could approve the draft Management Plan.

(90) The Committee commended Belgium for its responsiveness to feedback during the SGMP process. China raised a concern about using prohibited zones as a mechanism to protect two areas in the Pingvinane Nunataks by preventing any human presence, which in the view of China would impede or even stop scientific research and monitoring. China noted Annex V was intended to prevent human interference, not human presence, and suggested the use of a reference area as an alternative to prohibited zones to allow limited research and monitoring activities. Many Members noted that Annex V to the Environment Protocol provided for ASPAs to include areas kept inviolate from human interference, and for the designation of prohibited zones within ASPAs, and that there were prohibited zones within existing ASPAs. Many Members also recognised that the purpose for proposing these small sites at Pingvinane Nunataks as prohibited zones was to safeguard opportunities for future research by keeping these areas as pristine as possible, in particular, to study microbial environments with new molecular tools, and noted the size of the sites would not impede opportunities for scientific research to any substantial degree.

(91) Following changing "prohibited zones" to "restricted zones", the Committee agreed to the management plan for, and the establishment of, a new ASPA in parts of the Western Sør Rondane Mountains, Dronning Maud Land, East Antarctica.

(92) The Committee thanked Belgium for its work to put forward this proposal and for leading several rounds of discussion during the meeting on the drafting of the management plan. Many Members expressed their disappointment that consensus was not reached on the inclusion of prohibited zones within the ASPA. They urged Parties to respect the robust scientific rationale for the use of prohibited zones in the Area and refrain from entering these areas without full consultation with other Parties.

(93) Several Members also expressed their concern regarding the recent difficulty in achieving agreement on the use of the management tools available to the Committee, often due to the objections of one Member. Some Members suggested the Committee request legal advice from the ATCM regarding the relationship between text in the Antarctic Treaty concerning freedom of scientific investigation (Article II) and text in Annex V to the Environment Protocol on designation of areas kept inviolate from human interference and the identification of prohibited zones. Some Members noted that the CEP was not the correct forum for such discussions.

(94) China expressed its concern that it was important to consider the freedom of scientific investigation under the Antarctic Treaty when considering the use of management tools like prohibited areas. China noted that it was important that the Committee consider whether an area prohibited from all human activity would prevent scientific research and monitoring. It indicated that the importance of research and monitoring was emphasised throughout the Committee's meetings.

(95) Belgium thanked Members for their engagement during the meeting and intersessional period. It was heartened by the support for the proposed ASPA, and the flexibility shown by the Committee to reach compromise. Belgium noted that, like other Members, it regretted that the Committee could not reach consensus on the use of prohibited zones. Belgium reconfirmed its commitment to the Environment Protocol, and reiterated the importance of the CEP using the full range of measures and tools at its disposal to reach its objective of environmental protection.

(96) The convenor of the SGMP advised the Committee that the management plans for the

following three ASPAs were still under review by Chile:

- ASPA 125: Fildes Peninsula, King George (25 de Mayo) Island (Chile)
- ASPA 146: South Bay, Doumer Island, Palmer Archipelago (Chile)
- ASPA 150: Ardley Island (Ardley Peninsula), Maxwell Bay, King George Island (Chile)

(97) Chile noted that it would resume work on updates of these management plans and invited interested Members to contribute. Some Members offered to lend support in coordinating this effort and to contribute scientific expertise as relevant. The Committee expressed its appreciation for the collaborative nature of work on management plans, emphasising that ASPAs were a matter of joint interest for all Members.

ii) Revised draft Management Plans which have not been reviewed by the Subsidiary Group on Management Plans

(98) The Committee considered the report from the SGMP's pre-meeting review of 15 revised ASPA management plans and one revised ASMA management plan.

(99) The Committee thanked the convenor of the pre-meeting review, Polly Penhale (United States), for the excellent work undertaken during the intersessional period and the clear report on the status of draft management plans.

(100) The Committee further thanked the proponents for their efforts in submitting high-quality draft management plans.

(101) With respect to ASPA 156 (WP 28 rev. 1), ASPA 168 (WP 37 rev. 1) and ASPA 165 (WP 1), the Committee noted that the pre-meeting review had raised minor comments on these revised management plans, which had already been addressed by the proponents.

(102) With respect to ASPA 149 (WP 45), ASPA 123 (WP 23), ASPA 122 (WP 2 rev. 1), ASPA 172 (WP 24), ASPA 137 (WP 20), ASPA 138 (WP 26), ASPA 108 (WP 5), ASPA 117 (WP 6), ASPA 147 (WP 7), and ASPA 170 (WP 8), the Committee noted that the revised management plans had received no comments during the pre-meeting review.

(103) With respect to ASPA 145 (WP 51), the Committee noted that the draft management plan had already been discussed and approved by the Committee in 2022 and thereafter had been approved by SC-CAMLR, and that it now would move forward for adoption by the ATCM.

(104) With respect to ASPA 132 (WP 54 rev. 1) and ASMA 1 (WP 59), the Committee noted that minor technical issues had been identified. After minor amendments, the Committee approved these plans.

CEP advice to the ATCM on new and revised management plans for ASPAs and ASMAs

(105) The Committee agreed to forward the following revised and new management plans to the ATCM for approval by means of a Measure:

- ASMA 1, Admiralty Bay, King George Island
- ASPA 108, Green Island, Berthelot Islands, Antarctic Peninsula
- ASPA 117, Avian Island, Marguerite Bay, Antarctic Peninsula
- ASPA 122, Arrival Heights, Hut Point Peninsula, Ross Island
- ASPA 123, Barwick and Balham Valleys, Southern Victoria Land
- ASPA 132, Potter Peninsula, King George Island (Isla 25 de Mayo), South Shetland Islands

- ASPA 137, Northwest White Island, McMurdo Sound
- ASPA 138, Linnaeus Terrace, Asgard Range, Victoria Land
- ASPA 145, Port Foster, Deception Island, South Shetland Islands
- ASPA 147, Ablation Valley and Ganymede Heights, Alexander Island
- ASPA 149, Cape Shirreff and San Telmo Island, Livingston Island, South Shetland Islands
- ASPA 156, Lewis Bay, Mount Erebus, Ross Island
- ASPA 165, Edmonson Point, Wood Bay, Ross Sea
- ASPA 168, Mount Harding, Grove Mountains, East Antarctica
- ASPA 170, Marion Nunataks, Charcot Island, Antarctic Peninsula
- ASPA 172, Lower Taylor Glacier and Blood Falls, McMurdo Dry Valleys, Victoria Land
- ASPA 179, Parts of Western Sør Rondane Mountains, Dronning Maud Land, East Antarctica

---

iii) New draft management plans for protected/managed areas

(106) The Committee considered draft management plans for two proposed new ASPAs:

- WP 11 *Report on the informal ICG to develop an ASPA Draft Management Plan for Danger Islands Archipelago (North-eastern Antarctic Peninsula)* (Germany, United States)
- WP 60 rev. 1 *Draft Antarctic Specially Protected Area Management Plan for Farrier Col, Horseshoe Island, Marguerite Bay* (Belgium, Türkiye, United Kingdom)

(107) Germany introduced WP 11 *Report on the informal ICG to develop an ASPA Draft Management Plan for Danger Islands Archipelago (North-eastern Antarctic Peninsula)*, prepared jointly with the United States. It noted that the Danger Islands Archipelago was an area of exceptional ecological and scientific interest due to its outstanding number and diversity of seabirds. It recalled that CEP XXIV had agreed to a proposed prior assessment for the Danger Islands. The proponents had led an informal ICG to draft a management plan for the area and thanked all ICG participants for their useful comments and contributions, which had been incorporated into WP 11. The proponents recommended that the Committee take note of the draft management plan and refer it to the SGMP for further consideration.

(108) The Committee thanked Germany and the United States for their work on the proposed new ASPA and draft management plan, and commended the informal ICG participants for collaborating with the proponents toward the draft management plan. It agreed to forward the management plan for the proposed new ASPA to the SGMP for review in the coming intersessional period.

(109) IAATO expressed its appreciation for having been involved in the intersessional discussions, and noted that it had trialled draft site guidelines at Heroína Island to contribute to the discussions. IAATO reported that, although visits to the Danger Islands by IAATO operators were rare due to distance and local conditions, operators did visit the islands. It also reported that, in anticipation of the draft management plan for an ASPA for the Danger Islands Archipelago, IAATO had announced during its 2023 annual meeting that landings on Heroína Island would no longer be permitted.

(110) The United Kingdom introduced WP 60 rev. 1 *Draft Antarctic Specially Protected Area Management Plan for Farrier Col, Horseshoe Island, Marguerite Bay*, prepared jointly with Belgium and Türkiye, and recalled that CEP XXIV had agreed to a proposed prior assessment for the area. The United Kingdom explained that the region in the proposed ASPA was of environmental, scientific, wilderness and aesthetic value, highlighting that its lakes were likely refugia for species from the last glacial cycle and were rare examples of rockbound oligotrophic lakes. It noted that the proponents had prepared the draft management plan in accordance with Annex V of the Environment Protocol as well as the revised Guide to the Preparation of Management Plans for Antarctic Specially Protected Areas. The United Kingdom expressed its appreciation for the effective collaborative efforts of Türkiye and Belgium. It recommended that that CEP forward the draft management plan to the SGMP for intersessional review.

(111) Türkiye and Belgium also expressed their appreciation to the co-proponents for their cooperation towards the preparation of the draft management plan and further underscored the importance of the lakes.

(112) IAATO expressed thanks to Belgium, Türkiye and the United Kingdom for the draft Management Plan. IAATO noted that Horseshoe Island was a site that IAATO operators visited, mainly around HSM 63 following the ATCM Site Guidelines for Site No. 24. IAATO noted that it supported the draft recommendations and would notify its operators of the proposed ASPA for consideration during the 2023-24 season. IAATO offered to engage in further discussion of IAATO operator activities on Horseshoe Island.

(113) The Committee thanked the proponents for their work and highlighted the value of joint efforts to prepare management plans. Several Members offered support in collaborating on further work related to this management plan. Noting the important history of the lakes and the relevance of their protection to understanding processes such as dispersion across the continent, Members agreed that the area merited protection. The Committee agreed to forward the management plan for the proposed new ASPA to the SGMP for review in the coming intersessional period.

CEP advice to the ATCM on new draft management plans for protected/managed areas

(114) The Committee agreed to advise the ATCM that it had decided to forward the following draft management plans for protected areas to the SGMP for review:

- Proposal for a new Antarctic Specially Protected Area in Danger Islands Archipelago (North-eastern Antarctic Peninsula).
- Proposal for a new Antarctic Specially Protected Area in Farrier Col, Horseshoe Island, Marguerite Bay.

---

iv) Papers relating to prior assessment of proposed new protected areas

(115) The Committee considered one Working Paper relating to the prior assessment of a proposed new protected area, in accordance with the Guidelines: A prior assessment process for the designation of ASPAs and ASMAs.

(116) Ukraine introduced WP 58 *Prior assessment of a proposed Antarctic Specially Protected Area within the Argentine Islands and Kyiv Peninsula area, Antarctic Peninsula.* Ukraine explained that it had prepared a pre-assessment for a multi-site ASPA, which represented a range of values. It highlighted that protection of this area was also important for long-term research and for providing a control area against which to compare human impacts. Ukraine expressed its willingness to prepare a draft

management plan with all interested Members, if the CEP agreed that the area merited protection.

(117) The Committee thanked Ukraine for its work in preparing the prior assessment and recalled Ukraine's longstanding work to consider options for spatial protection and management of the area, including its long-term monitoring of the area. Members noted the use of the agreed prior assessment template and guidelines and commended the high level of detail contained in the document. Some Members raised concerns regarding a lack of clarity about the core values to be protected. They also noted that the number of sites incorporated might present some complexity in terms of implementation, while other Members noted the scattered nature of terrestrial biology in the area. Another Member commented on the lack of representativeness. While expressing general support for the prior assessment, the Committee noted the need for better clarity on these issues. The Committee encouraged Ukraine to take the Committee's comments into account to continue to develop a clearer framework for the area's protection.

(118) IAATO observed that several sites incorporated in the area were highly valued by IAATO operators and were some of the region's most visited sites. It suggested that more detailed maps would be useful and allow operators to zoom in on specific areas of the proposed ASPA. It also asked for further clarification on how the proposed ASPA would work in relation to existing site guidelines, on whether surface vessel travel would be allowed in marine-only areas, on yacht lines ashore, and on possible caveats around safety needs.

v) Other matters relating to management plans for protected/managed areas

(119) Chile introduced WP 50 *Status of Antarctic Specially Protected Area No. 144, Chile Bay (Discovery Bay)*, which provided an analysis of ASPA 144 and Chile's recommendation to delist the ASPA. Having completed its earlier long-term research project on benthic fauna, Chile had reviewed the area based on the Checklist to assist in the inspection of ASPAs and ASMAs, the Guidelines for Implementation of the Framework for Protected Areas, and the Guidelines for de-designation of ASPAs. This work had been supported by papers submitted to CEP XXI (WP 11, IP 9) and CEP XXIV (IP 127, IP 128), as well as IP 70 *Analysis of the current status of the Antarctic Specially Protected Area No. 144, Chile Bay (Discovery Bay), Greenwich Island* (Chile). Based on this analysis, Chile had determined that the Area's special interest as a control area for fauna restoration at Port Foster was no longer valid. Its research had not indicated the significant presence of other values that would support continuing with special protection. Chile therefore recommended that the CEP agree to the de-designation of ASPA 144.

(120) While supporting the proposal, one Member noted that the designation of protected areas should not be tied to specific projects or concrete activities. ASOC noted that the area could still hold scientific interest.

(121) The Committee thanked Chile for a thorough assessment in accordance with the de-designation guidelines. On the basis of this assessment, the Committee agreed that ASPA 144 could be de-designated. The Committee again underscored that such decisions should not be taken lightly and noted that the area would remain subject to the comprehensive general protections of the Environment Protocol that apply to all areas.

CEP advice to the ATCM on the de-designation of ASPA 144

(122) The Committee agreed to advise the ATCM that it had considered a thorough assessment of the status and values of ASPA 144 Chile Bay (Discovery Bay), presented in accordance with the Guidelines for de-designation of ASPAs (CEP XXIII Final Report,

Appendix 3), and had concluded on the basis of this assessment that the special protection status of this area could be removed, with the understanding that the area would remain under the comprehensive general protection provisions of the Environmental Protocol. Accordingly, the Committee agreed to recommend de-designation of ASPA 144 Chile Bay (Discovery Bay).

---

(123) Germany presented IP 60 *Elaboration of an ASPA Draft Management Plan for Otto-von-Gruber-Gebirge, Dronning Maud Land, East Antarctica,* prepared jointly with the United States. It reported on German and United States research expeditions into the Gruber Mountains in the 2022-23 Antarctic summer season. The main objective of the German team was to collect data to derive orthomosaics and digital elevation models of the proposed ASPA. The United States scientists continued both short- and long-term studies of ecological responses of the glacier, soil and lake ecosystems within the Untersee Oasis. The results of these investigations, which were still to be evaluated, would support the initial compilation of a draft management plan for the proposed ASPA. Germany and the United States reported that they would convene informal intersessional discussions with the aim of gathering input and comments to elaborate the first draft management plan for the Area, and encouraged participation from interested stakeholders and experts.

(124) The Russian Federation noted that the USSR had been carrying out scientific research in this area since 1969. The scientists of the Russian Antarctic Expedition were studying the flora of the area. Together with US scientists, a long-term scientific project was carried out in the Untersee Lake area. Russia was ready to join the US and Germany as one of the stakeholders in the proposal for this area as an ASPA.

(125) The Committee thanked the co-authors for their paper, and some Members expressed interest in participating in the intersessional discussions and noted willingness to contribute with data from scientific research they have done in this area.

9b) Historic Sites and Monuments

(126) New Zealand introduced WP 27 *Relocation of artefacts from HSM 68: Supply depot, Hell's Gate Moraine*, prepared jointly with the United Kingdom and Norway. It reported that the proponents had reviewed future storage and display options for artefacts from HSM 68, which had been stored in a container at New Zealand's Scott Base since being removed from their original location during the 1994-95 season. The proponents recommended that the CEP support the preferred long-term storage and safekeeping of the objects at Canterbury Museum in Christchurch, New Zealand. The objects would be conserved for possible future display as part of the museum's Antarctic collection or for a possible return to Antarctica. They also recommended that the CEP update the Conservation Status of HSM 68 listing on the Antarctic Protected Area database.

(127) The Committee thanked the proponents for assessing the future storage and display options of artefacts from HSM 68 and recognised that the decision to relocate the items had been difficult. The Committee agreed to update the Conservation Status of HSM 68. It also noted the utility of developing further guidance for managing and conserving HSMs that may need to be relocated outside of Antarctica, highlighting the provisions of Article 8.4 of Annex V of the Protocol.

CEP advice to the ATCM on the relocation of artefacts from HSM 68

(128) The Committee agreed to advise the ATCM that it supported the recommendation by New Zealand, the United Kingdom and Norway to relocate artefacts from HSM 68 outside of Antarctica for long-term storage and safekeeping.

(129) The Committee further agreed to update the Conservation Status on the HSM 68 listing on the Antarctic Protected Area database to read: "Sledge and supplies removed from site in 1994. The artefacts have been documented and conserved (2017) by the New Zealand-based Antarctic Heritage Trust. They are stored at Canterbury Museum, Christchurch, New Zealand as part of the Reserve Collection supported by the New Zealand Antarctic Heritage Trust. The artefacts are extremely fragile."

---

(130) The United Kingdom introduced WP 53 *HSM No. 93 The Wreck of Endurance: Conservation Management Plan and Future Protection.* It provided an update on progress with the Conservation Management Plan and future protection of the wreck of the *Endurance* following its discovery on 5 March 2022 and as described in ATCM XLIV - WP 47. The United Kingdom recommended that the Committee: note the progress on the Conservation Management Plan for HSM 93 and proposed next steps; note the proposed consultation during the development of the Conservation Management Plan for protecting HSM 93; and invite Members to share any initial views on the possible future proposal for seeking ASPA designation for the wreck site.

(131) The Committee once again commended the extraordinary feat of finding the wreck of the *Endurance* and the continued work of the United Kingdom to consider the appropriate level of protection for the wreck. It also thanked the United Kingdom for its progress in developing a Conservation Management Plan for the underwater site. While some Members noted with interest that the United Kingdom may seek ASPA designation for the wreck, some Members noted also that there may be practical and legal issues that may need further assessment when further considering the option of ASPA designation. Some Members also noted their interest in participating in the consultation process of the development of the Conservation Management Plan for protecting HSM 93.

(132) The Committee noted the following Information Papers submitted under this agenda item:

- IP 111 *Report on the work carried out at the "Swedish hut" on Snow Hill Island (HSM Nr. 38)* (Argentina, Sweden).
- IP 113 *State of conservation of the Casa Moneta Museum (HSM N°42)* (Argentina).

9c) Site Guidelines

(133) IAATO presented IP 53 *A Five-Year Overview and 2022-23 Season Report on IAATO Operator Use of Antarctic Peninsula Landing Sites and ATCM Visitor Site Guidelines*, which presented data collected from IAATO operator post-visit report forms. The report showed that, while overall tourism levels continued to rise after the hiatus during the COVID-19 pandemic, the increase was not uniform across all visitor sites. IAATO also noted collaboration with Parties on the development of new site guidelines and reviewing any of the existing IAATO site-specific guidelines would be welcomed.

(134) The Committee thanked IAATO for its paper. The Committee emphasised the value of having this information and receiving updates from IAATO and its members, and noted the importance of these updates for deliberations on matters relevant to tourism in light of the Environment Protocol.

9d) Marine Spatial Protection and Management

(135) ASOC introduced IP 118 rev. 1 *ASOC update on marine protected areas in the Southern Ocean.* ASOC noted that marine protection is a high-profile issue globally, and outside

the Antarctic Treaty system there is a growing international agreement that MPAs are an essential tool for preserving ocean biodiversity, including at the Convention on Biological Diversity and in the new Marine Biodiversity of Areas Beyond National Jurisdiction (BBNJ) agreement. ASOC also noted that CCAMLR had not adopted any new MPAs since 2019, but that there had been some positive developments, including a growing number of MPA co-proponents; further work on MPA proposals; and an expansion of the scientific literature. ASOC also encouraged the CEP to take action on issues relevant to MPAs and to the CEP's workplan, such as expanding the network of terrestrial and marine ASPAs and ASMAs in Antarctica, considering the designation of the emperor penguin as a Specially Protected Species, and taking action on climate change in the Antarctic.

(136) The Committee thanked ASOC for its work and noted its recommendations. Some Members stressed the importance of marine protection for biodiversity and in mitigating the impacts of climate change. Some Members called for continued efforts to strengthen the integration between ASPAs and ASMAs and CCAMLR's MPA network.

9e) Other Annex V Matters

(137) The SGMP convenor, Anoop Tiwari (India), introduced the second part of WP 47 *Subsidiary Group on Management Plans Report of activities during the intersessional period 2022-23* with respect to the SGMP's ToR 4 and 6. The SGMP had as a task under its ToR 6 to 'Review and revise where necessary existing management tools for protection and subsequent management of environments and habitats at risk from climate change,' and 'consider if and how they effectively consider climate change issues'. The SGMP had discussed this task through two rounds of discussions and concluded that it might be appropriate to prioritise in the first round the review of the Guidelines for implementation of the Framework for Protected Areas set forth in Article 3, Annex V of the Environment Protocol (Annex to Resolution 1 (2000)) and the (Revised) Guide to the Preparation of Management Plans for Antarctic Specially Protected Areas (Resolution 2 (2011)). The SGMP planned to initiate this work in the next intersessional period and report back to CEP 26 on progress.

(138) The SGMP also proposed a work plan for the 2023-24 intersessional period.

(139) The Committee thanked the SGMP for its advice, and agreed to adopt the SGMP's proposed work plan for 2023-24:

Terms of Reference	Suggested tasks
ToRs 1 to 3	Review draft management plans referred by CEP for intersessional review and provide advice to proponents (including the three pending plans from the previous intersessional period)
	Submit Working Paper to CEP 26 on SGMP ToR 1 to 3
ToRs 4 to 6	Work with relevant Parties to ensure progress on the review of management plans overdue for five-year review
	Pre-meeting review of all Management Plans with minor changes and submit a summary of recommendations to CEP during the discussion of revised Management Plans

Terms of Reference	Suggested tasks
	Continue work on CCRWP action 2(e) "Review and revise where necessary existing management tools for protection and subsequent management of environments and habitats at risk from climate change", consider if and how they effectively take climate change issues into consideration, and submit progress report to CEP 26
	Review and update the SGMP work plan

(140) SCAR presented IP 48 *Systematic Conservation Plan for the Antarctic Peninsula Project Updates and Next Steps,* prepared jointly with IAATO, which described a collaborative project to develop the first systematic conservation plan for the Antarctic Peninsula. SCAR reported that the project had primarily finished in 2021 and that, following the correction of some input data and additional requested analyses, the project had concluded in 2022. It also noted that the large amount of data generated by the project and the creation of a conservation planning decision-support tool tailored to the Antarctic Peninsula was likely to be of interest to a broad audience. SCAR explained that the decision-support tool was created in the form of R code, an open-source programming language and software environment for statistical analysis and graphics representation. This R code, together with the majority of input data used in the project, would be made available for public access and use prior to CEP 26. Outcomes from the project would also be made available in a peer-reviewed scientific publication.

(141) The Committee thanked SCAR and IAATO for their work on this project and tool. Some Members noted that it was not entirely clear how the tool could be used at a practical level and by policymakers, and asked whether more information or a demonstration could be provided in the future.

(142) SCAR thanked Members for their comments and reiterated that the open-source software used was the best platform for this valuable tool. SCAR reiterated the tool would be released before next year's meeting and would be open access, allowing any Member to test it. SCAR noted that the tool was likely to be of use in management discussions and encouraged Members to engage with and learn more about the tool once it was released.

(143) Argentina presented IP 22 *Contributions to the promotion and awareness of the care of palaeontological heritage in the Antarctic region*, which reported on an Argentine initiative to promote visitor awareness regarding Antarctic palaeontological heritage. Argentina reported that it had developed educational posters and brochures distributed in Ushuaia as well as the most visited Argentine scientific stations in Antarctica.

(144) The Committee thanked Argentina for its paper and for providing the material to the Members for further dissemination and feedback. It welcomed the valuable contribution to preserving paleontological heritage and encouraged further engagement around the topic. IAATO noted its efforts in fossil protection through the distribution of information through briefings with staff, visitors and crews.

(145) Spain presented IP 76 *Report of the management group for Antarctic Specially Managed Area (ASMA) No. 4 Deception Island for the period 2022/23*, prepared jointly with Argentina, Chile, Norway, United Kingdom and the United States. The paper reported on information exchange in relation to ASMA 4. It highlighted joint work conducted by Argentina and Spain, especially increasing observation of volcanic platforms. The co-authors thanked IAATO for its contributions to the work of the management group and reported on discussions regarding pollution in the Port Foster area and possible mitigation measures if the pollution levels increased.

(146) The Committee thanked the co-authors for the report and commended them for their work.

(147) New Zealand presented IP 90 *The need for increased protection of Antarctica's inland waters*, prepared jointly with Spain and the United Kingdom, which emphasised that the availability of liquid water was the most important physical driver of Antarctic terrestrial biodiversity. It noted that human activities had resulted in significant impacts on Antarctic inland waters both directly and indirectly, and highlighted the need for increased protection. It further noted that out of the management plans for all 75 current ASPAs, only two ASPAs had been designated explicitly to protect inland water systems, with fourteen additional ASPAs including some reference to them. The paper suggested that more strategic protection for inland waters could be enhanced through: the use of the Antarctic Conservation Biogeographic Regions (ACBRs) to ensure representative coverage; the use of Very High Resolution remote sensing products to identify likely areas for potential inclusion for inland water protection; setting goals to protect representative classes of inland water bodies; and considering designating new ASPAs by a collaborative approach, including areas where access is restricted for significant periods of time to act as strategic investments in habitat and biological diversity for future generations.

(148) The Committee thanked the co-authors and emphasised the vulnerability and importance of Antarctic inland water bodies and the need for their increased protection. The Committee welcomed the collaborative efforts on inland water ecosystems and research exchange that had taken place between Members.

(149) The Committee noted that the following additional Information Paper had been submitted under this agenda item:

- IP 130 rev. 1 *Deployment of the first permanent Argentine Volcano Monitoring Network in Deception Island* (Argentina).

Item 10: Conservation of Antarctic Flora and Fauna

10a) Quarantine and Non-native Species

(150) The United States introduced WP 3 *Surveillance and coordination for the prevention and detection of Highly Pathogenic Avian Influenza in Antarctica*, which raised concerns over the largest worldwide outbreak of Highly Pathogenic Avian Influenza (HPAI). The United States stressed that HPAI was a highly contagious viral disease which rapidly evolved and could have devastating consequences on Antarctic bird populations. It noted that the World Organization of Animal Health (WOAH) considered HPAI as a very serious threat and expected it to spread further. It stated that the risk of HPAI reaching Antarctica was very high. It noted the importance of reducing the threat of anthropogenic introduction or spread of HPAI through monitoring wildlife colonies for signs of HPAI, taking precautions when working around wildlife, and maintaining the highest biosecurity as recalled in the SCAR Antarctic Wildlife Health Working Group's (AWHWG) recommendations to national Antarctic programmes and tour operators. It also described procedures developed in the United States for detecting and preventing the introduction or spread of HPAI between seabird and marine mammal colonies. The United States encouraged Parties to develop and implement procedures for preventing the introduction or spread of HPAI by their national Antarctic programmes and to share information on HPAI detections in Antarctica. It further recommended that SCAR provide updates to the CEP on the potential impacts of HPAI to native birds and mammals in Antarctica.

(151) The Committee thanked the United States for its paper and for bringing this serious issue

to its attention. The Committee acknowledged the potential risks of HPAI spread in Antarctica and the great dangers it posed to Antarctic bird colonies and mammals. Many Members highlighted the need for coordinating efforts and developing a collective, timely and effective response to prevent the potential dramatic consequences of HPAI in Antarctica. Members stressed the importance of enhancing rapid information sharing and strengthening surveillance. The Committee encouraged Members to use the competent authorities sub-forum to exchange information to facilitate coordination and collaboration to meet this urgent challenge.

(152) SCAR noted that it would provide further updates on the potential impacts of HPAI on Antarctic birds and mammals, as requested by the Committee. It also referred to its IP 101 *Heightened Risk of Avian Influenza in the Antarctic Treaty Area,* prepared jointly with IAATO and COMNAP, which reported on work being undertaken to develop practical advice to identify suspected cases of HPAI and to mitigate or eliminate risks associated with direct human contact. It further noted the establishment of a collaborative group under the leadership of the SCAR Antarctic Wildlife Health Working Group to focus on these issues for the upcoming season, and encouraged wide participation of experts from the CEP in this work.

(153) Several Members shared their experiences with guidelines and protocols to prevent the introduction and spread of HPAI, as well as their national procedures for issuing permits, actions to avoid the spread of the virus, vessel monitoring, and possible mitigation actions. Members emphasised the importance of rapid coordination on sharing information about the early detection of suspicious cases, and suggested acting upon the assumption that the virus would inevitably spread in Antarctica. Members also welcomed further discussion on the mapping of outbreaks and noted that this should include suspected and confirmed outbreaks.

(154) Chile referred to its IP 122 *Implementation for Behavioral Protocol in Antarctica and Monitoring for the Highly Pathogenic Avian Influenza (HPAI) Virus in the Magallanes Region*, which provided a report on the occurrence of HPAI in Chile, with a particular focus on the Magallanes region, and its impact on wildlife, including skuas, marine mammals and penguins. Chile stressed the urgency of addressing this subject and called for collaboration between all relevant parties in preparing for and responding to potential outbreaks. Chile noted that it was developing preventive guidelines and measures which it would gladly share with other Members.

(155) The Republic of Korea referred to its IP 23 rev. 1 *Need for Rapid Detection of Avian Influenza Virus in Antarctic Wildlife*, which described its preventive protocols. It particularly highlighted that the rapid diagnosis kit would be used by the Korean Antarctic expeditions starting in the upcoming Antarctic season, and proposed a collaborative effort among the Parties. This kit could be used for preliminary detection of Avian Influenza Virus on site. Samples that were positive or suspected to be positive would be analysed, and potential outbreaks could be verified at appointed facilities within the space of one or two weeks.

(156) The United Kingdom drew the Committee's attention to its IP 39 *United Kingdom procedures for preventing the introduction or spread of Highly Pathogenic Avian Influenza in Antarctica*, which summarised the procedures followed by British expeditions during the 2022-23 season.

(157) The Committee welcomed all information shared on valuable national experiences and examples of procedures for preventing the introduction or spread of avian influenza in the Antarctic. It welcomed the contributions as particularly useful in the context of future collaboration between competent authorities and in promoting preventive procedures among national programmes and other stakeholders.

(158) COMNAP remarked that it continued to proactively share guidance on HPAI with national programmes that were preparing programme specific guidance. COMNAP informed that it would continue information sharing and that cooperative preventive protocols would be a focus at its upcoming annual meeting.

(159) IAATO noted that risks associated with HPAI also applied to seals. It also reported that IAATO had developed enhanced biosecurity procedures to avoid the spread of HPAI following discussions with the SCAR Antarctic Wildlife Health Working Group. These were in addition to existing biosecurity procedures in advance of the 2022/23 season. IAATO noted that it had also updated its procedures on the discovery of a high or unusual mortality event, attached to IP 51 *IAATO Operational Procedures for responsible wildlife watching – An update.*

(160) In supporting the recommendations of WP 3 the Committee encouraged Members to take necessary precautions to avoid the introduction and spread of HPAI in Antarctica and enhance information exchange, and welcomed SCAR's willingness to provide updated information on potential impacts of HPAI to native birds and mammals in Antarctica.

CEP advice to the ATCM on the prevention and detection of Highly Pathogenic Avian Influenza in Antarctica

(161) The Committee advised the ATCM that it considered that an outbreak of avian flu in Antarctica was likely and could be a detrimental threat to Antarctic wildlife.

(162) The Committee therefore advised the ATCM it had agreed to:

- encourage Parties and other stakeholders to develop and implement procedures for surveillance, prevention and response to the introduction, spread, or potential outbreaks of HPAI;
- encourage Parties to share information on HPAI detections in Antarctica, including the location of suspected and confirmed outbreaks, species, and approximate number of individuals affected, and the symptoms observed; and
- request that SCAR provide updates to the CEP on the potential impacts of HPAI to native birds and mammals in Antarctica.

---

(163) Australia introduced WP 14 *Review of International Maritime Organization (IMO) and Antarctic Treaty system (ATS) guidelines and agreements concerning ship biofouling and ballast water management* and referred to IP 9 *Topic Summary: CEP Discussions on Ship Biofouling and Ballast Water Management,* both prepared jointly with New Zealand and the United Kingdom. These papers presented the results of a review of IMO and ATS guidelines and agreements concerning ship biofouling and ballast water management, building on a progress report presented at CEP XXIV. The co-authors recommended that the CEP consider the information presented in the report, consider requesting COMNAP and IAATO to provide up-to-date advice on the ship biofouling and ballast water management practices employed by their members, and encourage monitoring for non-native marine species. Australia thanked COMNAP, IAATO and SCAR for their valuable input during discussions.

(164) The Committee thanked the co-authors for this information, noting that risks associated with marine non-native species were a high-priority issue for the CEP. The Committee called on Members to enhance understanding of such risks, and thanked Observers for continuing to provide up-to-date advice on the issue.

(165) IAATO and COMNAP agreed to report to CEP 27 (2025) on the ship biofouling and ballast water management practices and technologies of their members. SCAR confirmed that the editor of the Antarctic Environments Portal had been in contact with experts to develop a new Information Summary on pathways for the introduction of marine non-native species. COMNAP also commented that Parties had a key role to play especially but not exclusively as sea gateways, since domestic biosecurity protocols and inspection of vessels played a pivotal role in protection.

(166) The Committee endorsed the recommendations in WP 14 and thanked COMNAP, IAATO and SCAR for supporting its work on this important issue.

CEP advice to the ATCM on guidelines and agreements concerning ship biofouling and ballast water management

(167) The Committee advised the ATCM that, as part of its work on ship biofouling and ballast water management, it had considered a review of International Maritime Organization (IMO) and Antarctic Treaty system (ATS) guidelines and agreements concerning these matters, prepared jointly by Australia, New Zealand and the United Kingdom, and had agreed to:

- request COMNAP and IAATO to provide up-to-date advice by CEP 27 (2025) on the ship biofouling and ballast water management practices employed by their members;
- encourage monitoring for non-native marine species to enhance understanding of risks and to inform consideration of marine biosecurity measures, in line with needs identified in the Five-Year Work Plan, CCRWP and Non-native Species Manual; and
- bring the CEP's ongoing work on ship biofouling and ballast water management to the attention of the SC-CAMLR in light of shared objectives and responsibilities for managing marine non-native species risks in the Antarctic region.

---

(168) Poland presented IP 41 *Monitoring and eradication of a non-native grass,* Poa annua, *from the Western Shore of Admiralty Bay, King George Island, South Shetland Islands - 2022/2023 update.* The paper provided information on the monitoring and progress of eradication of the non-native grass *Poa annua* within the west coast of Admiralty Bay, King George Island, during the 2022/23 season. Poland drew attention to inspections of ASPA 128 that had not identified the presence of the grass.

(169) Poland presented IP 42 rev. 1 *Report of a finding of* Trichocera maculipennis *in Antarctic Specially Protected Area 128.* Recalling that *Trichocera maculipennis* (Diptera) imago individuals and larvae were first identified in the sewage system of Arctowski Polish Antarctic Station in 2017, Poland noted it had introduced systematic monitoring and control measures to eradicate the Diptera. Poland reported that it had identified Diptera individuals in two locations in ASPA 128 in the 2022/23 season. Poland noted that, in the next summer, it would monitor other locations to determine if Diptera were in other states of development in locations unrelated to station infrastructure. It also highlighted the need to develop procedures to take into account the scenario of non-native species beyond station areas, particularly among all Parties active on King George Island.

(170) Chile referred to its BP 16 *New findings on the presence of non-native insects on South Shetland Islands*, prepared jointly with the Republic of Korea and Uruguay. It noted that both *Trichocera maculipennis* and *Psychoda albipennis* were identified in semi-natural environments outside stations of King George Island. It also noted that an unidentified

beetle, a bedbug species *Lygaeus alboornatus* was found in the station, and that other insects had been collected from Doumer and Greenwich Islands. Chile noted this may imply a possible pathway for the expansion of these non-native insects, as well as a diversification of the species that could become established in the Antarctic Treaty Area. Chile urged Parties to reinforce measures for the prevention, monitoring, and control of non-native insects and to jointly define an eradication plan.

(171) The Committee thanked Poland, Chile, the Republic of Korea and Uruguay for their important papers. It drew attention to the concerning spread of non-native species, and the call to review domestic procedures and take collaborative action to prevent the spread of non-native species, particularly in King George Island.

10b) Specially Protected Species

(172) The United States introduced WP 9 *The United States Recognizes the Emperor Penguin as a Threatened Species and Provides Additional Protection for Emperor Penguins*. The United States recalled that, at CEP XXIV, many Members had expressed an intent to implement the draft Antarctic Specially Protected Species Action Plan (ATCM XLIV - WP 34) as a way to guide action on the management of emperor penguins. It reported that the United States Fish and Wildlife Service had conducted a review of the best available scientific, technological, and commercial advice, which had indicated that significant decreases in the global emperor penguin population by 2050 were likely. Declines were expected to vary across the continent, with colonies in some places projected to decline by over 90% due to sea-ice loss. The U.S. Fish and Wildlife Service had therefore determined that the emperor penguin met the definition of a threatened species under the Endangered Species Act, and the United States had listed the emperor penguin as a threatened species in November 2022. In light of this, the United States recommended that the CEP encourage Members:

1) to note that their domestic legislation may contribute to the protection of Antarctic species under threat;
2) to implement the draft Antarctic Specially Protected Species Action Plan for the emperor penguin, attached to ATCM XLIV - WP 34; and
3) to report recent research results on the status of the emperor penguin to CEP 26 with the aim to reconsider recommending to the ATCM the designation of the emperor penguin as a Specially Protected Species under Annex II to the Protocol.

(173) The Committee thanked the United States for its paper. Many Members also congratulated the United States on its action to use domestic legislation to list the emperor penguin as a threatened species. Most Members expressed disappointment that the Committee had been unable to list the emperor penguin as a Specially Protected Species during CEP XXIV. These Members noted that the best available science, previously presented by SCAR (ATCM XLIII - WP 37), as well as other available scientific data, demonstrated that the emperor penguin was vulnerable and warranted designation as a Specially Protected Species in accordance with Annex II to the Environment Protocol and agreed procedures.

(174) India informed the CEP about the Indian Antarctic Act, which had been passed by the Parliament but had yet to come into force, and had provisions for the protection of current Antarctic Specially Protected Species as well as any Antarctic Specially Protected Species that might be agreed by the CEP in the future.

(175) China noted that conclusions it had drawn from the draft Antarctic Specially Protected Action Plan for Emperor Penguins did not support the designation as specially protected species, specifically: the population of the emperor penguin had been stable in the past 20-30 years; the emperor penguin was influenced by the reduction of sea ice because of

climate change, which we have limited ability to manage for, rather than human activity in Antarctica; and the emperor penguin faced very low threat from human activities both in the marine and terrestrial environment.

(176) Several Members emphasised that despite fluctuations in emperor penguin population trends, the best available science, and the draft Antarctic Specially Protected Species Action Plan for Emperor Penguins indicated that the population was projected to decline significantly, particularly due to the loss of sea ice due to climate change. Many Members therefore called for continued efforts to protect the species under Annex II to the Environment Protocol. Some Members also called for ratification of the High Seas Treaty as in their view it could be another means of protecting the emperor penguin.

(177) Members agreed that domestic legislation may contribute to the protection of Antarctic species under threat. Some Members noted limitations in their legal instruments and the need to consider other approaches. Many Members encouraged those Members who were able to do so, to work toward domestic legislation contributing to the protection of threatened Antarctic species. Australia referred to its IP 89 *Draft Specially Protected Species Action Plan for the Emperor Penguin: complementary actions by Australia*. The paper outlined actions by Australia that were consistent with the draft Action Plan (ATCM XLIV - WP 34). In keeping with the recommendations in WP 9, it also indicated that preliminary work was underway to consider listing the emperor penguin as a threatened species under Australia's national environmental legislation.

(178) IAATO reported that a routine review of its own procedures for visiting emperor penguin colonies was in process, as noted in IP 51, which had also been informed by the draft action plan. IAATO had reinforced relevant procedures for both deep field and vessel-based operations, including procedures related to distance from wildlife and for biosecurity, flight operations and visitor management. It welcomed continued sharing of information to promote conservation, noting that this also helped to inform the responsible management of IAATO's own activities.

(179) Many Members expressed their appreciation that numerous Members and Observers had been using the draft action plan to guide actions related to the species, and encouraged continued and increased efforts by Members and Observers to advance the actions in the draft Action Plan.

(180) Members agreed to report recent research results on the status of the emperor penguin and thanked SCAR for its ongoing contributions in this regard.

(181) The United Kingdom introduced WP 52 *A five-year assessment of the impacts on emperor penguins of low sea-ice extent*, prepared jointly with France, Germany and the United States. Noting that land-fast sea ice was crucial for emperor penguins as a breeding and moulting platform, the proponents indicated that current models linked to IPCC projections suggested emperor penguin populations would decline dramatically by the end of the century, and may become quasi-extinct. The United Kingdom highlighted that over the five-year period assessed (2018-2022), 42% of emperor penguin colonies had likely experienced total or partial breeding failure due to fast-ice break-up in at least one year. The United Kingdom noted that elements of the assessment would soon be published in the *Nature* journal *Communications Earth and Environment*, and that further publications were in preparation. In light of the assessment's findings, the proponents recommended that: the CEP encourage Members to report on their implementation of the draft Antarctic Specially Protected Species Action Plan, attached to ATCM XLIV - WP 34, along with their existing and planned steps to enhance the conservation of the emperor penguin; and SCAR and/or interested Members report recent research results on the status of the emperor penguin population and sea-ice extent around Antarctica to inform the future consideration by the ATCM of the designation of the emperor penguin as a Specially Protected Species under Annex II to the Protocol.

(182) ASOC noted that its member World Wide Fund for Nature (WWF) had been pleased to support the work presented in WP 52 for many years, and underscored that it was critical that emperor penguins should be designated as a Specially Protected Species.

(183) The Committee thanked the proponents of WP 52 for bringing the paper to its attention. It also thanked them for sharing the results of the study presented in the paper, which supported the conclusions shared by SCAR in ATCM XLIII - WP 37. Many Members noted that the study clearly demonstrated that changes in sea ice were a threat to the emperor penguin species and indicated a need to take a precautionary approach and to consider the species as one under threat. Most Members supported the recommendations of the paper and, recalling the discussion on WP 9, encouraged continued work toward designation of the emperor penguin as a Specially Protected Species at the earliest opportunity. The Committee expected that the issue would be revisited in the near future.

(184) The Russian Federation referred to monitoring of emperor penguins near Mirny station. It noted that the reduction in the area of the ice cover and the earlier breakup of fast ice had a negative impact on the survival of birds, as well as on the number of nesting birds. Thus, local observations had shown that the determining factors affecting the colony were not anthropogenic, but natural.

(185) SCAR noted that sea ice had reached a record low in 2023, as indicated in WP 42. It also highlighted its assessment of the emperor penguin as vulnerable to ongoing and projected climate change, and therefore warranting protection as a Specially Protected Species. SCAR called attention to the Antarctic Environments Portal, which had recently published three relevant summaries on sea ice, including on its biological importance, trends, and future projections. It noted that the SCAR lecture also had contained relevant information on the use of satellite technology for monitoring both emperor penguin populations and sea ice. SCAR noted that while the recent discovery of new emperor penguin colonies had provided updated population estimates, this did not change the projected downward trend in population. SCAR indicated that it would continue to report recent research to inform future discussion around designation of the emperor penguin as a Specially Protected Species.

10c) Other Annex II Matters

(186) Argentina presented IP 124 *Comprehensive approach to the study of the Emperor Penguin colony in Snow Hill Island*, which reported on work carried out by Argentina to better support the study, and to further develop tools for the protection, of the emperor penguin colony on Snow Hill Island. Argentina noted that such scientific activity had previously been challenging due to logistical constraints, but that advances had recently become possible thanks to the establishment of a new refuge. Argentina also indicated its interest to further develop a guideline for visitors to the Snow Hill Island penguin colony, and invited collaboration on this by other Members.

(187) The Committee thanked Argentina for the information presented and for its invitation to work collaboratively on the issue.

(188) IAATO noted that it had established specific guidelines for visits to the Snow Hill Island penguin colony, as noted in IP 51. It highlighted that these guidelines had been developed based on ATCM XL - WP 44, which also had been authored by Argentina, and expressed its gratitude for Argentina's assistance in developing them.

(189) The Committee noted the following Information Papers had been submitted under this agenda item:

- IP 33 *Scientific use of Remotely Piloted Aircraft Systems (RPAS) in Antarctica: a review* (Portugal, Germany, United Kingdom).

- IP 51 *IAATO Operational Procedures for responsible wildlife watching – An update* (IAATO).
- IP 52 *IAATO Deep Field and Air Operations Biosecurity Procedures – An update* (IAATO).
- IP 63 *Update: Managing the Effects of anthropogenic noise in the Antarctic – Steps towards the development of an underwater noise protection concept for Antarctica* (Germany).
- IP 139 *Cuantificación de la Contaminación por Macro y Microplásticos en el Área de Influencia de la Estación Científica Pedro Vicente Maldonado-Isla Greenwich (2023-2025)* (Ecuador).

Item 11: Environmental Monitoring and Reporting

(190) The Netherlands introduced WP 17 *Environmental monitoring: an international framework*, prepared jointly with France and Belgium. Noting that monitoring had long been identified as key to better assessing possible environmental changes and identifying impacts of human activities, and that environmental monitoring was an obligation under Article 3.2 of the Environment Protocol, the Netherlands drew the Committee's attention to the need for an international monitoring framework. The Netherlands noted that several Parties had undertaken monitoring efforts but observed that efforts to date might not provide an adequate overview of developments in the Antarctic environment. It noted the lack of a coordinating mechanism and adequate resources on monitoring as contributing issues. The proponents recommended that the Committee discuss the matter and establish an ICG to develop a concrete proposal for an international framework for environmental monitoring, laying out the parameters of what and where to monitor and taking into account the important issue of accumulation.

(191) The Committee thanked the Netherlands, France and Belgium for their paper. It underscored the importance of environmental monitoring programmes to assess environmental changes and human impacts, and several Members highlighted their experience in this regard. Members noted that coordinated monitoring would enable better-informed decisions, both nationally and internationally. Members also noted that a coordinated and systematic approach was beneficial to overall monitoring in Antarctica and environmental impact assessments.

(192) Several Members suggested that an integrated monitoring system for the entire continent might be challenging to achieve, highlighting that environmental monitoring was time-consuming and costly, and that there were differences in approaches and types of monitoring undertaken by different Members. Considering possible ways forward, Members raised a range of considerations including: the importance of reviewing past and current monitoring efforts and defining specific objectives; identifying knowledge gaps and appropriate monitoring indicators and tools; and holding workshops to promote inclusive engagement by Members.

(193) ASOC suggested that a way forward could be to develop an ASPA network through systematic conservation planning, noting that ASPAs could serve as reference areas for monitoring as well as support efforts toward disentangling multiple impacts.

(194) IAATO noted that it had supported long-term monitoring programmes for many years and that separating out direct impacts of tourism from possible impacts caused by other human activities or climate change was challenging. It reported that it was expanding its own monitoring capabilities, including implementing a site monitoring programme to collect baseline data that would evolve over the coming years.

(195) Following further consideration, the Committee agreed to establish an ICG to discuss development of an international framework for environmental monitoring. The Committee agreed that the convener and supporting Members could consider whether an informal workshop, either virtual or in-person, could be helpful for the ICG discussions in an effort to increase participation of Members and Observers.

CEP advice to the ATCM on an international framework for environmental monitoring

(196) The Committee agreed to advise the ATCM that it had established an ICG to discuss development of an international framework for environmental monitoring with the following Terms of Reference:

- Agree on work methods;
- Identify and analyse existing monitoring activities and the data available;
- Discuss objectives for environmental monitoring needed to fulfil the requirements of the Environment Protocol and develop an initial framework of parameters that, based on environmental values and cumulative impact, would require monitoring to meet those objectives;
- Report on an initial gap analysis between the existing monitoring portfolio and what is required; and
- The ICG would work intersessionally and report to CEP 26.

(197) The Committee welcomed the offer from Uruguay to act as ICG convener.

---

(198) The United Kingdom introduced WP 41 *Monitoring the impacts of human activity in Antarctica*. It recalled that CEP XXIV had agreed to the recommendations of ATCM XLIV - WP 22, which had recommended that Parties promote the establishment of monitoring programmes to assess human impacts related to tourism. In response, WP 41 summarised some of the programmes the United Kingdom had undertaken or supported to inform the development of approaches and tools for the management of activities to protect the Antarctic environment. The paper highlighted a project that had been undertaken to assess the utility of satellite imagery to monitor human impacts at some of Antarctica's most visited sites. Based on this, the United Kingdom outlined proposed next steps for developing an approach to assess the use of RPAS imagery to monitor human impacts at highly-visited tourist sites. It recommended that the CEP: note the summary of United Kingdom-led or supported programmes that could contribute data for the future monitoring of impacts of human activities in Antarctica; continue to share information about their own programmes relevant to the monitoring of human impacts on the Antarctic environment; discuss how to best collate information on existing monitoring programmes; and note the results of a recent project to assess the use of satellite imagery for monitoring human impacts and consider contributing to the proposed continuation project to assess the use of RPAS imagery to monitor human impacts at multiple highly-visited tourist sites.

(199) The Committee thanked the United Kingdom for its work in preparing WP 41 and for its efforts to monitor human impacts in Antarctica. The Committee generally supported the paper's recommendations. Several Members emphasised the need for clear definition of what was being monitored as well as the importance of both remote and *in situ* methodological approaches. Many Members shared experience with ongoing monitoring activities, referring to relevant initiatives outlined in WP 17, IP 61, IP 62, and ATCM

XLII - IP 154 and ATCM XLIV - WP 22, among others, as well as the SCAR lecture on satellite-based science. The Committee emphasised the importance of ongoing information sharing related to monitoring and collation of data related to human impacts in Antarctica, and the value of monitoring as a basis for environmental impact assessments.

(200) SCAR and several Members noted that an important first step would be to understand current monitoring work being undertaken by Members, and to identify how this could be used to understand gaps and achieve objectives. SCAR highlighted that the use of satellite imagery would be increasingly important to monitoring efforts moving forward and stated that it would continue to engage with Members on this issue.

(201) SCAR introduced WP 18 *Contribution of information to inform State of the Antarctic Environment Reporting (SAER): a potential new SCAR initiative*, which described the outcomes of a recent SCAR workshop to consider the potential provision of information to inform elements of State of the Antarctic Environment Reporting (SAER). It proposed that the resulting new SAER initiative would bring together a variety of relevant existing knowledge which could be used to make web-based maps, identify knowledge gaps and perform assessments, and it noted that the SCAR Antarctic Environments Portal could be a suitable platform for such a tool. SCAR recommended that the Committee: note the recent SCAR workshops held to consider how best the scientific community might contribute to SAER; consider the proposal by SCAR to develop a mechanism for the provision of information relevant to SAER; and request the view of CEP Members regarding (i) the usefulness of this proposal and (ii) if considered beneficial, what information would be most useful for supporting the Committee in its provision of advice to the ATCM on the state of the Antarctic environment.

(202) The Committee thanked SCAR for its paper. It welcomed SCAR's proposal to develop a mechanism for SAER, noting its relevance to the CEP's work including with respect to environmental monitoring and providing advice to the ATCM. Members highlighted the usefulness of this initiative for the CEP's entire work agenda, including to develop a systematic approach to environmental monitoring, as well as to further develop the Antarctic Protected Area System.

(203) Members noted that the SCAR Antarctic Environments Portal could be a useful platform for the dissemination of reports and highlighted that reports should be in a format that was easily understood by policymakers.

(204) The Committee noted that it would be useful to receive an example report from SCAR to fully assess the practicality and usefulness of its proposed mechanism for providing information on SAER.

(205) SCAR introduced WP 49 rev. 1 *Antarctic Near-shore and Terrestrial Observing System (ANTOS)*, prepared jointly with New Zealand, Australia, Italy, the Republic of Korea and the United States. The paper noted that the Antarctic Near-shore and Terrestrial Observing System (ANTOS) aimed to establish a continent-wide network of instruments to collect data on a range of parameters that could be used to identify and track environmental variability and change, with a biological focus. ANTOS sites were being established in a number of environments around the Antarctic, with 13 potential sites identified so far, and results would be collected at an open-source database developed by the Korean Polar Research Institute. SCAR explained that the valuable information gathered via ANTOS would help ensure the most up-to-date understanding of change in near-shore and terrestrial environments and ecosystems, and provide a more complete understanding of changes occurring in the Antarctic region.

(206) The Committee thanked the co-authors and warmly welcomed the goals of ANTOS, recognising it as a valuable monitoring tool with significant potential. Several Members

voiced enthusiasm for the news of progress made on the development of ANTOS and recalled their long-standing support for and participation in the project. Members expressed their willingness to engage in ANTOS and outlined various ways in which their national Antarctic programmes and research projects were contributing to, and would continue to contribute to, the system.

(207) Portugal presented IP 32 *Mercury in Antarctic marine ecosystems,* prepared jointly with Bulgaria, France, Germany, Japan, and the United Kingdom. The paper described the most recent scientific information on total mercury in Antarctic marine food webs. Portugal highlighted that mercury was one of the most toxic existing elements, which was highly bioaccumulative in organisms and biomagnified along food webs, but noted that information for the Antarctic region was lacking. It encouraged greater information exchange between Members, more monitoring research and increased use of coordinated methodologies related to mercury and other trace contaminants.

(208) Germany presented IP 59 *International Science & Infrastructure for Synchronous Observation (Antarctica InSync),* prepared jointly with Australia, France, Italy, Norway, the United Kingdom and the United States. It proposed a synchronous scientific observation mission to allow for a circumpolar assessment of the connections between ice, ocean, climate and environment, including human pressures and their solutions such as marine protection. Germany noted that current important science questions and needs had been identified in the SCAR Horizon Scan and Southern Ocean Action Plan, and that these could be addressed by a joint ambitious and coordinated effort. Germany welcomed all interested Members to support this international science initiative aimed to enhance collaboration, knowledge, data sharing and outreach to raise awareness of the role of Antarctica and the Southern Ocean for humanity's future.

(209) France added that, although the Antarctica InSync initiative focused on the Southern Ocean, all infrastructures, marine or terrestrial, could be included in the initiative, irrespective of their size, type or location. It noted that Antarctica InSync provided an excellent opportunity for early career researchers and encouraged Members to facilitate their involvement.

(210) SCAR welcomed the important proposal for a synchronous scientific observation mission. It noted SCAR's plans to host a UN Decade Collaborative Centre (DCC), as described in IP 104, which would create an international network for groups including Antarctica InSync to communicate and collaborate in support of the goals of the UN Ocean Decade.

(211) The Committee thanked the proponents for this initiative and noted the enthusiasm of Members and Observers to contribute to its development.

(212) The United States presented IP 65 *Environmental Field Reviews: Supporting Monitoring Obligations and the Environmental Impact Assessment Feedback Process*, which described an environmental field review programme that evaluated active projects and field camps to identify potential issues, areas for improvement, and mitigation alternatives. It included a table to assist in prioritisation and some relevant follow-up activities.

(213) SCAR presented IP 75 *Antarctic Environments Portal* (SCAR), which provided an update on the management and operation of the Antarctic Environments Portal, including examples of how Portal articles were linked to issues of priority interest for the CEP. SCAR also thanked those Members who provided financial support for the development of the Portal, welcomed feedback on Portal content and encouraged discussion with Members on how to develop and support the Portal in the future.

(214) The Committee thanked SCAR for its valuable work in managing the Portal and

encouraged it to continue the good work. It noted that there had been several references to the Portal throughout the Committee's discussions and it encouraged Members to continue to support the Portal, including through financial contributions when possible.

(215) SCAR presented IP 100 *Anthropogenic noise in Antarctic terrestrial environments*, which reported on sources, methods of monitoring and wildlife impacts of terrestrial anthropogenic noise as an emerging area of Antarctic research. It noted that the preparation of this work had been supported by the SCAR ANT-ICON-SCATS Fellowship programme. SCAR noted that although there was a substantial body of research concerning noise from anthropogenic sources in Antarctica, the overwhelming majority of this work focused on marine environments and issues such as the impacts of underwater noise on marine wildlife. In contrast, much less attention had been given to the specific effects of terrestrial anthropogenic noise on the Antarctic soundscape and its environmental, scientific, wilderness and aesthetic values, including for example impacts on flying birds, penguins and seals. SCAR noted that such impacts could potentially be significant, ranging from behavioural and physiological responses in organisms to cases of mortality in some extreme circumstances. Stressing the potential significance of the topic for Antarctic conservation and the assessment of environmental impacts and effects, SCAR invited all Members to draw their attention to the subject and the potential field of research.

(216) The Committee thanked SCAR for the paper and for drawing its attention to this knowledge gap, and welcomed the establishment of programmes such as the SCAR ANT-ICON-SCATS Fellowship in furthering the integration between science and management. Noting positively Poland's example of monitoring terrestrial noise levels (BP 11), various participants affirmed the importance of this subject and offered their support to further research on this field.

(217) Spain presented IP 135 *Monitorización de embarcaciones turísticas y no gubernamentales en el entorno de la Isla Decepción*, which summarised the results of an analysis of the movement of tourist and non-governmental vessels using three different tools around Deception Island. It demonstrated that the detection of yachts could be significantly improved by combining data from multiple monitoring systems.

(218) The Committee noted the following Information Papers had been submitted under this agenda item:

- IP 61 *Current initiatives for a structured sample and data collection of environmental contamination in the Antarctic* (Germany, Australia, Italy, Portugal, Sweden, United Kingdom, United States).
- IP 62 *Tourism monitoring in Antarctica – Report on the progress in developing a concept for the analysis of the impacts of tourism on the assets to be protected in the Antarctic* (Germany).
- IP 78 *Plastic Pollution in the Southern Ocean* (SCAR).

(219) The Committee noted the following Background Papers had been submitted under this agenda item:

- BP 8 *Report on the RPAS monitoring program at Arctowski Station for 2021-2023* (Poland).
- BP 11 *Scope of environmental monitoring conducted in relation to the ongoing renovation of the Arctowski Polish Antarctic Station* (Poland).
- BP 15 *Ongoing Italian projects on the assessment of chemical contamination in Antarctica* (Italy).

Item 12: Inspection Reports

(220) The Committee noted the following Information Paper had been submitted under this agenda item:

- IP 46 *Report of Informal UK Government Inspection of Base A, Port Lockroy* (United Kingdom).

Item 13: General Matters

(221) Finland introduced WP 36 *Towards gender-neutral language in the Antarctic Treaty System*, prepared jointly with the United Kingdom, Spain, Germany, New Zealand, Norway and France. It noted the significant increase in participation by women in Antarctic science and research. It also recalled that, on several occasions, Members had emphasised the importance of equality and inclusiveness, and reported on their commitment to promoting inclusivity and diversity in their Antarctic programmes. The co-sponsors proposed that the CEP request the Secretariat to review all relevant CEP documents that pertained to current and future cooperation with a view to ensure the use of gender-neutral language across these documents.

(222) The Committee thanked the co-authors for this important paper. It acknowledged the importance of using a gender-neutral approach to language and noted that the changes the Committee had agreed at this meeting to the CEP Rules of Procedure included modifications to ensure gender-inclusive language. Many Members noted that this proposal aligned with their national policies, programmes and objectives. Some Members pointed out that contextual differences among the official languages should be acknowledged when gender neutrality was applied to texts. The Russian Federation noted that the United Nations had prepared a manual for inclusivity in all of its six official languages and that such documents could provide good guidance for the Secretariat in its review.

CEP advice to ATCM on improving gender-neutral language in the Antarctic Treaty System

(223) The Committee agreed to advise the ATCM that it encouraged Members and Observers to continue promoting inclusivity, equity and diversity in their Antarctic activities, and to use gender-neutral, respectful and inclusive language in spoken and written documentation, reporting and other forms of communication.

(224) The Committee also agreed to task the Secretariat to review, within existing resources, all CEP-relevant documents that pertained to current and future cooperation, with a view to ensuring gender-neutral language across these documents.

---

(225) WMO presented IP 28 *Further Plans of the Year of Polar Prediction in the Southern Hemisphere (YOPP-SH) and Completion of the Polar Prediction Project,* which summarised recent activities undertaken in the Antarctic region as part of the World Weather Research Programme's Polar Prediction Project (PPP). Although PPP had formally concluded on 31 December 2022, activities would continue in 2023 in three key areas: the Year of Polar Prediction in the Southern Hemisphere (YOPP-SH); the Model Intercomparison and Improvement Project (MIIP); and the PPP Societal and Environmental Research Applications group (PPP-SERA). Furthermore, the Research Programme had a new activity approved, the Polar Coupled Analysis and Prediction for Services, which would commence in 2024.

(226) Portugal presented IP 34 *Topics and target audiences on education and outreach*

activities by the Antarctic Treaty Parties: a review, prepared jointly with Belgium, Bulgaria, Chile, Spain, the United Kingdom and WMO. The review found that, since 1961, 200 ATCM papers had been produced relating to education and outreach with key topics including science, wildlife, biodiversity and environment, with the main target audience being the general public including schools and universities. Since the first ATCM workshop on education and outreach in 2015, and the subsequent establishment of the ICG on education and outreach, the number of ATCM papers on education and outreach had further increased, as had the level of information sharing by Parties. The review further noted that current ATCM papers addressed new relevant topics including equity, diversity and inclusion, and engaged the next generations of scientists and educators.

(227) Portugal presented IP 35 *Conclusions of the UN Ocean Conference 2022 in Lisbon, Portugal*, prepared jointly with France, Sweden and WMO, which reported on the second UN Ocean Conference in support of the implementation of UN Sustainable Development Goal 14. The Conference, which adopted a declaration entitled "Our ocean, our future, our responsibility", included several events relating to the Antarctic and Southern Ocean. France and Costa Rica had declared their availability to host the third UN Oceans Conference and welcomed contributions relating to the Antarctic region and the work of the Antarctic Treaty system for future UN Oceans conferences.

(228) France presented IP 74 *The Ice Memory Programme*, prepared jointly with Italy, which provided an update on the Ice Memory Programme and addressed questions raised by Parties during previous meetings. In response to questions raised previously by the Committee, the co-sponsors reported *inter alia* on its assessments of risks and existing procedures related to the avoidance of non-native species introduction into the Antarctic environment. They also noted that the carbon footprint of the Ice Memory Programme logistics in Antarctica was estimated to be three times lower than storing the ice cores in commercial freezers.

(229) The Committee noted the following Information Papers had been submitted under this agenda item:

- IP 20 *Renewal of the Norwegian Troll Research Station, Dronning Maud Land* (Norway).
- IP 104 *Update on the Southern Ocean contribution to the United Nations Decade of Ocean Science for Sustainable Development* (SCAR, Belgium, Netherlands, WMO).

(230) The Committee noted the following Secretariat Papers had been submitted under this agenda item:

- SP 8 *Review of the utilisation of the EIES* (Secretariat).
- SP 9 *Developments on the ATS website related to meeting paper preparation and submission* (Secretariat).

Item 14: Election of Officers

(231) The Committee re-elected Anoop Kumar Tiwari from India as Vice-chair for a second two-year term and congratulated him on his reappointment to the role. Tiwari was also reappointed convenor of the SGMP.

(232) The Committee elected Patricia Ortúzar from Argentina as Chair of the CEP and congratulated her on her appointment.

(233) The Committee warmly thanked and congratulated Birgit Njåstad for her excellent work and significant contributions during her two terms as Chair.

Item 15: Preparation for the Next Meeting

(234) The Committee adopted the Preliminary Agenda for CEP 26 (Appendix 3).

Item 16: Adoption of the Report

(235) The Committee adopted its Report.

Item 17: Closing of the Meeting

(236) The Chair closed the Meeting on Thursday, 1 June 2023.

Appendix 1

CEP Five-year Work Plan

<table>
<tr><td colspan="2">Issue / Environmental Pressure: Introduction of non-native species</td></tr>
<tr><td colspan="2">Priority: 1</td></tr>
<tr><td colspan="2">Actions:
1. Continue developing practical guidelines & resources for all Antarctic operators.
2. Implement related actions identified in the Climate Change Response Work Programme.
3. Consider the spatially explicit, activity-differentiated risk assessments to mitigate the risks posed by terrestrial non-native species.
4. Develop a surveillance strategy for areas at high risk of non-native species establishment.
5. Give additional attention to the risks posed by intra-Antarctic transfer of propagules.</td></tr>
<tr><td>Intersessional period 2023/24</td><td>• Initiate work to develop a non-native species response strategy, including appropriate responses to diseases of wildlife
• To help the Committee in assessing the effectiveness of the Non-native Species Manual, request a report from COMNAP on the implementation of quarantine and biosecurity measures by its members</td></tr>
<tr><td>CEP 26 2024</td><td>• Discuss the intersessional work concerning the development of a response strategy for inclusion in the Non-native Species Manual, and the implementation of quarantine and biosecurity measures by COMNAP members.
• SCAR to present information on existing mechanism to assist with the identification of non-native species</td></tr>
<tr><td>Intersessional period 2024/25</td><td>• Ask SCAR to compile a list of available biodiversity information sources and databases to help Parties establish which native species are present at Antarctic sites and thereby assist with identifying the scale and scope of current and future introductions
• Develop generally applicable monitoring guidelines. More detailed or site-specific monitoring may be required for particular locations
• Request a report from Parties and Observers on the application of biosecurity guidelines by their members</td></tr>
<tr><td>CEP 27 2025</td><td>• Discuss the intersessional work concerning the development of monitoring guidelines for inclusion in the NNS Manual.
• Consider the reports from Parties and Observers on the application of biosecurity guidelines by their members</td></tr>
</table>

Intersessional period 2025/26	• Initiate work to assess the risk of marine non-native species introductions
CEP 28 2026	• Discuss the intersessional work concerning the risks of marine non-native species
Intersessional period 2026/27	• Develop specific guidelines to reduce non-native species release with wastewater discharge • Review the progress and contents of the CEP Non-native Species Manual
CEP 29 2027	• CEP to consider if intersessional work is required to review/update the Non-native Species Manual
Intersessional period 2027/28	• As appropriate, intersessional work to review the Non-native Species Manual
CEP 30 2028	• CEP to consider report of ICG, if established, and consider adoption of revised Non-native Species Manual by the ATCM through a resolution

Science knowledge and information needs:

- Identify terrestrial and marine regions and habitats at risk of introduction
- Identify native species at risk of relocation and vectors and pathways for intra-continental transfer
- Synthesise knowledge of Antarctic biodiversity, biogeography and bioregionalisation and undertake baseline studies to establish which native species are present
- Identify pathways for the introduction of marine species (including risks associated with wastewater discharge)
- Assess risks and pathways for introduction of microorganisms that might impact on existing microbial communities
- Monitor for non-native species in the terrestrial and marine environments (including microbial activity near sewage treatment plant discharges)
- Identify techniques to rapidly respond to non-native species introductions
- Identify pathways for introduction of non-native species without any direct human intervention

Issue / Environmental Pressure: Tourism and NGO activities

Priority: 1

Actions:

1. Provide advice to ATCM as requested.
2. Advance recommendations from ship-borne tourism ATME.

Intersessional period 2023/24	• Work on framework for pre-assessment relating to new, novel or particularly concerning activities

	• Continued work on site sensitivity methodology
CEP 26 2024	• Consider outcomes of discussions relating to pre-assessment relating to new, novel or particularly concerning activities • Discuss the trial site sensitivity methodology • Consider report from SCAR and others on wilderness values and their practical application • Report from SCAR on carrying capacity
Intersessional period 2024/25	
CEP 27 2025	
Intersessional period 2025/26	
CEP 28 2026	
Intersessional period 2026/27	
CEP 29 2027	
Intersessional period 2027/28	
CEP 30 2028	
Science knowledge and information needs: • Consistent and dedicated monitoring of tourism impacts • Monitor visitor sites covered by Site Guidelines	

Issue / Environmental Pressure: Climate Change Implications for the Environment	
Priority: 1	
Actions: 1. Consider implications of climate change for management of Antarctic environment. 2. Implement the Climate Change Response Work Programme.	
Intersessional period 2023/24	• Subsidiary group conducts work in accordance with agreed work plan • Plan for five-yearly joint SC-CAMLR CEP workshop
CEP 26 2024	• Standing agenda item • Consider subsidiary group report, including CCRWP updates

Intersessional period 2024/25	• Five-yearly joint SC-CAMLR CEP workshop
CEP 27 2025	• Consider outcomes of joint SC-CAMLR/CEP workshop during 2024/25 intersessional period
Intersessional period 2025/26	
CEP 28 2026	
Intersessional period 2026/27	
CEP 29 2027	
Intersessional period 2027/28	
CEP 30 2028	

Science knowledge and information needs:

- Improve understanding of current and future change to the terrestrial (including aquatic) biotic and abiotic environment due to climate change
- Long-term monitoring of change to the terrestrial (including aquatic) biotic and abiotic environment due to climate change
- Continue to develop biogeographic tools to provide a sound basis for informing Antarctic area protection and management at regional and continental scales in light of climate change, including identifying the need to set aside reference areas for future research and identifying areas resilient to climate change
- Identify and prioritise Antarctic biogeographic regions most vulnerable to climate change
- Understand and predict near-shore marine changes and impacts of the change
- Long-term monitoring of change to the near-shore marine biotic and abiotic environment due to climate change
- Assessment on impact of ocean acidification to marine biota and ecosystems
- Understand population status, trends, vulnerability and distribution of key Antarctic species
- Understand habitat status, trends, vulnerability and distribution
- Southern Ocean observations and modelling to understand climate change
- Identify areas that may be resilient to climate change
- Monitor emperor penguin colonies, including using remote sensing and complementary techniques, to identify trends in populations and potential climate change *refugia*

<table>
<tr><td colspan="2">Issue / Environmental Pressure: Processing new and revised protected / managed area management plans</td></tr>
<tr><td colspan="2">Priority: 1</td></tr>
<tr><td colspan="2">Actions:
1. Refine the process for reviewing new and revised management plans.
2. Update existing guidelines.
3. Develop guidelines to ASMA preparation.</td></tr>
<tr><td>Intersessional period 2023/24</td><td>• SGMP conducts work as per agreed work plan</td></tr>
<tr><td>CEP 26 2024</td><td>• Consider SGMP report</td></tr>
<tr><td>Intersessional period 2024/25</td><td>• SGMP conducts work as per agreed work plan</td></tr>
<tr><td>CEP 27 2025</td><td>• Consider SGMP report</td></tr>
<tr><td>Intersessional period 2025/26</td><td>• SGMP conducts work as per agreed work plan</td></tr>
<tr><td>CEP 28 2026</td><td>• Consider SGMP report</td></tr>
<tr><td>Intersessional period 2026/27</td><td>• SGMP conducts work as per agreed work plan</td></tr>
<tr><td>CEP 29 2027</td><td>• Consider SGMP report</td></tr>
<tr><td>Intersessional period 2027/28</td><td>• SGMP conducts work as per agreed work plan</td></tr>
<tr><td>CEP 30 2028</td><td>• Consider SGMP report</td></tr>
<tr><td colspan="2">Science knowledge and information needs:
• Monitoring to assess the status of values at ASPA 107 Emperor Island
• Use remote sensing techniques to monitor changes in vegetation within ASPAs
• Long-term monitoring of biological values in ASPAs</td></tr>
</table>

Issue / Environmental Pressure: Implementing and improving the EIA provisions of Annex I	
Priority: 1	
Actions: **1. Refine the process for considering CEEs and advising the ATCM accordingly.** **2. Develop guidelines for assessing cumulative impacts.** **3. Review EIA guidelines and consider wider policy and other issues.** **4. Consider application of strategic environmental assessment in Antarctica.**	
Intersessional period 2023/24	• Discuss changes to the EIA database with a view to giving proposals to the Secretariat. Discuss the mechanisms to provide answers to the comments that are transmitted through the intersessional contact groups or other means on the global environmental impact assessments • Consider potential changes required to EIA database to improve its utility • Establish ICG to review draft CEEs as required • Members and Observers work to progress and coordinate information that will assist development of guidance on identifying and assessing cumulative impacts • Members to work on further guidance with regards to commenting processes related to CEEs • Informal intersessional discussions to take forward work to improve effectiveness of the Antarctic EIA system
CEP 26 2024	• Consideration of ICG reports on draft CEEs, as required • Consider outcomes of intersessional discussions to take forward work to improve effectiveness of the Antarctic EIA system • Consideration of topic summary on CEP discussions on cumulative impacts • Consider Secretariat assessment of implementation of Article 3 (6) on the uptake of comments received in Final CEEs
Intersessional period 2024/25	• Establish ICG to review draft CEEs as required • Members and Observers work to progress and coordinate information that will assist development of guidance on identifying and assessing cumulative impacts
CEP 27 2025	• Ask SCAR to provide guidance on how to do an environmental baseline condition survey, and consider their advice in due course • Consideration of ICG reports on draft CEE, as required
Intersessional period 2025/26	• Establish ICG to review draft CEEs as required

	• Members and Observers work to progress and coordinate information that will assist development of guidance on identifying and assessing cumulative impacts
CEP 28 2026	• Encourage Parties to provide feedback on the utility of the revised set of *Guidelines for Environmental Impact Assessment in Antarctica* in the preparation of EIAs • Consideration of the options for preparing guidance on identifying and assessing cumulative impacts • Consideration of ICG reports on draft CEE, as required
Intersessional period 2026/27	• Establish ICG to review draft CEEs as required
CEP 29 2027	• Consideration of ICG reports on draft CEE, as required
Intersessional period 2027/28	• Establish ICG to review draft CEEs as required
CEP 30 2028	• Consideration of ICG reports on draft CEE, as required

Issue / Environmental Pressure: Operation of the CEP and Strategic Planning	
Priority: 2	
Actions: 1. Keep the five-year work plan up to date based on changing circumstances and ATCM requirements. 2. Identify opportunities for improving the effectiveness of the CEP. 3. Consider long-term objectives for Antarctica (50-100 years' time). 4. Consider opportunities for enhancing the working relationship between the CEP and the ATCM.	
Intersessional period 2023/24	• ICG to continue discussions relating to strategic priorities and 5YWP
CEP 26 2024	• Consider the outcomes of ICG on strategic priorities and 5YWP
Intersessional period 2024/25	
CEP 27 2025	
Intersessional period 2025/26	
CEP 28 2026	

Intersessional period 2026/27	
CEP 29 2027	
Intersessional period 2027/28	
CEP 30 2028	

Issue / Environmental Pressure: Repair or Remediation of Environmental Damage	
Priority: 2	
Actions: 1. Respond to further request from the ATCM related to repair and remediation, as appropriate. 2. Monitor progress on the establishment of Antarctic-wide inventory of sites of past activity. 3. Consider guidelines for repair and remediation. 4. Members develop practical guidelines and supporting resources for inclusion in the Clean-up Manual. 5. Continue developing bioremediation and repair practices for inclusion in the Clean-up Manual.	
Intersessional period 2023/24	• Continuous review of the Manual. Parties to work on the development of new techniques or guidelines
CEP 26 2024	• Insertion of new tools and guidelines as they become available and agreed by the Committee
Intersessional period 2024/25	• Continuous review of the Manual. Parties to work on the development of new techniques or guidelines
CEP 27 2025	• Continuous review of the Manual and insertion of new tools and guidelines as they become available
Intersessional period 2025/26	• Continuous review of the Manual. Parties to work on the development of new techniques or guidelines
CEP 28 2026	• Continuous review of the Manual and insertion of new tools and guidelines as they become available
Intersessional period 2026/27	• Continuous review of the Manual. Parties to work on the development of new techniques or guidelines
CEP 29 2027	• Continuous review of the Manual and insertion of new tools and guidelines as they become available

Intersessional period 2027/28	• Continuous review of the Manual. Parties to work on the development of new techniques or guidelines
CEP 30 2028	• Continuous review of the Manual and insertion of new tools and guidelines as they become available
Science knowledge and information needs: • Research to inform the establishment of appropriate environmental quality targets for the repair or remediation of environmental damage in Antarctica • Techniques to prevent mobilisation of contaminants such as melt water diversion and containment barriers • Techniques for *in situ* and *ex situ* remediation of sites contaminated by fuel spills or other hazardous substances	

Issue / Environmental Pressure: Monitoring and state of the environment reporting	
Priority: 2	
Actions: 1. Identify key environmental indicators and tools. 2. Establish a process for reporting to the ATCM. 3. SCAR to support information to COMNAP and CEP.	
Intersessional period 2023/24	• SCAR to consider systematic sampling and data collection of chemical contamination in the Antarctic • ICG – building blocks international monitoring framework
CEP 26 2024	• Consider monitoring report by UK on ASPA 107 • Consider SCAR's advice on systematic sampling and data collection of chemical contamination in the Antarctic • Consider the outcomes of the ICG – building blocks international monitoring framework
Intersessional period 2024/25	
CEP 27 2025	
Intersessional period 2025/26	
CEP 28 2026	
Intersessional period 2026/27	
CEP 29 2027	

<table>
<tr><td>Intersessional period 2027/28</td><td></td></tr>
<tr><td>CEP 30 2028</td><td></td></tr>
<tr><td colspan="2">Science knowledge and information needs:
• Long-term monitoring of change to the terrestrial (including aquatic) biotic and abiotic environment due to climate change
• Long-term monitoring of change to the near-shore marine biotic and abiotic environment due to climate change
• Monitor bird populations to inform future management actions
• Use remote sensing techniques to monitor changes in vegetation within ASPAs and more widely
• Monitor emperor penguin colonies, using remote sensing and complementary techniques, to identify potential climate change refugia
• Long-term monitoring of biological values in ASPAs
• Long-term monitoring to verify or detect environmental impacts associated with human activities
• Long-term monitoring and sustained observations of environmental change
• Consistent and dedicated monitoring of tourism impacts
• Systematic and regular monitoring of visitor sites covered by Site Guidelines
• Long-term monitoring of biological indicators at sites visited by tourists</td></tr>
</table>

<table>
<tr><td colspan="2">Issue / Environmental Pressure: Marine spatial protection and management</td></tr>
<tr><td colspan="2">Priority: 2</td></tr>
<tr><td colspan="2">Actions:
1. Cooperation between the CEP and SC-CAMLR on common interest issues.
2. Cooperate with CCAMLR on Southern Ocean bioregionalisation and other common interests and agreed principles.
3. Identify and apply processes for spatial marine protection.
4. Consider connectivity between land and ocean, and complementary actions that could be taken by Parties with respect to MPAs.</td></tr>
<tr><td>Intersessional period 2023/24</td><td></td></tr>
<tr><td>CEP 26 2024</td><td>• Continue to consider advice relating to Resolution 5 (2017)</td></tr>
<tr><td>Intersessional period 2024/25</td><td></td></tr>
<tr><td>CEP 27 2025</td><td></td></tr>
</table>

Intersessional period 2025/26	
CEP 28 2026	
Intersessional period 2026/27	
CEP 29 2027	
Intersessional period 2027/28	
CEP 30 2028	

Issue / Environmental Pressure: Site specific guidelines for tourist-visited sites	
Priority: 2	
Actions: 1. Periodically review the list of sites subject to Site Guidelines and consider whether development of guidelines is needed for additional sites. 2. Regular review of all existing Site Guidelines to ensure that they are accurate and up to date, including precautionary updates where appropriate. 3. Provide advice to ATCM as required. 4. Review the format of the Site Guidelines.	
Intersessional period 2023/24	• Consider developing guidelines for short overnight stays to ensure consistent application of best practices and minimise impacts to the Antarctic environment
CEP 26 2024	• Committee to consider outcome of discussions on a new layout template for Visitor Site Guidelines • Standing agenda item; Parties to report on their reviews of Site Guidelines
Intersessional period 2024/25	• Development of a repository of pictures to aid in the regular review of Site Guidelines
CEP 27 2025	• Standing agenda item; Parties to report on their reviews of Site Guidelines
Intersessional period 2025/26	
CEP 28 2026	
Intersessional period 2026/27	

CEP 29 2027	
Intersessional period 2027/28	
CEP 30 2028	
Science knowledge and information needs: • Long-term monitoring to assess the status and recovery of vegetation at Barrientos Island • Systematic and regular monitoring of visitor sites covered by Site Guidelines	

Issue / Environmental Pressure: Overview of the protected areas system	
Priority: 2	
Actions: 1. Apply the Environmental Domains Analysis (EDA) and Antarctic Conservation Biogeographic Regions (ACBR) to enhance the protected areas system. 2. Maintain and develop Protected Area database. 3. Assess the extent to which Antarctic IBAs are or should be represented within the series of ASPAs.	
Intersessional period 2023/24	• Undertake work to advance actions agreed by the Committee from discussions on the protected areas workshop • SCAR to provide advice on selection criteria that might be applied to identified IBAs or other bird areas when considering ASPA designation
CEP 26 2024	• Committee to consider advice from SCAR on selection criteria that might be applied to identified IBAs or other bird areas when considering ASPA designation • Review progress on the work to advance actions agreed by the Committee from discussions on the protected areas workshop
Intersessional period 2024/25	• Undertake work to advance actions agreed by the Committee from discussions on the protected areas workshop
CEP 27 2025	• Review progress on the work to advance actions agreed by the Committee from discussions on the protected areas workshop
Intersessional period 2025/26	
CEP 28 2026	
Intersessional period 2026/27	
CEP 29 2027	

Intersessional period 2027/28	
CEP 30 2028	
Science knowledge and information needs: • Continue to develop biogeographic tools to provide a sound basis for informing Antarctic area protection and management at regional and continental scales in light of climate change, including identifying the need to set aside reference areas for future research and identifying areas resilient to climate change • Use remote sensing techniques to monitor changes in vegetation within ASPAs and more widely, to inform the further development of the Antarctic protected areas system	

Issue / Environmental Pressure: Designation and management of Historic Sites and Monuments	
Priority: 2	
Actions: 1. Maintain the list and consider new proposals as they arise. 2. Consider strategic issues as necessary, including issues relating to designation of HSM versus clean-up provisions of the Protocol. 3. Review the presentation of the HSM list with the aim to improve information availability.	
Intersessional period 2023/24	• Develop further guidance with regard to the listing of HSMs with no known location • Consider how environmental impact assessments can form a part of Historic Site and Monument assessment
CEP 26 2024	• Consider guidance concerning the listing of HSMs with no known location • Review proposals relating to EIAs and the HSM listing process
Intersessional period 2024/25	
CEP 27 2025	
Intersessional period 2025/26	
CEP 28 2026	
Intersessional period 2026/27	
CEP 29 2027	
Intersessional period	

2027/28	
CEP 30 2028	

Issue / Environmental Pressure: Biodiversity knowledge	
Priority: 2	
Actions: 1. Maintain awareness of threats to existing biodiversity. 2. CEP to consider further scientific advice on wildlife disturbance.	
Intersessional period 2023/24	• Informal intersessional discussions relating to assessing the protection of Antarctic seals • Continue informal discussions on the recommendations in CEP XXIV - WP 34
CEP 26 2024	• Report on informal intersessional discussions relating to assessing the protection of Antarctic seals
Intersessional period 2024/25	
CEP 27 2025	
Intersessional period 2025/26	
CEP 28 2026	
Intersessional period 2026/27	
CEP 29 2027	
Intersessional period 2027/28	
CEP 30 2028	
Science knowledge and information needs: • Research on the environmental impacts of remotely piloted aircraft systems (RPAS), particularly on wildlife responses including: o a range of species including flying seabirds and seals; o both behavioural and physiological responses; o demographic effects, including breeding numbers and breeding success; o ambient environmental conditions, for example, wind and noise; o the effects of RPAS of different sizes and specifications;	

- the contribution of RPAS noise to wildlife disturbance;
- comparisons with control sites and human disturbance; and
- habituation effects.

- Collection and submission of further spatially explicit biodiversity data
- Research on the impacts of underwater noise on Antarctic marine mammals
- Synthesis of available knowledge on the biogeography, bioregionalisation and endemism within Antarctica
- Site-specific, timing-specific and species-specific studies to understand the impacts arising from interactions between human activities and wildlife and support evidence-based guidelines to avoid disturbance
- Inventory of Mt Erebus ice caves and microbial communities
- Regular population counts and research to understand the status and trends in the southern giant petrel population

<table>
<tr><td colspan="2">Issue / Environmental Pressure: Outreach and education</td></tr>
<tr><td colspan="2">Priority: 3</td></tr>
<tr><td colspan="2">Actions:
1. Review current examples and identify opportunities for greater education and outreach.
2. Encourage Members to exchange information regarding their experiences in this area.
3. Establish a strategy and guidelines for exchanging information between Members on Education and Outreach for long-term perspective.</td></tr>
<tr><td>Intersessional period 2023/24</td><td></td></tr>
<tr><td>CEP 26 2024</td><td></td></tr>
<tr><td>Intersessional period 2024/25</td><td></td></tr>
<tr><td>CEP 27 2025</td><td></td></tr>
<tr><td>Intersessional period 2025/26</td><td></td></tr>
<tr><td>CEP 28 2026</td><td></td></tr>
<tr><td>Intersessional period 2026/27</td><td></td></tr>
<tr><td>CEP 29 2027</td><td></td></tr>
<tr><td>Intersessional period 2027/28</td><td></td></tr>
</table>

CEP 30 2028	

Issue / Environmental Pressure: Protection of outstanding geological values	
Priority: 3	
Actions: 1. Consider further mechanisms for protection of outstanding geological values.	
Intersessional period 2023/24	
CEP 26 2024	
Intersessional period 2024/25	
CEP 27 2025	
Intersessional period 2025/26	
CEP 28 2026	
Intersessional period 2026/27	
CEP 29 2027	
Intersessional period 2027/28	
CEP 30 2028	

Appendix 2

Procedure for CEP consideration of draft CEEs

1. The agenda of each CEP meeting shall include an item relating to the consideration of draft CEEs forwarded to the CEP in accordance with Paragraph 4 of Article 3 of Annex I to the Protocol.
2. The CEP shall, under this agenda item, consider any draft CEE and provide advice to the ATCM on such drafts in accordance with Article 12 and Annex I of the Protocol.
3. Proponents are encouraged to inform the CEP Chair, as early as possible, of their intention to submit a draft CEE, so that the CEP Chair can make the necessary arrangements for intersessional discussions of the draft CEE in a timely manner.
4. In accordance with Paragraph 4 of Article 3 of Annex I to the Protocol, proponents shall circulate draft CEEs at least 120 days before the next Antarctic Treaty Consultative Meeting (ATCM). To facilitate translation in accordance with the provisions of paragraph 8 of these guidelines, proponents are encouraged to circulate draft CEEs as soon as practicable and preferably 165 days before the next ATCM.
5. Proponents shall submit the draft CEE (or a link to it) to the Secretariat by e-mail and make it publicly available, in one of the four official languages, on a website of their preference.
6. The Secretariat will immediately notify the CEP Chair and then post the draft CEE (or a link to it) on the CEP section of its website.
7. Upon receipt of the notification by the Secretariat, the CEP Chair shall immediately notify the CEP contact points of the availability of the draft CEE and provide details of the website at which the documents can be accessed.
8. Also upon receipt of the draft CEE, the Secretariat shall immediately send it for translation into all other official languages and post these versions in the CEP section of its website as soon as possible, and as far as practical at least 120 days before the next ATCM.
9. The Chair shall suggest a convenor for an open-ended intersessional contact group (ICG) to consider the draft CEE. The convenor should preferably not be from the proponent Party.
10. The Chair shall allow a period of 15 days for Members to object or offer comments, suggestions or proposals concerning:
    i. the proposed convenor.
    ii. additional terms of reference beyond the following generic issues:
        - the extent to which the CEE conforms to the requirements of Article 3 of Annex I of the Environment Protocol.
        - whether the CEE: a) has identified all the environmental impacts of the proposed activity; and b) suggests appropriate methods of mitigating (reducing or avoiding) those impacts.
        - whether the conclusions of the draft CEE are adequately supported by the information contained within the document.
        - the clarity, format and presentation of the draft CEE.

11. If the Chair does not receive a reply within 15 days, it will be considered that the Members agree with the proposed convenor and the generic terms of reference. If the Chair receives comments on i) or ii) listed above within the 15-day limit the Chair shall, as appropriate, circulate a revised suggestion for one or both items. A further 15-day limit applies for Members to respond.
12. All ICG discussions shall be open to CEP Members and Observers and shall take place on the CEP Discussion Forum.
13. The right of a CEP Member to raise an issue on a draft CEE at the CEP and the right of a Party to raise an issue at the ATCM is not affected by its participation or lack thereof in the open-ended intersessional contact group.
14. The outcome of the ICG's deliberations, indicating areas of agreement and areas where differing views are expressed, shall be reported in a Working Paper submitted by the convenor to the next CEP meeting.

Appendix 3

Preliminary Agenda for CEP 26 (2024)

1. Opening of the Meeting
2. Adoption of the Agenda
3. Strategic Discussions on the Future Work of the CEP
4. Operation of the CEP
5. Cooperation with other Organisations
6. Repair and Remediation of Environment Damage
7. Climate Change Implications for the Environment:
    a. Strategic Approach
    b. Implementation and Review of the Climate Change Response Work Programme
8. Environmental Impact Assessment (EIA):
    a. Draft Comprehensive Environmental Evaluations
    b. Other EIA Matters
9. Area Protection and Management Plans:
    a. Management Plans
    b. Historic Sites and Monuments
    c. Site Guidelines
    d. Marine Spatial Protection and Management
    e. Other Annex V Matters
10. Conservation of Antarctic Flora and Fauna:
    a. Quarantine and Non-native Species
    b. Specially Protected Species
    c. Other Annex II Matters
11. Environmental Monitoring and Reporting
12. Inspection Reports
13. General Matters
14. Election of Officers
15. Preparation for the Next Meeting
16. Adoption of the Report
17. Closing of the Meeting

3. Appendices

Changes to mining ban text on ATS website

It is sometimes publicly reported that the Protocol 'expires' in 2048. This is a misinterpretation and is not correct. Neither the Protocol, nor the Antarctic Treaty, have a termination date. For the first fifty years from the Protocol's entry into force (1998), it can only be modified by the unanimous agreement of all Consultative Parties to the Antarctic Treaty. After this point (from 2048), any of the Antarctic Treaty Consultative Parties can call for a review conference into the Protocol's operation (Art. 25.2).

The Protocol provides that if a review conference is called, it can be modified or amended by a majority of all Parties, including three-quarters of the Consultative Parties at the time of the Protocol's adoption. Any modifications or amendments will only enter into force with the agreement of all 26 Consultative Parties that adopted the Protocol in 1991. Additionally, the prohibition on Antarctic mineral resource activities in Article 7 cannot be removed or amended unless a binding legal regime on Antarctic mineral resource activities is in force. The introduction of such a regime would require consensus.

XLV ANTARCTIC TREATY CONSULTATIVE MEETING
May 29 – June 8, 2023 | Helsinki – Finland

XLV ANTARCTIC TREATY CONSULTATIVE MEETING
HELSINKI 28.5.-8.6.2023

HOST COUNTRY COMMUNIQUÉ
9 JUNE 2023

From May 28 to June 8, Finland hosted the XLV Antarctic Treaty Consultative Meeting (ATCM) as well as the XXV meeting of the Committee for Environmental Protection (CEP). The meetings, organized by the Ministry for Foreign Affairs of Finland, took place in Helsinki and were held in in-person format after the virtual and hybrid meetings in Paris and Berlin in 2021 and 2022. A total of 500 delegates were registered for the ATCM XLV of which 400 attended in person.

The ATCM brought together the 56 States Parties to the Antarctic Treaty, as well as Observers and Experts and was chaired by Ms. Päivi Kaukoranta, the Director of the National Security Authority of Finland at the Ministry for Foreign Affairs. The CEP was chaired by Ms. Birgit Njåstad (Norway). Ms. Tiina Jortikka-Laitinen acted as the Head of Host Country Secretariat.

Ms. Johanna Sumuvuori, Deputy Foreign Minister of Finland, Ms. Terhi Lehtonen, State Secretary of the Ministry of the Environment, and Helena Gualinga, climate and environmental activist, officially opened the conference. Ms. Sumuvuori condemned Russia's breach of international law and illegal war of one Consultative Party against another, noting it to be contrary to the spirit of the Antarctic Treaty. Ms. Sumuvuori and Ms. Lehtonen highlighted the importance of acting in accordance with the slogan of the Helsinki meeting "From Urgency to Action" and called on the international community to intensify action against climate change and its impacts in Antarctica. Ms. Gualinga, representing the Youth, emphasized the dramatic global effects of climate change, from the Amazon rainforest to the Arctic and Antarctic, and reminded of the responsibility of today's decision-makers for future generations.

In accordance with the decision of the ATCM-44 in Berlin, the first joint ATCM-CEP session on Climate Change was held in Helsinki on June 2. The day started with the inspirational kick-off session, during which the Secretary General of the World Meteorological Organization, Dr. Petteri Taalas and the Executive Secretary of UNFCCC, Mr. Simon Stiell highlighted the central role of the Antarctic in the global climate system and the importance of Greenhouse Gas (GHG) emissions reductions. The Key Note Speaker Dr. Valérie Masson-Delmotte, Co-Chair of IPCC Working Group 1, emphasized seriousness, urgency and action and underlined the need for rapid environmental governance responses and research advances to inform decision-making.

Concluding the climate discussions, the Consultative Parties adopted the Helsinki Declaration on Climate Change in the Antarctic highlighting the global implications of climate change and the need for urgent action to protect Antarctica.

Parties expressed concerns about the rapidly growing tourism in Antarctica and decided to establish a dedicated process to develop a comprehensive framework for regulation of tourism in Antarctica. They also highlighted the importance to implement the already approved ATCM Measures M4 (2004) and M15 (2009).

Throughout the discussions, Parties highlighted the importance of Article 7 of the Protocol on Environmental Protection, which prohibits any activity relating to mineral resources, other than scientific research. It was emphasized that the ban on mining is one of the core provisions of the Protocol, which does not have an expiry date.

The Committee for Environmental Protection (CEP) considered a wide array of issues, and through its advice to the Parties contributed to strengthening the implementation of the Environmental Protocol. Its advice included management of protected areas, efficiency of the environmental impact assessment system, climate change response, environmental monitoring and conservation of Antarctic flora and fauna. The Committee expressed great concern that an outbreak of avian flu in Antarctica could be a detrimental threat to Antarctic wildlife, and advised the Parties on the importance of developing and implementing appropriate preventive actions. The CEP will continue to work to promote the effectiveness and enhance the work of the Committee.

Finland and Argentina co-hosted the Topical Session on the harmonized implementation of the IMO Polar Code. There were engaged discussions on the need to continue prioritizing the harmonized implementation and effective enforcement of the IMO Polar Code in the Multi-year Strategic Work Plan. Furthermore, ship owners and operators of vessels in Arctic and Antarctic waters were called to recognize and thoroughly implement the requirements of the Polar Code.

The Helsinki meeting acknowledged the growing number of women in Antarctic policy-making, science and operations and highlighted the importance of equality and inclusiveness in the implementation of the Antarctic Treaty. Many Parties announced their commitment to promoting inclusivity and diversity in their national Antarctic programs. The meeting also emphasized the importance of gender-neutral and respectful inclusive language in spoken and written documentation, reporting and other forms of communication.

The next ATCM will be hosted by India from 20 to 30 May 2024.

Preliminary Agenda for ATCM 46, Working Groups and Allocation of Items

Plenary

1) Opening of the Meeting
2) Election of Officers and Creation of Working Groups
3) Adoption of the Agenda, Allocation of Items to Working Groups and Consideration of the Multi-year Strategic Work Plan
4) Operation of the Antarctic Treaty System: Reports by Parties, Observers and Experts
5) Report of the Committee for Environmental Protection
6) Operation of the Antarctic Treaty System:
   a. Request from Canada to become a Consultative Party

Working Group 1: Policy, Legal, Institutional

6) Operation of the Antarctic Treaty System:
   b. General matters
7) Operation of the Antarctic Treaty System: Matters related to the Secretariat
8) Liability
9) Biological Prospecting in Antarctica
10) Exchange of Information
11) Education Issues
12) Multi-year Strategic Work Plan
    a. Policy, Legal and Institutional priorities

Working Group 2: Science, Operations, Tourism

12) Multi-year Strategic Work Plan
    b. Science, Operations and Tourism priorities
13) Safety and Operations in Antarctica
14) Inspections under the Antarctic Treaty and Environment Protocol
15) Science issues, future science challenges, scientific cooperation and facilitation
16) Implications of Climate Change for Management of the Antarctic Treaty Area
17) Tourism and Non-governmental Activities in the Antarctic Treaty Area, including Competent Authorities Issues

Special Working Group 3: Development of a Tourism Framework

18) Development of a Tourism Framework

Plenary

19) Preparation of the 47th Meeting
20) Any other Business
21) Adoption of the Final Report
22) Close of the Meeting

PART II

Measures, Decisions and Resolutions

1. Measures

Measure 1 (2023)

Antarctic Specially Managed Area No 1 (Admiralty Bay, King George Island): Revised Management Plan

The Representatives,

Recalling Articles 4, 5 and 6 of Annex V to the Protocol on Environmental Protection to the Antarctic Treaty, providing for the designation of Antarctic Specially Managed Areas ("ASMA") and approval of Management Plans for those Areas;

Recalling

- Recommendation X-5 (1979), which designated the Western shore of Admiralty Bay as Site of Special Scientific Interest ("SSSI") No 8, and Decision 1 (2002), which renamed and renumbered the Site as Antarctic Specially Protected Area ("ASPA") No 128;
- Recommendation XIII-16 (1985), which added Historic Site and Monument ("HSM") No 51 Puchalski Grave to the List of Historic Sites and Monuments ("the List");
- Measure 2 (2006) which designated Admiralty Bay, King George Island as ASMA 1, within which ASPA 128 and HSM 51 are located, and adopted a Management Plan for the Area;
- Measure 14 (2014), which adopted a revised Management Plan for ASMA 1;

Noting Measure 4 (2014), which adopted a revised Management Plan for ASPA 128;

Noting that the Committee for Environmental Protection has endorsed a revised Management Plan for ASMA 1;

Desiring to replace the existing Management Plan for ASMA 1 with the revised Management Plan;

Recommend to their Governments the following Measure for approval in accordance with paragraph 1 of Article 6 of Annex V to the Protocol on Environmental Protection to the Antarctic Treaty:

That:

1. the revised Management Plan for Antarctic Specially Managed Area No 1 (Admiralty Bay, King George Island), which is annexed to this Measure, be approved; and

2. the Management Plan for Antarctic Specially Managed Area No 1 annexed to Measure 14 (2014) be revoked.

Measure 2 (2023)

Antarctic Specially Protected Area No 108 (Green Island, Berthelot Islands, Antarctic Peninsula): Revised Management Plan

The Representatives,

Recalling Articles 3, 5 and 6 of Annex V to the Protocol on Environmental Protection to the Antarctic Treaty providing for the designation of Antarctic Specially Protected Areas ("ASPA") and approval of Management Plans for those Areas;

Recalling

- Recommendation IV-9 (1966), which designated Green Island, Berthelot Islands, Antarctic Peninsula as Specially Protected Area ("SPA") No 9;
- Recommendation XVI-6 (1991), which annexed a Management Plan for the Area;
- Decision 1 (2002), which renamed and renumbered SPA 9 as ASPA 108;
- Measures 1 (2002), 1 (2013) and 1 (2018), which adopted revised Management Plans for ASPA 108;

Recalling that Recommendation IV-9 (1966) was designated as no longer current by Decision 1 (2011) and that Recommendation XVI-6 (1991) did not become effective and was withdrawn by Decision 3 (2017);

Noting that the Committee for Environmental Protection has endorsed a revised Management Plan for ASPA 108;

Desiring to replace the existing Management Plan for ASPA 108 with the revised Management Plan;

Recommend to their Governments the following Measure for approval in accordance with paragraph 1 of Article 6 of Annex V to the Protocol on Environmental Protection to the Antarctic Treaty:

That:

1. the revised Management Plan for Antarctic Specially Protected Area No 108 (Green Island, Berthelot Islands, Antarctic Peninsula), which is annexed to this Measure, be approved; and

2. the Management Plan for the Antarctic Specially Protected Area No 108 annexed to Measure 1 (2018) be revoked.

Measure 3 (2023)

Antarctic Specially Protected Area No 117 (Avian Island, Marguerite Bay, Antarctic Peninsula): Revised Management Plan

The Representatives,

Recalling Articles 3, 5 and 6 of Annex V to the Protocol on Environmental Protection to the Antarctic Treaty providing for the designation of Antarctic Specially Protected Areas ("ASPA") and approval of Management Plans for those Areas;

Recalling

- Recommendation XV-6 (1989), which designated Avian Island, North-West Marguerite Bay as Site of Special Scientific Interest ("SSSI") No 30 and annexed a Management Plan for the Site;
- Recommendation XVI-4 (1991), which redesignated SSSI 30 as Specially Protected Area ("SPA") No 21 and annexed a revised Management Plan for the Area;
- Decision 1 (2002), which renamed and renumbered SPA 21 as ASPA 117;
- Measures 1 (2002), 2 (2013) and 2 (2018), which adopted revised Management Plans for ASPA 117;

Recalling that Recommendations XV-6 (1989) and XVI-4 (1991) did not become effective and were designated as no longer current by Decision 1 (2011);

Noting that the Committee for Environmental Protection has endorsed a revised Management Plan for ASPA 117;

Desiring to replace the existing Management Plan for ASPA 117 with the revised Management Plan;

Recommend to their Governments the following Measure for approval in accordance with paragraph 1 of Article 6 of Annex V to the Protocol on Environmental Protection to the Antarctic Treaty:

That:

1. the revised Management Plan for Antarctic Specially Protected Area No 117 (Avian Island, Marguerite Bay, Antarctic Peninsula), which is annexed to this Measure, be approved; and
2. the Management Plan for Antarctic Specially Protected Area No 117 annexed to Measure 2 (2018) be revoked.

Measure 4 (2023)

Antarctic Specially Protected Area No 122 (Arrival Heights, Hut Point Peninsula, Ross Island): Revised Management Plan

The Representatives,

Recalling Articles 3, 5 and 6 of Annex V to the Protocol on Environmental Protection to the Antarctic Treaty providing for the designation of Antarctic Specially Protected Areas ("ASPA") and approval of Management Plans for those Areas;

Recalling

- Recommendation VIII-4 (1975), which designated Arrival Heights, Hut Point Peninsula, Ross Island as Site of Special Scientific Interest ("SSSI") No 2 and annexed a Management Plan for the Site;
- Recommendations X-6 (1979), XII-5 (1983), XIII-7 (1985), XIV-4 (1987), Resolution 3 (1996) and Measure 2 (2000), which extended the expiry date of SSSI 2;
- Decision 1 (2002), which renamed and renumbered SSSI 2 as ASPA 122;
- Measures 2 (2004), 3 (2011), 3 (2016) and 8 (2022), which adopted revised Management Plans for ASPA 122;

Recalling that Measure 2 (2000) was withdrawn by Measure 5 (2009);

Recalling that Recommendations VIII-4 (1975), X-6 (1979), XII-5 (1983), XIII-7 (1985), XIV-4 (1987) and Resolution 3 (1996) were designated as no longer current by Decision 1 (2011);

Noting that the Committee for Environmental Protection has endorsed a revised Management Plan for ASPA 122;

Desiring to replace the existing Management Plan for ASPA 122 with the revised Management Plan;

Recommend to their Governments the following Measure for approval in accordance with paragraph 1 of Article 6 of Annex V to the Protocol on Environmental Protection to the Antarctic Treaty:

That:

1. the revised Management Plan for Antarctic Specially Protected Area No 122 (Arrival Heights, Hut Point Peninsula, Ross Island), which is annexed to this Measure, be approved; and

2. the Management Plan for Antarctic Specially Protected Area No 122 annexed to Measure 8 (2022) be revoked.

Measure 5 (2023)

Antarctic Specially Protected Area No 123 (Barwick and Balham Valleys, Southern Victoria Land): Revised Management Plan

The Representatives,

Recalling Articles 3, 5 and 6 of Annex V to the Protocol on Environmental Protection to the Antarctic Treaty providing for the designation of Antarctic Specially Protected Areas ("ASPA") and approval of Management Plans for those Areas;

Recalling

- Recommendation VIII-4 (1975), which designated Barwick Valley, Victoria Land as Site of Special Scientific Interest ("SSSI") No 3 and annexed a Management Plan for the Site;
- Recommendations X-6 (1979), XII-5 (1983), XIII-7 (1985), Resolution 7 (1995) and Measure 2 (2000), which extended the expiry date of SSSI 3;
- Decision 1 (2002), which renamed and renumbered SSSI 3 as ASPA 123;
- Measures 1 (2002), 6 (2008), 3 (2013) and 1 (2019), which adopted revised Management Plans for ASPA 123;

Recalling that Recommendations VIII-4 (1975), X-6 (1979), XII-5 (1983), XIII-7 (1985) and Resolution 7 (1995) were designated as no longer current by Decision 1 (2011);

Recalling that Measure 2 (2000) did not become effective and was withdrawn by Measure 5 (2009);

Noting that the Committee for Environmental Protection has endorsed a revised Management Plan for ASPA 123;

Desiring to replace the existing Management Plan for ASPA 123 with the revised Management Plan;

Recommend to their Governments the following Measure for approval in accordance with paragraph 1 of Article 6 of Annex V to the Protocol on Environmental Protection to the Antarctic Treaty:

That:

1. the revised Management Plan for Antarctic Specially Protected Area No 123 (Barwick and Balham Valleys, South Victoria Land), which is annexed to this Measure, be approved; and

2. the Management Plan for Antarctic Specially Protected Area No 123 annexed to Measure 1 (2019) be revoked.

Measure 6 (2023)

Antarctic Specially Protected Area No 132 (Potter Peninsula, King George Island (Isla 25 de Mayo), South Shetland Islands): Revised Management Plan

The Representatives,

Recalling Articles 3, 5 and 6 of Annex V to the Protocol on Environmental Protection to the Antarctic Treaty providing for the designation of Antarctic Specially Protected Areas ("ASPA") and approval of Management Plans for those Areas;

Recalling

- Recommendation XIII-8 (1985), which designated Potter Peninsula, King George Island (Isla 25 de Mayo), South Shetland Islands as Site of Special Scientific Interest ("SSSI") No 13 and annexed a Management Plan for the Site;
- Measure 3 (1997), which annexed a revised Management Plan for SSSI 13;
- Decision 1 (2002), which renamed and renumbered SSSI 13 as ASPA 132;
- Measures 2 (2005), 4 (2013) and 3 (2018), which adopted revised Management Plans for ASPA 132;

Recalling that Measure 3 (1997) has not become effective and was withdrawn by Measure 6 (2011);

Noting that the Committee for Environmental Protection has endorsed a revised Management Plan for ASPA 132;

Desiring to replace the existing Management Plan for ASPA 132 with the revised Management Plan;

Recommend to their Governments the following Measure for approval in accordance with paragraph 1 of Article 6 of Annex V to the Protocol on Environmental Protection to the Antarctic Treaty:

That:

1. the revised Management Plan for Antarctic Specially Protected Area No 132 (Potter Peninsula, King George Island (Isla 25 de Mayo), South Shetland Islands), which is annexed to this Measure, be approved; and

2. the Management Plan for Antarctic Specially Protected Area No 132 annexed to Measure 3 (2018) be revoked.

Measure 7 (2023)

Antarctic Specially Protected Area No 137 (Northwest White Island, McMurdo Sound): Revised Management Plan

The Representatives,

Recalling Articles 3, 5 and 6 of Annex V to the Protocol on Environmental Protection to the Antarctic Treaty providing for the designation of Antarctic Specially Protected Areas ("ASPA") and approval of Management Plans for those Areas;

Recalling

- Recommendation XIII-8 (1985), which designated Northwest White Island, McMurdo Sound as Site of Special Scientific Interest ("SSSI") No 18 and annexed a Management Plan for the Site;
- Recommendation XVI-7 (1991) and Measure 3 (2001), which extended the expiry date of SSSI 18;
- Decision 1 (2002), which renamed and renumbered SSSI 18 as ASPA 137;
- Measures 1 (2002), 9 (2008) and 7 (2013), which adopted revised Management Plans for ASPA 137;

Recalling that Measure 3 (2001) did not become effective and was withdrawn by Measure 4 (2011);

Recalling that Recommendation XVI-7 (1991) did not become effective and was designated as no longer current by Decision 1 (2011);

Recalling that the Committee for Environmental Protection ("CEP") XXI (2018) reviewed and continued without changes the Management Plan for ASPA 137, which is annexed to Measure 7 (2013);

Noting that the CEP has endorsed a revised Management Plan for ASPA 137;

Desiring to replace the existing Management Plan for ASPA 137 with the revised Management Plan;

Recommend to their Governments the following Measure for approval in accordance with paragraph 1 of Article 6 of Annex V to the Protocol on Environmental Protection to the Antarctic Treaty:

That:

1. the revised Management Plan for Antarctic Specially Protected Area No 137 (Northwest White Island, McMurdo Sound), which is annexed to this Measure, be approved; and

2. the Management Plan for Antarctic Specially Protected Area No 137 annexed to Measure 7 (2013) be revoked.

Measure 8 (2023)

Antarctic Specially Protected Area No 138 (Linnaeus Terrace, Asgard Range, Victoria Land): Revised Management Plan

The Representatives,

Recalling Articles 3, 5 and 6 of Annex V to the Protocol on Environmental Protection to the Antarctic Treaty providing for the designation of Antarctic Specially Protected Areas ("ASPA") and approval of Management Plans for those Areas;

Recalling

- Recommendation XIII-8 (1985), which designated Linnaeus Terrace, Asgard Range, Victoria Land as Site of Special Scientific Interest ("SSSI") No 19 and annexed a Management Plan for the Site;
- Resolution 7 (1995), which extended the expiry date of SSSI;
- Measure 1 (1996), which annexed a revised Management Plan for SSSI 19;
- Decision 1 (2002), which renamed and renumbered SSSI 19 as Antarctic Specially Protected Area No 138;
- Measures 10 (2008) and 8 (2013), which adopted revised Management Plans for ASPA 138;

Recalling that Resolution 7 (1995) was designated as no longer current by Decision 1 (2011);

Recalling that Measure 1 (1996) has not become effective and was withdrawn by Measure 10 (2008);

Recalling that the Committee for Environmental Protection ("CEP") XXI (2018) reviewed and continued without changes the Management Plan for ASPA 138, which is annexed to Measure 8 (2013);

Noting that the Committee for Environmental Protection has endorsed a revised Management Plan for ASPA 138;

Desiring to replace the existing Management Plan for ASPA 138 with the revised Management Plan;

Recommend to their Governments the following Measure for approval in accordance with paragraph 1 of Article 6 of Annex V to the Protocol on Environmental Protection to the Antarctic Treaty:

That:

1. the revised Management Plan for Antarctic Specially Protected Area No 138 (Linnaeus Terrace, Asgard Range, Victoria Land), which is annexed to this Measure, be approved; and

2. the Management Plan for Antarctic Specially Protected Area No 138 annexed to Measure 8 (2013) be revoked.

Measure 9 (2023)

Antarctic Specially Protected Area No 144 (Chile Bay (Discovery Bay), Greenwich Islands, South Shetland Islands): Revoked Management Plan

The Representatives,

Recalling Articles 3, 5 and 6 of Annex V to the Protocol on Environmental Protection to the Antarctic Treaty providing for the designation of Antarctic Specially Protected Areas ("ASPA") and approval of Management Plans for those Areas;

Recalling

- Recommendation XIV-5 (1987), which designated Chile Bay (Discovery Bay), Greenwich Islands, South Shetland Islands as Site of Special Scientific Interest ("SSSI") No 26, and annexed a Management Plan for the Site;
- Resolution 3 (1996) and Measure 2 (2000), which extended the date of expiry of SSSI 26;
- Decision 4 (1998), which listed SSSI 26 as a SSSI with marine areas of interest to the Commission for the Conservation of Antarctic Marine Living Resources;
- Decision 1 (2002), which renamed and renumbered SSSI 26 as ASPA 144;
- Measure 4 (2005), which extended the date of expiry of the Management Plan for ASPA 144;

Recalling that Recommendation XIV-5 (1987) was designated as no longer current by Measure 13 (2014);

Recalling that Resolution 3 (1996) was designated as no longer current by Decision 1 (2011) and that Measure 2 (2000) did not become effective and was withdrawn by Measure 5 (2009);

Recalling that Decision 4 (1998) was designated as no longer current by Decision 9 (2005);

Noting that the Committee for Environmental Protection has reviewed the appropriateness of additional protection afforded by ASPA status for Chile Bay (Discovery Bay);

Desiring to update the status of ASPA 144;

Recommend to their Governments the following Measure for approval in accordance with paragraph 1 of Article 6 of Annex V to the Protocol on Environmental Protection to the Antarctic Treaty:

That:

1. the Management Plan for Antarctic Specially Protected Area No 144 annexed to Recommendation XIV-5 (1987) be revoked; and
2. Antarctic Specially Protected Area No 144 shall not be used as a future designation.

Measure 10 (2023)

Antarctic Specially Protected Area No 145 (Port Foster, Deception Island, South Shetland Islands): Revised Management Plan

The Representatives,

Recalling Articles 3, 5 and 6 of Annex V to the Protocol on Environmental Protection to the Antarctic Treaty providing for the designation of Antarctic Specially Protected Areas ("ASPA") and approval of Management Plans for those Areas;

Recalling

- Recommendation XIV-5 (1987) which designated Port Foster, Deception Island as Site of Special Scientific Interest ("SSSI") No 27 and annexed a Management Plan for the Site;
- Resolution 3 (1996) and Measure 2 (2000), which extended the date of expiry of the Management Plan for SSSI 27;
- Decision 1 (2002) which renamed and renumbered SSSI 27 as ASPA 145;
- Measure 3 (2005), which incorporated ASPA 145 into Antarctic Specially Managed Area No 4 (Deception Island) and adopted a revised Management Plan for ASPA 145;

Recalling that Recommendation XIV-5 (1987) was designated as no longer current by Measure 13 (2014);

Recalling that Resolution 3 (1996) was designated as no longer current by Decision 1 (2011);

Noting that the Committee for Environmental Protection has endorsed a revised Management Plan for ASPA 145;

Desiring to replace the existing Management Plan for ASPA 145 with the revised Management Plan;

Recommend to their Governments the following Measure for approval in accordance with paragraph 1 of Article 6 of Annex V to the Protocol on Environmental Protection to the Antarctic Treaty:

That:

1. the revised Management Plan for Antarctic Specially Protected Area No 145 (Port Foster, Deception Island, South Shetland Islands), which is annexed to this Measure, be approved; and

2. the Management Plan for Antarctic Specially Protected Area No 145 annexed to Measure 3 (2005) be revoked.

Measure 11 (2023)

Antarctic Specially Protected Area No 147 (Ablation Valley and Ganymede Heights, Alexander Island): Revised Management Plan

The Representatives,

Recalling Articles 3, 5 and 6 of Annex V to the Protocol on Environmental Protection to the Antarctic Treaty providing for the designation of Antarctic Specially Protected Areas ("ASPA") and approval of Management Plans for those Areas;

Recalling

- Recommendation XV-6 (1989), which designated Ablation Valley and Ganymede Heights, Alexander Island as Site of Special Scientific Interest ("SSSI") No 29 and annexed a Management Plan for the Site;
- Resolution 3 (1996), which extended the expiry date for SSSI 29;
- Measure 2 (2000), which extended the expiry date for the Management Plan for SSSI 29;
- Decision 1 (2002), which renamed and renumbered SSSI 29 as ASPA 147;
- Measures 1 (2002), 10 (2013) and 4 (2018), which adopted revised Management Plans for ASPA 147;

Recalling that Recommendation XV-6 (1989) and Resolution 3 (1996) were designated as no longer current by Decision 1 (2011);

Recalling that Measure 2 (2000) did not become effective and was withdrawn by Measure 5 (2009);

Noting that the Committee for Environmental Protection has endorsed a revised Management Plan for ASPA 147;

Desiring to replace the existing Management Plan for ASPA 147 with the revised Management Plan;

Recommend to their Governments the following Measure for approval in accordance with paragraph 1 of Article 6 of Annex V to the Protocol on Environmental Protection to the Antarctic Treaty:

That:

1. the revised Management Plan for Antarctic Specially Protected Area No 147 (Ablation Valley and Ganymede Heights, Alexander Island), which is annexed to this Measure, be approved; and
2. the Management Plan for Antarctic Specially Protected Area No 147 annexed to Measure 4 (2018) be revoked.

Measure 12 (2023)

Antarctic Specially Protected Area No 149 (Cape Shirreff and San Telmo Island, Livingston Island, South Shetland Islands): Revised Management Plan

The Representatives,

Recalling Articles 3, 5 and 6 of Annex V to the Protocol on Environmental Protection to the Antarctic Treaty providing for the designation of Antarctic Specially Protected Areas ("ASPA") and approval of Management Plans for those Areas;

Recalling

- Recommendation IV-11 (1966), which designated Cape Shirreff, Livingston Island, South Shetland Islands as Specially Protected Area ("SPA") No 11;
- Recommendation XV-7 (1989), which terminated SPA 11 and redesignated the Area as Site of Special Scientific Interest ("SSSI") No 32 and annexed a Management Plan for the Site;
- Resolution 3 (1996) and Measure 2 (2000), which extended the expiry date of SSSI 32;
- Decision 1 (2002), which renamed and renumbered SSSI 32 as ASPA 149;
- Measures 2 (2005), 7 (2011), 7 (2016) and 16 (2022), which adopted revised Management Plans for ASPA 149;

Recalling that Recommendation XV-7 (1989) and Measure 2 (2000) did not become effective, and that Measure 2 (2000) was withdrawn by Measure 5 (2009);

Recalling that Recommendation XV-7 (1989) and Resolution 3 (1996) were designated as no longer current by Decision 1 (2011);

Noting that the Committee for Environmental Protection has endorsed a revised Management Plan for ASPA 149;

Desiring to replace the existing Management Plan for ASPA 149 with the revised Management Plan;

Recommend to their Governments the following Measure for approval in accordance with paragraph 1 of Article 6 of Annex V to the Protocol on Environmental Protection to the Antarctic Treaty:

That:

1. the revised Management Plan for Antarctic Specially Protected Area No 149 (Cape Shirreff and San Telmo Island, Livingston Island, South Shetland Islands), which is annexed to this Measure, be approved; and

2. the Management Plan for Antarctic Specially Protected Area No 149 annexed to Measure 16 (2022) be revoked.

Measure 13 (2023)

Antarctic Specially Protected Area No 156 (Lewis Bay, Mount Erebus, Ross Island): Revised Management Plan

The Representatives,

Recalling Articles 3, 5 and 6 of Annex V to the Protocol on Environmental Protection to the Antarctic Treaty providing for the designation of Antarctic Specially Protected Areas ("ASPA") and approval of Management Plans for those Areas;

Recalling

- Measure 2 (1997), which designated Lewis Bay, Mount Erebus, Ross Island as Specially Protected Area ("SPA") No 26 and adopted a Management Plan for the Area;
- Decision 1 (2002), which renamed and renumbered SPA 26 as ASPA 156;
- Measures 2 (2003) and 13 (2013), which adopted revised Management Plans for ASPA 156;

Recalling that the Committee for Environmental Protection ("CEP") XI (2008) reviewed and continued without changes the Management Plan for ASPA 156, which is annexed to Measure 2 (2003);

Recalling that Measure 2 (1997) has not become effective and was withdrawn by Measure 8 (2010);

Recalling that the CEP XXI (2018) reviewed and continued without changes the Management Plan for ASPA 156, which is annexed to Measure 13 (2013);

Noting that the CEP has endorsed a revised Management Plan for ASPA 156;

Desiring to replace the existing Management Plan for ASPA 156 with the revised Management Plan;

Recommend to their Governments the following Measure for approval in accordance with paragraph 1 of Article 6 of Annex V to the Protocol on Environmental Protection to the Antarctic Treaty:

That:

1. the revised Management Plan for Antarctic Specially Protected Area No 156 (Lewis Bay, Mount Erebus, Ross Island), which is annexed to this Measure, be approved; and

2. the Management Plan for Antarctic Specially Protected Area No 156 annexed to Measure 13 (2013) be revoked.

Measure 14 (2023)

Antarctic Specially Protected Area No 165 (Edmonson Point, Wood Bay, Ross Sea): Revised Management Plan

The Representatives,

Recalling Articles 3, 5 and 6 of Annex V to the Protocol on Environmental Protection to the Antarctic Treaty providing for the designation of Antarctic Specially Protected Areas ("ASPA") and approval of Management Plans for those Areas;

Recalling

- Measure 1 (2006), which designated Edmonson Point, Wood Bay, Ross Sea as ASPA 165 and annexed a Management Plan for the Area;
- Measures 8 (2011) and 7 (2017), which adopted revised Management Plans for ASPA 165;

Noting that the Committee for Environmental Protection has endorsed a revised Management Plan for ASPA 165;

Desiring to replace the existing Management Plan for ASPA 165 with the revised Management Plan;

Recommend to their Governments the following Measure for approval in accordance with paragraph 1 of Article 6 of Annex V to the Protocol on Environmental Protection to the Antarctic Treaty:

That:

1. the revised Management Plan for Antarctic Specially Protected Area No 165 (Edmonson Point, Wood Bay, Ross Sea), which is annexed to this Measure, be approved; and

2. the Management Plan for Antarctic Specially Protected Area No 165 annexed to Measure 7 (2017) be revoked.

Measure 15 (2023)

Antarctic Specially Protected Area No 168 (Mount Harding, Grove Mountains, East Antarctica): Revised Management Plan

The Representatives,

Recalling Articles 3, 5 and 6 of Annex V to the Protocol on Environmental Protection to the Antarctic Treaty providing for the designation of Antarctic Specially Protected Areas ("ASPA") and approval of Management Plans for those Areas;

Recalling

- Measure 2 (2008), which designated Mount Harding, Grove Mountains, East Antarctica as ASPA 168 and annexed a Management Plan for the Area;
- Measure 17 (2015), which adopted a revised Management Plan for ASPA 168;

Noting that the Committee for Environmental Protection has endorsed a revised Management Plan for ASPA 168;

Desiring to replace the existing Management Plan for ASPA 168 with the revised Management Plan;

Recommend to their Governments the following Measure for approval in accordance with paragraph 1 of Article 6 of Annex V to the Protocol on Environmental Protection to the Antarctic Treaty:

That:

1. the revised Management Plan for Antarctic Specially Protected Area No 168 (Mount Harding, Grove Mountains, East Antarctica), which is annexed to this Measure, be approved; and
2. the Management Plan for Antarctic Specially Protected Area No 168 annexed to Measure 17 (2015) be revoked.

Measure 16 (2023)

Antarctic Specially Protected Area No 170 (Marion Nunataks, Charcot Island, Antarctic Peninsula): Revised Management Plan

The Representatives,

Recalling Articles 3, 5 and 6 of Annex V to the Protocol on Environmental Protection to the Antarctic Treaty providing for the designation of Antarctic Specially Protected Areas ("ASPA") and approval of Management Plans for those Areas;

Recalling

- Measure 4 (2008) which designated Marion Nunataks, Charcot Island, Antarctic Peninsula as ASPA 170 and adopted a Management Plan for the Area;
- Measures 16 (2013) and 5 (2018), which adopted revised Management Plans for ASPA 170;

Noting that the Committee for Environmental Protection has endorsed a revised Management Plan for ASPA 170;

Desiring to replace the existing Management Plan for ASPA 170 with the revised Management Plan;

Recommend to their Governments the following Measure for approval in accordance with paragraph 1 of Article 6 of Annex V to the Protocol on Environmental Protection to the Antarctic Treaty:

That:

1. the revised Management Plan for Antarctic Specially Protected Area No 170 (Marion Nunataks, Charcot Island, Antarctic Peninsula), which is annexed to this Measure, be approved; and
2. the Management Plan for Antarctic Specially Protected Area No 170 annexed to Measure 5 (2018) be revoked.

Measure 17 (2023)

Antarctic Specially Protected Area No 172 (Lower Taylor Glacier and Blood Falls, McMurdo Dry Valleys, Victoria Land): Revised Management Plan

The Representatives,

Recalling Articles 3, 5 and 6 of Annex V to the Protocol on Environmental Protection to the Antarctic Treaty providing for the designation of Antarctic Specially Protected Areas ("ASPA") and approval of Management Plans for those Areas;

Recalling Measure 9 (2012) which designated Lower Taylor Glacier and Blood Falls, McMurdo Dry Valleys, Victoria Land as ASPA 172 and annexed a Management Plan for the Area;

Recalling Measure 6 (2018), which adopted a revised Management Plan for ASPA 172;

Noting that that the Committee for Environmental Protection has endorsed a revised Management Plan for ASPA 172;

Desiring to replace the existing Management Plan for ASPA 172 with the revised Management Plan;

Recommend to their Governments the following Measure for approval in accordance with paragraph 1 of Article 6 of Annex V to the Protocol on Environmental Protection to the Antarctic Treaty:

That:

1. the revised Management Plan for Antarctic Specially Protected Area No 172 (Lower Taylor Glacier and Blood Falls, McMurdo Dry Valleys, Victoria Land), which is annexed to this Measure, be approved; and

2. the Management Plan for Antarctic Specially Protected Area No 172 annexed to Measure 6 (2018) be revoked.

Measure 18 (2023)

Antarctic Specially Protected Area No 179 (Parts of Western Sør Rondane Mountains, Dronning Maud Land, East Antarctica): Management Plan

The Representatives,

Recalling Articles 3, 5 and 6 of Annex V to the Protocol on Environmental Protection to the Antarctic Treaty providing for the designation of Antarctic Specially Protected Areas ("ASPA") and approval of Management Plans for those Areas;

Noting that the Committee for Environmental Protection ("CEP") has endorsed a Management Plan for ASPA 179;

Recognising that this area supports outstanding environmental, scientific, historic, aesthetic or wilderness values, or ongoing or planned scientific research, and would benefit from special protection;

Desiring to designate Parts of Western Sør Rondane Mountains, Dronning Maud Land, East Antarctica as ASPA 179, and to approve the Management Plan for this Area;

Recommend to their Governments the following Measure for approval in accordance with paragraph 1 of Article 6 of Annex V to the Protocol on Environmental Protection to the Antarctic Treaty:

That:

1. Parts of Western Sør Rondane Mountains, Dronning Maud Land, East Antarctica, be designated as Antarctic Specially Protected Area No 179; and

2. the Management Plan, which is annexed to this Measure, be approved.

2. Decisions

Decision 1 (2023)

Revised Rules of Procedure for the Committee for Environmental Protection (2023)

The Representatives,

Recalling Decision 2 (2011) which adopted Revised Rules of Procedure for the Committee for Environmental Protection ("the Revised Rules");

Recalling that Rule 15 of the Revised Rules provides that the Committee for Environmental Protection ("CEP") shall elect a Chair and two Vice-chairs from among the Consultative Parties;

Desiring to update the Revised Rules to include procedures for nominating and electing the Chair and Vice-chairs, and to clarify the serving terms for these positions;

Decide that the Revised Rules of Procedure for the Committee for Environmental Protection (2023) annexed to this Decision shall replace the Revised Rules of Procedure for the Committee for Environmental Protection (2011) annexed to Decision 2 (2011).

Revised Rules of Procedure for the Committee for Environmental Protection (2023)

Rule 1

Where not otherwise specified the Rules of Procedure for the Antarctic Treaty Consultative Meeting shall be applicable.

Rule 2

For the purposes of these Rules of Procedure:

a) the expression "Protocol" means the Protocol on Environmental Protection to the Antarctic Treaty, signed in Madrid on 4 October, 1991;

b) the expression "the Parties" means the Parties to the Protocol;

c) the expression "Committee" means the Committee for Environmental Protection as defined in Article 11 of the Protocol;

d) the expression "Secretariat" means the Secretariat of the Antarctic Treaty.

Part I Representatives and Experts

Rule 3

Each Party to the Protocol is entitled to be a member of the Committee and to appoint a representative who may be accompanied by experts and advisers with suitable scientific, environmental or technical competence.

Before each meeting of the Committee each member of the Committee shall, as early as possible, notify the Host Government of that meeting of the name and designation of each representative, and before or at the beginning of the meeting, the name and designation of each expert and adviser.

Part II Observers and Consultation

Rule 4

Observer status in the Committee shall be open to:

a) any Contracting Party to the Antarctic Treaty which is not a Party to the Protocol;

b) the President of the Scientific Committee on Antarctic Research, the Chair of the Scientific Committee for the Conservation of Antarctic Marine Living Resources and the Chair of the Council of Managers of National Antarctic Programmes, or their nominated Representatives;

c) subject to the specific approval of the Antarctic Treaty Consultative Meeting, other relevant scientific, environmental and technical organisations which can contribute to the work of the Committee.

Rule 5

Before each meeting of the Committee each observer shall, as early as possible, notify the Host Government of that meeting of the name and designation of its representative attending the meeting.

Rule 6

Observers may participate in the discussions, but shall not participate in the taking of decisions.

Rule 7

In carrying out its functions the Committee shall, as appropriate, consult with the Scientific Committee on Antarctic Research, the Scientific Committee for the Conservation of Antarctic Marine Living Resources, the Council of Managers of National Antarctic Programmes and other relevant scientific, environmental and technical organisations.

Rule 8

The Committee may seek the advice of experts as required on an *ad hoc* basis.

Part III Meetings

Rule 9

The Committee shall meet once a year, generally and preferably in conjunction with the Antarctic Treaty Consultative Meeting and at the same location. With the agreement of the ATCM, and in order to fulfill its functions, the Committee may also meet between annual meetings.

The Committee may establish informal open-ended contact groups to examine specific issues and report back to the Committee.

Open-ended contact groups established to undertake work during intersessional periods shall operate as follows:

a) where appropriate, the contact group coordinator shall be agreed by the Committee during its meeting and noted in its final report;

b) where appropriate, the terms of reference for the contact group shall be agreed by the Committee and included in its final report;

c) where appropriate, the modes of communication for the contact group, such as e-mail, the online discussion forum maintained by the Secretariat and informal meetings, shall be agreed by the Committee and included in its final report;

d) representatives who wish to be involved in a contact group shall register their interest with the coordinator through the discussion forum, by e-mail or by other appropriate means;

e) the coordinator shall use appropriate means to inform all group members of the composition of the contact group;

f) all correspondence shall be made available to all members of the contact group in a timely manner; and

g) when providing comments, members of the contact group shall state for whom they are speaking.

The Committee may also agree to establish other informal sub-groups or to consider other ways of working such as, but not limited to, workshops and video-conferences.

Rule 10

The Committee may establish, with the approval of the Antarctic Treaty Consultative Meeting, subsidiary bodies, as appropriate.

Such subsidiary bodies shall operate on the basis of the Rules of Procedure of the Committee as applicable.

Rule 11

The Rules of Procedure for the preparation of the Agenda of the Antarctic Treaty Consultative Meeting shall apply with necessary changes to Committee meetings.

Before each meeting of any subsidiary body the Secretariat, in consultation with the Chair of both the Committee and of the subsidiary body, shall prepare and distribute a preliminary annotated Agenda.

Part IV Submission of Documents

Rule 12

1. Working Papers shall refer to papers submitted by Members of the Committee that require discussion and action at a Meeting and papers submitted by Observers referred to in Rule 4(b).

2. Secretariat Papers shall refer to papers prepared by the Secretariat pursuant to a mandate established at a Meeting, or which would, in the view of the Executive Secretary, help inform the Meeting or assist in its operation.

3. Information Papers shall refer to:
- Papers submitted by Members of the Committee or Observers referred to in Rule 4(b) that provide information in support of a Working Paper or that are relevant to discussions at a Meeting;
- Papers submitted by Observers referred to in Rule 4(a) that are relevant to discussions at a Meeting; and
- Papers submitted by Observers referred to in Rule 4(c) that are relevant to discussions at a Meeting.

4. Background Papers shall refer to papers submitted by any participant that will not be introduced in a Meeting, but that are submitted for the purpose of formally providing information.

5. Procedures for the submission, translation and distribution of documents are annexed to the ATCM Rules of Procedure.

Part V Advice and Recommendations

Rule 13

The Committee shall try to reach consensus on the recommendations and advice to be provided by it pursuant to the Protocol.

Where consensus cannot be achieved the Committee shall set out in its report all views advanced on the matter in question.

Part VI Decisions

Rule 14

Where decisions are necessary, decisions on matters of substance shall be taken by a consensus of the members of the Committee participating in the meeting. Decisions on matters of procedure shall be taken by a simple majority of the members of the Committee present and voting. Each member of the Committee shall have one vote. Any question as to whether an issue is a procedural one shall be decided by consensus.

Part VII Chair and Vice-chairs

Rule 15

The Committee shall elect a Chair and two Vice-chairs from among the Consultative Parties. The Chair and the Vice-chairs shall be elected for a period of two annual meetings of the Committee and, where possible, their terms shall be staggered.

The Chair and the Vice-chairs shall not be re-elected to their post for more than one additional two-meeting term. The Chair and Vice-chairs shall not be representatives from the same Party.

The Vice-chair who has been a Vice-chair for the longer period of time (in total, counting any previous term of office) shall be first Vice-chair.

In the event that both Vice-chairs are appointed for the first time at the same meeting, the Committee shall determine which Vice-chair is elected as first Vice-chair.

The candidates for Chair and Vice-chairs shall be nominated in accordance with the following procedure.

a) At least 180 days before the opening of the meeting of the Committee in which an election will be required, the Chair shall issue a circular to:
   - remind Members that there will be an election;
   - if the current Chair or Vice-chairs are at the end of their first term, notify Members of their willingness to serve for a second term; and
   - invite nominations for the position(s).

b) Members should preferably submit nominations to the Secretariat at least 60 days before the start of the meeting of the Committee. Candidates should:
   - be from among the Antarctic Treaty Consultative Parties;
   - have sound working knowledge of the Antarctic Treaty system, the practices and the work of the Committee and the issues under consideration by the Committee;
   - have the support of their Party to serve in the role for at least one term covering two annual meetings of the Committee; and
   - reflect the requirement that the Chair and Vice-chairs be from different Parties.

c) Before the Meeting, the Chair will issue a circular summarising the results of any call for nominations.

The following procedure shall be followed during elections:

a) A quorum will be required for a valid election.

b) Each Member will be entitled to one vote (in each round of voting, if multiple rounds are required).

c) The outcome of the election will be decided by simple majority of the Members present and voting.

d) In the event that there are more than two candidates for a position, rounds of voting shall be conducted, eliminating the candidate with the least votes in each round.

Rule 16

Amongst other duties the Chair shall have the following powers and responsibilities:

a) convene, open, preside at and close each meeting of the Committee;

b) make rulings on points of order raised at each meeting of the Committee provided that each representative retains the right to request that any such decision be submitted to the Committee for approval;

c) approve a provisional agenda for the meeting after consultation with Representatives;

d) sign, on behalf of the Committee, the report of each meeting;

e) present the report referred to in Rule 22 on each meeting of the Committee to the Antarctic Treaty Consultative Meeting;

f) as required, initiate intersessional work; and

g) as agreed by the Committee, represent the Committee in other forums.

Rule 17

Whenever the Chair is unable to act, the first Vice-chair shall assume the powers and responsibilities of the Chair.

Whenever both the Chair and first Vice-chair are unable to act, the second Vice-chair shall assume the powers and responsibilities of the Chair.

Rule 18

In the event of the office of the Chair falling vacant between meetings, the first Vice-chair shall exercise the powers and responsibilities of the Chair until a new Chair is elected.

If the offices of both the Chair and first Vice-chair fall vacant between meetings, the second Vice-chair shall exercise the powers and responsibilities of the Chair until a new Chair is elected.

Rule 19

The Chair and Vice-chairs shall begin to carry out their functions on the conclusion of the meeting of the Committee at which they have been elected.

Part VIII Administrative Facilities

Rule 20

As a general rule the Committee, and any subsidiary bodies, shall make use of the administrative facilities of the Government which agrees to host its meetings.

Part IX Languages

Rule 21

English, French, Russian and Spanish shall be the official languages of the Committee and, as applicable, the subsidiary bodies referred to in Rule 10.

Part X Records and Reports

Rule 22

The Committee shall present a report on each of its meetings to the Antarctic Treaty Consultative Meeting. The report shall cover all matters considered at the meeting of the Committee, including at its intersessional meetings and by its subsidiary bodies as appropriate, and shall reflect the views expressed. The report shall also include a comprehensive list of the officially circulated Working Papers, Information Papers and Background Papers. The report shall be presented to the Antarctic Treaty Consultative Meeting in the official languages. The report shall be circulated to the Parties, and to observers attending the meeting, and shall thereupon be made publicly available.

Part XI Amendments

Rule 23

The Committee may adopt amendments to these Rules of Procedure, which shall be subject to approval by the Antarctic Treaty Consultative Meeting.

Decision 2 (2023)

Secretariat Report, Programme and Budget

The Representatives,

Recalling Measure 1 (2003) on the establishment of the Secretariat of the Antarctic Treaty ("the Secretariat");

Bearing in mind the Financial Regulations for the Secretariat of the Antarctic Treaty annexed to Decision 4 (2003) and amended by Decision 6 (2005);

Recalling Decision 4 (2009) concerning, amongst other matters, the Translation Contingency Fund;

Noting increased translation expenses;

Decide:

1. to approve the audited Financial Report for 2021/22 annexed to this Decision (Annex 1);
2. to take note of the Secretariat Report 2022/23, which includes the Provisional Financial Report for 2022/23, annexed to this Decision (Annex 2);
3. to take note of the Five Year Forward Budget Profile 2024/25-2028/29 and approve the Secretariat Programme 2023/24, including the Budget for 2023/24 and the Forecast Budget 2024/25, annexed to this Decision (Annex 3);
4. to increase the level of the Translation Contingency Fund to $50,000; and
5. to request that the Executive Secretary of the Secretariat open at the Antarctic Treaty Consultative Meeting Forum a topic to report to the Consultative Parties on financial issues.

"2023 – 1983/2023 – 40 YEARS OF DEMOCRACY"

Presidencia de la Nación
Sindicatura General de la Nación

ANNEX I

Opinion of the Auditor

Secretary
of the Secretariat of the Antarctic Treaty
Maipú 757, 4° piso
CUIT (Tax No.) 30-70892567-1
Re: ATCM XLV - CPA XXV Antarctic Treaty Consultative Meeting, 2023 – Helsinki, Finland

1. Report on Financial Statements

We have audited the attached Financial Statements of the Antarctic Treaty Secretariat, which include the following: Statement of Income and Expenditure, Statement of Financial Position, Statement of Equity, Cash Flow Statement and Explanatory Notes for the financial period commencing 1 April 2021 and ending 31 March 2022.

2. Management Responsibility for Financial Statements

The Antarctic Treaty Secretariat, constituted under Argentine Law No. 25.888 of 14 May 2004, is responsible for the preparation and reasonable presentation of the attached financial statements according to accounting methods based on cash movements in accordance with International Accounting Standards and the specific Standards for Antarctic Treaty Consultative Meetings. Such responsibility includes: designing, implementing and maintaining internal controls for the preparation and presentation of the Financial Statements such that they are free of misstatements, due to error or fraud, selecting and implementing appropriate accounting policies, and preparing accounting estimates which are reasonable under the circumstances.

3. Auditor's Responsibility

Our responsibility is to express our opinion on these Financial Statements based on our audit.

The audit was conducted in accordance with International Auditing Standards and the Annex to Decision 3 (2012) of the XXXI Antarctic Treaty Consultative Meeting, which describes the tasks to be carried out by the external auditor.

These standards require compliance with ethical requirements, and planning and execution of the audit so as to provide reasonable assurance that the Financial Statements are free of material errors.

An audit includes the execution of procedures in order to obtain evidence of the amounts and the exposure reflected in the Financial Statements. The procedures selected depend on the auditor's judgement, including an assessment of the risks of material errors in the Financial Statements.

In conducting such a risk assessment, the auditor considers the internal control relevant to the preparation and reasonable presentation of the Financial Statements by the organisation, in order to design suitable procedures that are appropriate to the circumstances.

An audit also includes an assessment of appropriateness of the accounting principles used, an opinion on whether the accounting estimates made by management are reasonable, as well as an assessment of the general presentation of the Financial Statements.

We believe that the audited evidence we have obtained is sufficient and appropriate to provide a basis for our opinion as auditors.

"2023 – 1983/2023 – 40 YEARS OF DEMOCRACY"

Presidencia de la Nación
Sindicatura General de la Nación

4. Opinion

In our opinion, the attached Financial Statements of the Antarctic Treaty Secretariat corresponding to the financial period ending 31 March 2022 have been prepared, in all material aspects, in accordance with International Accounting Standards, the specific standards for Antarctic Treaty Consultative Meetings, and methods of accounting based on cash flow.

5. Other Matters

The information contained in Note 1 to the attached financial statements, indicates that they have been prepared by the Antarctic Treaty Secretariat following the guidelines established in the Financial Regulations, Annexed to Decision 4 (2003), which differ in certain aspects related to valuation and presentation from the professional accounting standards in force in the Autonomous City of Buenos Aires, Argentina.

In addition, the information mentioned in the preceding paragraph reflects the currency conversion differences generated over a financial year in a context of strong devaluation of the legal tender of the Argentine Republic.

6. Additional information required by law

Pursuant to the analysis described in point 3, I report that the above-mentioned Financial Statements are based on accounting records that are not transcribed into books in accordance with current Argentine standards.

We also report that, according to the accounting entries as of 31 March 2022, the liabilities accrued in favour of the Argentine Single Social Security System in Argentine pesos and pursuant to settlements made by the Secretariat amounting to ARS 1 361 317.5 (USD 11 200.39), there was no debt due and payable in Argentine pesos as of that date.

It is worth noting that labour relations are governed by Antarctic Treaty Secretariat Staff Regulations.

Autonomous City of Buenos Aires, 3 April 2023

SINDICATURA GENERAL DE LA NACIÓN

Ariel Maximiliano Bozzano
Contador Público (U.B.A.)
C.P.C.E.C.A.B.A. – T°379 – F°044

Annex I - Final Report for 2021/22

1. Income and Expenditure Statement for all funds for the period 1 April 2021 to 31 March 2022 and comparison with the previous period.

		Budget	
INCOME	**31/3/2021**	**31/3/2022**	**31/3/2022**
Contributions (Note 10)	1 378 097	1 378 097	1 378 097
General Fund (Note 1.11)	-	-	-
Other income (Note 2)	734	1 000	975
Total income	1 378 831	1 379 097	1 379 072
EXPENDITURE			
Salaries and wages	678 136	706 510	707 463
Translation and interpretation services	22 840	220 000	240 184
Travel and accommodation	10 230	30 000	26 532
Information technology	46 011	53 850	45 873
Printing, editing and copying	1 801	16 500	12 517
General services	35 295	48 808	34 206
Communications	13 827	19 900	16 543
Office expenses	12 711	18 500	14 618
Administration	6 750	9 000	6 228
Representation expenses	169	4 000	770
Financing (Note 9)	54 571	55 000	19 104
Total expenditure	882 340	1 182 068	1 124 040
ALLOCATION OF FUNDS			
Staff termination fund	25 813	26 768	26 768
Staff replacement fund	-	-	-
Operating fund	-	-	-
Translation contingency fund	-	-	-
Total allocation of funds	25 813	26 768	26 768
Total expenditure and allocations	908 153	1 208 836	1 150 808
(Loss) / Profit for the period	470 678	170 261	228 264

This statement must be read in conjunction with the accompanying Notes 1 to 10

Annex I - Final Report for 2021/22

2. Statement of Financial Position as of 31 March 2022 and comparison with the previous period

ASSETS	31/3/2021	31/3/2022
Current assets		
Cash and cash equivalents (Note 3)	1 541 947	2 131 016
Contributions due (Note 10)	128 674	141 963
Other receivables (Note 4)	31 971	1 122
Other current assets (Note 5)	86 424	49 953
Total current assets	1 789 016	2 324 055
Non-current assets		
Fixed assets (Notes 1.3 and 6)	88 999	89 722
Total non-current assets	88 999	89 722
Total Assets	1 878 015	2 413 777
LIABILITIES		
Current liabilities		
Accounts payable (Note 7)	36 748	29 232
Contributions received in advance (Note 10)	387 197	660 495
Special voluntary fund for specific purposes (Note 1.9)	9 461	24 171
Remuneration and contributions payable (Note 8)	33 096	32 611
Total current liabilities	466 502	746 509
Non-current liabilities		
Staff termination fund (Note 1.4)	70 129	96 897
Staff replacement fund (Note 1.5)	50 000	50 000
Translation contingency fund (Note 1.6)	30 000	30 000
Involuntary separation from service fund (Note 1.7)	80 291	80 291
Fixed assets replacement fund (Note 1.8)	22 702	23 426
Total non-current liabilities	253 122	280 614
Total Liabilities	719 624	1 027 123
NET ASSETS	1 158 391	1 386 655

This statement must be read in conjunction with the accompanying Notes 1 to 10

Annex I - Final Report for 2021/22

3. Statement of Changes in Net Assets as of 31 March 2022 and comparison with the previous period.

Represented by	Net assets 31/3/2021	Income	Expenditure and Appropriations	Other income	Net assets 31/3/2022
General fund	928 439	1 378 097	(1 150 808)	975	1 156 703
- for staff appraisal					0 00
- to cover translation contingency fund					0 00
- to set up an involuntary separation from service fund					0 00
Operating fund (Note 1.9)	229 952				229 952
Net assets	1 158 391				1 386 655

This statement must be read in conjunction with the accompanying Notes 1 to 10

Annex I - Final Report for 2021/22

4 Cash flow statement for the period 1 April 2021 to 31 March 2022 and comparison with the previous period.

Variations in cash and cash equivalents		**31/3/2022**			**31/3/2021**
Cash and cash equivalents at year-start		1 541 947		1 203 852	
Cash and cash equivalents at year-end		2 131 016		1 541 947	
Net increase in cash and cash equivalents			589 069		338 095
Causes of the variations in cash and cash equivalents					
Operating activities					
Contributions received	977 611			816 731	
Payment of remunerations and salaries	(707 064)			(676 725)	
Payment of translation services	(233 224)			(15 880)	
Payment of travel, accommodation, etc.	(21 731)			-	
Payment of printing, editing and copying services	(12 517)			(1 801)	
Payment of general services	(27 721)			(38 692)	
Other payments to suppliers	(85 316)			(67 207)	
Net cash and cash equivalent flow from operating activities		(109 964)			16 426
Investment activities					
Purchase of fixed assets	(1 983)			(16 172)	
Net cash and cash equivalent flow from investment activities		(1 983)			(16 172)
Financing activities					
Contributions received in advance	660 495			387 197	
Payment of severance and replacement expenses	-			-	
Preparation for ATCM	-			-	
Collection pt. 5.6 Staff Regulations	208 453			167 620	
Payment pt. 5.6 Staff Regulations	(170 370)			(165 545)	
Net advance rent	15 200			13 532	
Net movement AFIP	17 445			(38 593)	
Sundry income / (expenditure)	975			4 272	
Net cash and cash equivalent flow from financing activities		732 198			368 483
Foreign currency activities					
Net loss	(31 182)			(30 643)	
Net cash and cash equivalent flow from foreign currency activities		(31 182)			(30 643)
Net increase in cash and cash equivalents			589 069		338 095

This statement must be read in conjunction with the accompanying Notes 1 to 10

Notes to the Financial Statements as of 31 March 2021 and 2022

1 BASIS FOR PREPARATION OF FINANCIAL STATEMENTS

These financial statements are expressed in US dollars, in compliance with the guidelines established in the Financial Regulations, Annex to Decision 4 (2003). These statements were prepared in accordance with the International Financial Reporting Standards (IFRS) of the International Accounting Standards Board (IASB). The accounting method used is accrual-based.

1,1 Historical Cost

The financial statements have been prepared under the historical cost convention, unless indicated otherwise.

1,2 Office

The office of the Secretariat is provided by the Ministry of Foreign Affairs, Foreign Trade and Worship of the Argentine Republic. Its use is free of rent and common expenses.

1,3 Fixed assets

All items are valued at historical cost, less accumulated depreciation. Depreciation is calculated on a straight-line basis at annual rates appropriate to extinguish their values at the end of their estimated useful life. The aggregate residual value of fixed assets does not exceed their economic utilisation value.

1,4 Staff termination fund

In accordance with Staff Regulation 10.4, the fund shall be sufficiently funded to compensate executive staff members at a rate of one month basic pay for each year of service.

1,5 Staff replacement fund

The fund is used to cover the travel costs of the Secretariat's executive staff to and from the headquarters of the Secretariat.

1,6 Translation contingency fund

In accordance with Decision 4 (2009), the Fund was set up to cover translation expenses, which may be incurred by the unforeseen increase in the volume of documents submitted to the ATCM for translation.

1,7 Involuntary separation from service fund

Compliant with Article 10.5 of the Antarctic Treaty Secretariat's Staff Regulations for general services staff.

1,8 Fixed assets replacement fund

In accordance with the IAS, assets whose useful life exceeds one financial year must be disclosed as an asset in the Statement of Financial Position. Up to March 2010, the balancing entry was an adjustment to the General Fund. As of April 2010 the balancing entry of these assets will be shown in liabilities under this item.

1,9 Operating fund

In accordance with Financial Regulation Article 6.2 (a), this must not exceed one-sixth (1/6) of the budget for the current financial year. In the current financial year, this fund was unallocated.

1,10 Special voluntary fund for specific purposes

Pt (82) of the XXXV ATCM Final Report, to receive voluntary contributions by the parties. The Voluntary Fund is money to meet the payment of rent and common expenses for the financial year.

1,11 General fund

This Fund was set up to account for the Secretariat's income and expenditure.

Notes to the Financial Statements as of 31 March 2021 and 2022

		31/3/2021	31/3/2022
2 Other Income			
	Interest earned	-	-
	Discounts obtained	734	975
	Total	734	975
3 Cash and cash equivalents			
	Cash in dollars	1 530	1 480
	Cash in Argentine pesos	150	159
	BNA special account in dollars	1 521 302	2 116 254
	BNA account in Argentine pesos	18 964	13 123
	Investments	-	-
	Total	1 541 947	2 131 016
4 Other receivables			
	Staff regulations pt. 5.6	31 971	1 122
5 Other current assets			
	Advance payments	31 738	18 178
	VAT receivable	50 456	27 500
	Other expenses to be recovered	4 230	4 275
	Total	86 424	49 953
6 Fixed assets			
	Books and subscriptions	16 704	17 341
	Office equipment	40 227	40 227
	Furniture	52 436	52 436
	Computer hardware and software	143 719	150 937
	Total original cost	253 086	260 940
	Accumulated depreciation	(164 087)	(171 218)
	Total	88 999	89 722
7 Accounts payable			
	Commercial suppliers	3 219	3 503
	Accrued expenditure	33 359	25 742
	Other	170	-13
	Total	36 748	29 232
8 Remuneration and contributions payable			
	Remuneration	9 500	9 900
	Contributions	23 596	22 711
	Total	33 096	32 611
9 Financing			
	Exchange rate difference due to payments	22 723	13 328
	Exchange rate difference disbursement Argentina	15 264	2 056
	Exchange rate difference VAT refund	16 584	3 720
	Total	54 571	19 104

Notes to the Financial Statements as of 31 March 2021 and 2022

10 Contributions due, committed, cancelled and received in advance.

Contributions Parties	Due 31/3/2021	Com-mitted	Cancelled $	Due 31/3/2022	Advanced 31/3/2022
Argentina		60 347	60 347		-
Australia		60 347	60 372		60 335
Belgium		40 021	40 021		40 009
Brazil	100 749	40 021	84 948	55 822	-
Bulgaria		33 923	33 923		-
Chile		46 119	-	46 119	-
China		46 119	46 144		-
Czech Republic		40 021	40 021		-
Ecuador		33 923	33 923		-
Finland		40 021	40 021		-
France		60 347	60 347		60 347
Germany		52 217	52 229		-
India		46 119	46 119		-
Italy		52 217	52 217		52 216
Japan		60 347	60 347		-
Netherlands		46 119	46 119		46 119
New Zealand		60 347	60 347		60 322
Norway		60 347	60 347		60 327
Peru	27 926	33 923	61 849		33 965
Poland		40 021	40 021		40 021
Republic of Korea		40 021	40 021		40 021
Russian Federation		46 119	46 119		-
South Africa		46 119	46 119		46 119
Spain		46 119	46 119		-
Sweden		46 119	46 129		-
Ukraine		40 021	40 033		-
United Kingdom		60 347	60 347		60 347
United States		60 347	60 347		60 347
Uruguay		40 021	-	40 021	-
Total	128 674	1 378 097	1 364 894	141 962	660 495

Albert Lluberas Bonaba
Executive Secretary

Roberto A. Fennell
Financial Manager

Provisional Financial Report FY 2022/23

APPROPRIATION LINES	Audited Statement 2021/22	Budget 2022/23	Prov Statement 2022/23
INCOME			
Contributions pledged	$ 1 378 097	$ 1 378 097	$ 1 378 097
Voluntary contributions	$ -	$ -	$ -
Other income	$ 975	$ 3 500	$ 2 069
Total Income	**$ 1 379 072**	**$ 1 381 597**	**$ 1 380 166**
EXPENSES			
SALARIES			
Executive	$ 303 468	$ 313 825	$ 313 825
General staff	$ 388 841	$ 405 842	$ 406 124
ATCM support staff	$ 8 900	$ 15 220	$ 13 288
Trainee	$ -	$ 1 200	$ -
Overtime	$ 6 254	$ 12 000	$ 9 081
Total Salaries	$ 707 463	$ 748 087	$ 742 318
TRANSLATION AND INTERPRETATION			
Translation and Interpretation	$ 240 184	$ 310 000	$ 337 155
TRAVEL			
Travel, lodging, allowance, misc.	$ 26 532	$ 108 500	$ 95 853
INFORMATION TECHNOLOGY			
Hardware	$ 9 799	$ 11 000	$ 12 826
Software	$ 3 451	$ 3 500	$ 2 945
Development	$ 22 752	$ 26 000	$ 24 117
Hardware & software maintenance	$ 3 870	$ 3 500	$ 3 156
Support	$ 6 000	$ 8 000	$ 4 880
Total Information Technology	$ 45 873	$ 52 000	$ 47 924
PRINTING, EDITING & COPYING			
Final Report	$ 11 401	$ 12 000	$ 8 356
Other publications	$ 1 117	$ 2 500	$ 1 465
Total Printing Editing & Copying	$ 12 517	$ 14 500	$ 9 821
GENERAL SERVICES			
Legal advice & counselling	$ 571	$ 3 500	$ 4 725
Payroll services	$ 8 194	$ 8 400	$ 8 400
External audit	$ 11 619	$ 11 618	$ 11 428
Cleaning, maintenance & security	$ 2 774	$ 8 000	$ 7 354
Training	$ 2 599	$ 7 000	$ 3 712
Banking	$ 7 558	$ 7 900	$ 7 380
Rental of equipment	$ 892	$ 1 000	$ 740
Total General Services	$ 34 206	$ 47 418	$ 43 739
COMMUNICATION			
Telephone	$ 3 068	$ 2 500	$ 4 045
Internet	$ 4 091	$ 4 500	$ 4 822
Web hosting	$ 9 180	$ 10 000	$ 5 991
Postage	$ 204	$ 1 000	$ 299
Total Communication	$ 16 543	$ 18 000	$ 15 157

	Audited Statement 2021/22	Budget 2022/23	Prov Statement 2022/23
OFFICE			
Stationery & consumables	$ 3 111	$ 2 500	$ 3 342
Books & subscriptions	$ 303	$ 1 000	$ 795
Insurance	$ 3 198	$ 3 500	$ 2 800
Furniture	$ 1 476	$ 1 500	$ 2 130
Office equipment	$ 1 100	$ 3 000	$ 150
Office improvement	$ 5 430	$ 4 500	$ 3 800
Total Office	$ 14 618	$ 16 000	$ 13 017
ADMINISTRATIVE			
Office supplies	$ 741	$ 2 500	$ 750
Local transport	$ 2 380	$ 1 000	$ 70
Miscellaneous	$ 1 197	$ 2 200	$ 2 378
Utilities	$ 1 910	$ 2 500	$ 2 194
Total Administrative	$ 6 228	$ 8 200	$ 5 392
REPRESENTATION			
Representation	$ 770	$ 4 000	$ 1 365
FINANCING			
Expenditures exchange (gain)/loss	$ 13 328	$ 11 500	$ 23 460
Host Country Payments exchange (gain)/loss	$ 2 033	$ 5 800	$ 22 184
VAT Refunds net (gain)/loss	$ 3 720	$ 8 000	$ 10 760
Total Financing (gain)/loss	$ 19 081	$ 25 300	$ 56 404
SUBTOTAL EXPENSES	**$ 1 124 017**	**$ 1 352 005**	**$ 1 368 145**
FUND APPROPRIATIONS			
Working Capital Fund	$ -	$ -	$ -
Staff Replacement Fund	$ -	$ -	$ -
Staff Termination Fund	$ 26 768	$ 29 592	$ 29 592
Involuntary Separation from Service	$ -	$ -	$ -
Translation Contingency Fund	$ -	$ -	$ -
Total Fund Appropriation	$ 26 768	$ 29 592	$ 29 592
TOTAL EXPENSES & APPROPRIATIONS	**$ 1 150 785**	**$ 1 381 597**	**$ 1 397 737**
Surplus / (Deficit) for the period	**$ 228 287**	**$ -**	**$ (17 571)**

	Audited Statement 2021/22	Net Movements 2022/23	Prov Statement 2022/23

FUND ACTIVITY

GENERAL FUND

	Audited Statement 2021/22	Net Movements 2022/23	Prov Statement 2022/23
Audited start balance	$ 1 156 703		
To Involuntary Separation from Service Fund		$ (1 204)	
To Translation Contingency Fund		$ (30 000)	
Surplus/(Deficit) for the current period		$ (17 571)	
Provisional end balance			**$ 1 107 928**

WORKING CAPITAL FUND

	Audited Statement 2021/22	Net Movements 2022/23	Prov Statement 2022/23
Audited start balance	$ 229 952		
Provisional end balance		$ -	**$ 229 952**

*) **STAFF REPLACEMENT FUND**

	Audited Statement 2021/22	Net Movements 2022/23	Prov Statement 2022/23
Audited start balance	$ 50 000		
Provisional end balance		$ -	**$ 50 000**

*) **STAFF TERMINATION FUND**

	Audited Statement 2021/22	Net Movements 2022/23	Prov Statement 2022/23
Audited start balance	$ 96 897		
Appropriation in the current period		$ 29 592	
Provisional end balance			**$ 126 489**

) **INVOLUNTARY SEPARATION FROM SERVICE

	Audited Statement 2021/22	Net Movements 2022/23	Prov Statement 2022/23
Audited start balance	$ 80 291		
From General Fund		$ 1 204	
Provisional end balance			**$ 81 495**

***) **TRANSLATION CONTINGENCY FUND**

	Audited Statement 2021/22	Net Movements 2022/23	Prov Statement 2022/23
Audited start balance	$ 30 000		
Translation of CEE "Base Petrel"		$ (30 000)	
From General Fund		$ 30 000	
Provisional end balance			**$ 30 000**

FINANCIAL REGULATION 6.3

	Audited Statement 2021/22	Net Movements 2022/23	Prov Statement 2022/23
General Fund	$ 1 156 703	$ (48 775)	$ 1 107 928
****) Unpaid Contributions	$ (141 962)		$ (181 983)
Cash Surplus	**$ 1 014 741**		**$ 925 945**

*) Decision 1 (2006)

**) Decision 3 (2019)

***) Decision 4 (2009)

****) Unpaid contributions as of 31 March 2022 and 31 March 2023

Secretariat Programme 2023/2024

Introduction

This work programme outlines the activities proposed for the Secretariat in the Financial Year 2023/24 (from 1 April 2023 to 31 March 2024).

The programme focuses on the Secretariat's regular activities, such as the preparation of ATCM 46, the publication of Reports, tasks assigned to the Secretariat under Measure 1 (2003), and the various tasks requested by the latest ATCMs. The programme and the accompanying budget figures for 2023/24 are based on the approved Forecast Budget for the Financial Year 2023/2024 (D1 (2022)).

Support for intersessional activities

During recent years, both the ATCM and the CEP have produced a substantial amount of intersessional work, mainly through Intersessional Contact Groups (ICGs) and informal discussion forums. The Secretariat will continue to provide support to these discussions, issue regular reminders of discussions in progress, and regularly provide detailed updates on the status of these discussions on the forum. The Secretariat will maintain close contact with ATCM Working Group Chairs to provide assistance for the preparation of the next meeting.

Concerning the CEP, the Secretariat will continue to work with the CEP Chair and the conveners of the Subsidiary Group on Climate Change Response (SGCCR) and the Subsidiary Group on Management Plans (SGMP). The Secretariat will also continue to take part in regular video calls coordinated by the CEP Chair to facilitate the intersessional work of the CEP and prepare for the next meeting.

Planned support for ATCM 46 (2024) and ATCM 47 (2025)

The Government of India and the Secretariat of the Antarctic Treaty will jointly organise ATCM 46 and CEP 26, which will take place in 2024. The responsibilities of the Host Country Secretariat and the Antarctic Treaty Secretariat are described in the Organisational Manual, updated annually by the Antarctic Treaty Secretariat. The main tasks of the Secretariat at the meeting are document management, supervision of technical services, organisation of translation and interpretation services, assistance to Chairs and support for the compilation and publication of the Final Report. The Host Country Secretariat is responsible for the organisation of the venue, the provision of technical services, the contracting of rapporteur services and the social functions.

The translation and interpretation services comprise the translation of documents before, during and after the meeting, and interpretation during sessions. The Secretariat will also organise the note-taking services during the meeting and is responsible for the compilation and editing of the reports of the ATCM and CEP Meeting. The Secretariat will establish a section of its website to make documents and other relevant materials available for delegates and to provide online registration to the meeting.

The Secretariat will also continue assisting the Government of Italy in relation to the organisation of ATCM 47 (2025), including issues such as office and meeting room layouts and capacity, IT and audio-visual support and planning of events.

Coordination and contact

In addition to maintaining regular contact via email and telephone with the Parties and international institutions of the Antarctic Treaty system, attendance at meetings is an important tool to maintain coordination and communication. Therefore, the Executive Secretary will attend the CCAMLR-42 (2023) meeting, and the Deputy Executive Secretary will participate in the COMNAP AGM 35 (2023) meeting, both to take place in Hobart, Australia.

Based on the valuable experiences of the past year, the Secretariat will be ready to perform virtual training and discussion sessions with delegates, at Parties' request, to support the use of the EIES, explain new features and exchange views on how to continue enhancing it. The Secretariat also stands ready to assist Parties at any time in relation to the services provided through the website, the management of information, documents, contacts and intersessional activities, among others.

Website and Information Systems

Development of the Secretariat website

The Secretariat will start a process of refinement of the categories and topics currently used to classify ATCM measures in the Antarctic Treaty database with the aim of facilitating the search and filtering of measures. Based on user feedback and surveys provided at the meeting, the Secretariat will also make improvements to the platform for the submission of documents to the ATCM and the CEP as well as the meeting page tools such as notifications and events.

Mapping tools

The Secretariat will continue to explore the possibility of using the existing web-based geographical information platform for representing a variety of georeferenced content already existing in its databases or that could result from new information exchange requirements. In this sense, it is planned to develop maps to display scientific cooperation and Antarctic sites affected by past activities.

Information Exchange and the Electronic Information Exchange System (EIES)

The Secretariat will continue to assist Parties in posting their information exchange materials, as well as to process information uploaded using the File Upload functionality. In addition, the Secretariat will increase the production of tutorials and/or training programmes about the EIES to facilitate Parties' engagement, encourage the utilization of the EIES products, and understand Parties' particular needs when using the system.

The Secretariat will also develop new tools to clearly and quickly visualize the status of the information uploaded/published by Parties in each EIES section.

Redesign and improvement of the Contacts Database

This newly redesigned interface, including new features for online registration to meetings, will continue to be improved, taking into account the valuable feedback received from users.

The Secretariat will continue to offer direct assistance to the Parties in order to facilitate keeping the database updated, modifying or removing contact points that have changed or become obsolete.

Publications

ATCM Final Report and CEP Report

For ATCM XLV in Helsinki, the Secretariat has prepared for the timely translation in the four Treaty languages of the CEP Chair's non-paper on the CEP advice to the ATCM. After the meeting, the Secretariat will translate, publish and distribute the ATCM XLV Final Report and its Annexes in the four Treaty languages pursuant to the Procedures for the Submission, Translation and Distribution of Documents for the ATCM and the CEP Meeting, and other requirements established by the ATCM (ATCM XXXII Final Report, paragraph 72).

The Final Report will be available on the Secretariat's website and hard copies will be distributed by courier and diplomatic channels. Hard copies will also be available for purchase through online retailers. The Secretariat will adjust its internal procedures to continue to improve the editorial quality of the report, including pre-meeting and post-meeting document formatting.

Other Publications

The Secretariat will publish an updated edition of the *Rules of Procedure of the Antarctic Treaty Consultative Meeting and the Committee for Environmental Protection* in the four Treaty languages. This book will be available on the Secretariat website and hard copies will also be available from online retailers worldwide. The Secretariat is ready to produce a new edition of the *Compilation of Key Documents of the Antarctic Treaty System* in the four Treaty languages, if needed.

Documentation and Public Information

Documents of the ATCM

The Secretariat will continue its efforts to complete its archive of the Final Reports and other records of the ATCM and other meetings of the Antarctic Treaty system in the four Treaty languages. We would like to reiterate our invitation to the Parties to search for their files to achieve a complete archive at the Secretariat. Please contact the Secretariat for a detailed list of missing papers.

The Secretariat will make available on its website additional documents arising from ATCM XLV, including reports from Observers and Experts and other documents, in line with the provisions established by the ATCM (ATCM XXXII Final Report, paragraph 72).

Glossaries and Editorial Guidelines

The Secretariat will continue to maintain the glossary of terms and expressions of the ATCM to generate a nomenclature in the four Treaty languages. The Secretariat will update its editorial guidelines, aimed at standardising the work of rapporteurs, translators, proofreaders and Secretariat staff. The Secretariat will update its web-based technical glossary for internal use, with the aim of improving consistency in the translation of ATCM documents.

Image Bank

The Secretariat plans to improve the interface of the current image bank, with the purpose of providing it with a renewed visual aspect and new tools for searching, selecting and downloading existing photographic material.

We would like to reiterate our invitation to provide the Secretariat with original photographic material to be published in the image bank under a Creative Commons license. We would especially appreciate receiving photographs corresponding to Antarctic Treaty Meetings before the establishment of the Secretariat, as well as those related to field work carried out by Parties in Antarctica in pursuit of compliance with the regulations established by the ATCM and the CEP, such as inspection activities.

Likewise, the Secretariat enabled a section of the image bank aimed at the collection and public dissemination of videos in digital format. With a criterion like that applied for the bank of still images, we would appreciate receiving videos related to the Consultative Meetings, such as the presentation videos displayed each year by the host country of the following meeting during the closing plenary session.

The Tools for Delegates section of the Secretariat Website offers to delegates a form for submitting photographic material.

Personnel

On 1 April 2023 the Secretariat staff consisted of the following personnel:

Position	Since	Rank	Step	Term
Executive staff				
Executive Secretary	1-09-2017	E1	5	31-08-2025
Deputy Executive Secretary	15-07-2019	E3	3	31-07-2023
General staff				
Information Officer	1-11-2004	G1	6	
Support Officer (part time)	1-02-2020	G2	3	
Finance Officer (part time)	1-12-2008	G2	6	
Editor	1-02-2006	G2	6	
IT Specialist	1-02-2019	G3	4	
Communications Specialist (part time)	1-10-2010	G4	6	
Office Manager	15-11-2012	G4	6	
Cleaning Assistant (part time)	1-07-2015	G7	6	

On 30 June 2023 the Finance Officer (G2-IV) Mr. Alan Fennel will retire and will be replaced by the Accountant (G3-I) Mrs. Gabriela Russo. This planned change was explained in the "Roadmap for further actions" section of the "Report on the review process of roles and responsibilities of the Secretariat of the Antarctic Treaty staff" distributed to Parties during the ATCM XLIV (2022) in Berlin. Due to some necessary overlapping this change will result in a slight increase in the General Staff salaries line for FY 2023/24 but a larger decrease for the same line for the FY 2024/25 onwards considering the lower salary level and the first step of seniority of the new position.

No further changes are foreseen in the staff positions of the Secretariat.

Financial Matters

The Budget for the Financial Year 2023/24 and the Forecast Budget for the Financial Year 2024/25 are included in Appendix 1.

Draft Budget for the Financial Year 2023/24

Allocation to the appropriation lines follows closely the proposed forecast from last year. Only smaller adjustments to the foreseen expenses in the Financial Year 2023/24 have been introduced to reflect rising costs in US dollars both locally and internationally, and the possible impact of further devaluations in the Financing line.

As explained above some overlapping in the Accountant position will result in a slight increase in the General Staff salaries line for FY 2023/24 but a larger decrease for the same line for the FY 2024/25.

The cost of living continued to rise sharply in Argentina in the year 2022. The inflation rate (Índice de Precios al Consumidor) for 2022 published by INDEC (Instituto Nacional de Estadística y Censos de la República Argentina) was 94.80% and was only partially compensated by a rise of the US Dollar against the Argentine Peso of 70.07%. Global inflation has also surged in this period affecting the economy and triggering salary rises in all Consultative Parties.[1]

[1] IMF Global inflation data up to October 2022

For this reason and keeping an extremely conservative approach below the average wage rises for most Consultative Parties for 2022, the Executive Secretary proposes to increase the salaries by 2.9%.

The proposed salary scale is provided in Appendix 3.

Despite the impact of these factors, due to conservative and precautionary management, a budget with a moderate deficit of only 27 920 USD was attained that could easily be covered by the existing surplus in the General Fund.

Quarterly reports of budget implementation will be provided to the Parties in accordance with Decision 1 (2022).

Funds

Working Capital Fund

According to Financial Regulation 6.2 (a), the Working Capital Fund must be maintained at 1/6 of the Secretariat's budget (currently 229 952 USD).

Staff Termination Fund

The Staff Termination Fund will be credited with 33 620 USD in accordance with Staff Regulation 10.4 (see Appendix 1).

Translation Contingency Fund

The Secretariat will request that the level of 30 000 USD assigned to this Fund by D4 (2009) be increased to an updated level of 50 000 USD to better cover unforeseen increases in the volume of documents submitted to the ATCM for translation, considering current costs and volume, and the requirement for translation of large documents such as draft CEEs.

Forecast Budget for the Financial Year 2024/25

It is expected that most of the regular activities of the Secretariat will continue in the Financial Year 2023/24 including meetings in person in 2024 in India and therefore, unless the programme undergoes major changes, no major change in appropriation lines is foreseen.

However, rise adjustments in USD for local costs in Argentina are expected to affect operational costs while global inflation would bring rising costs to Travel and Translation & Interpretation.

Therefore, the Forecast Budget for this period is expected to show a deficit of approximately 45 000 USD which would be covered by accumulated surplus in the General Fund.

The contributions for the Financial Year 2024/25 will not rise. Appendix 2 shows the contribution scale for the Financial Year 2024/25.

Five-Year Forward Budget profile 2024/25 - 2028/29

Under reasonable assumptions the budget profile allows a zero-nominal increase in contributions until 2028/29 as explained in the Five-Year Budget Profile document presented separately by the Secretariat.

Budget FY 2023/24 and Forecast FY 2024/25

APPROPRIATION LINES	Prov Statement 2022/23	Forecast 2023/24	Budget 2023/24	Forecast 2024/25
INCOME				
Contributions pledged	$ 1 378 097	$ 1 378 097	$ 1 378 097	$ 1 378 097
Voluntary contributions	$ -	$ -	$ -	$ -
Other income	$ 2 069	$ 3 500	$ 6 500	$ 6 000
Total Income	**$ 1 380 166**	**$ 1 381 597**	**$ 1 384 597**	**$ 1 384 097**
EXPENSES				
SALARIES				
Executive	$ 313 825	$ 319 574	$ 328 898	$ 332 909
General staff	$ 406 124	$ 410 187	$ 420 371	$ 407 819
ATCM support staff	$ 13 288	$ 16 000	$ 14 900	$ 16 000
Trainee	$ -	$ 1 200	$ 600	$ 1 200
Overtime	$ 9 081	$ 12 000	$ 10 000	$ 10 500
Total Salaries	**$ 742 318**	**$ 758 961**	**$ 774 769**	**$ 768 428**
TRANSLATION AND INTERPRETATION				
Translation and Interpretation	**$ 337 155**	**$ 312 000**	**$ 313 500**	**$ 325 000**
TRAVEL				
Travel, lodging, allowance, misc.	**$ 95 853**	**$ 111 300**	**$ 106 900**	**$ 114 000**
INFORMATION TECHNOLOGY				
Hardware	$ 12 826	$ 11 000	$ 11 000	$ 11 000
Software	$ 2 945	$ 3 500	$ 3 500	$ 3 500
Development	$ 24 117	$ 27 500	$ 25 500	$ 26 500
Hardware & software maintenance	$ 3 156	$ 3 500	$ 3 500	$ 3 500
Support	$ 4 880	$ 8 000	$ 7 000	$ 7 500
Total Information Technology	**$ 47 924**	**$ 53 500**	**$ 50 500**	**$ 52 000**
PRINTING, EDITING & COPYING				
Final Report	$ 8 356	$ 12 500	$ 10 000	$ 11 000
Other publications	$ 1 465	$ 3 000	$ 2 500	$ 3 000
Total Printing Editing & Copying	**$ 9 821**	**$ 15 500**	**$ 12 500**	**$ 14 000**
GENERAL SERVICES				
Legal advice & counselling	$ 4 725	$ 4 000	$ 3 000	$ 3 500
Payroll services	$ 8 400	$ 8 400	$ 8 400	$ 8 400
External audit	$ 11 428	$ 11 618	$ 11 428	$ 11 428
Cleaning, maintenance & security	$ 7 354	$ 8 000	$ 8 000	$ 8 000
Training	$ 3 712	$ 7 000	$ 6 000	$ 7 000
Banking	$ 7 380	$ 8 000	$ 8 000	$ 8 500
Rental of equipment	$ 740	$ 1 000	$ 1 000	$ 1 000
Total General Services	**$ 43 739**	**$ 48 018**	**$ 45 828**	**$ 47 828**
COMMUNICATION				
Telephone	$ 4 045	$ 2 500	$ 3 500	$ 4 000
Internet	$ 4 822	$ 4 500	$ 4 500	$ 5 000
Web hosting	$ 5 991	$ 10 000	$ 8 500	$ 9 000
Postage	$ 299	$ 1 000	$ 700	$ 700
Total Communication	**$ 15 157**	**$ 18 000**	**$ 17 200**	**$ 18 700**

	Prov Statement 2022/23	Forecast 2023/24	Budget 2023/24	Forecast 2024/25
OFFICE				
Stationery & consumables	$ 3 342	$ 2 500	$ 3 000	$ 3 300
Books & subscriptions	$ 795	$ 1 000	$ 1 000	$ 1 000
Insurance	$ 2 800	$ 3 500	$ 3 300	$ 3 700
Furniture	$ 2 130	$ 1 500	$ 1 500	$ 2 000
Office equipment	$ 150	$ 3 500	$ 3 000	$ 3 500
Office improvement	$ 3 800	$ 4 000	$ 4 000	$ 4 000
Total Office	**$ 13 017**	**$ 16 000**	**$ 15 800**	**$ 17 500**
ADMINISTRATIVE				
Office supplies	$ 750	$ 3 000	$ 2 000	$ 2 500
Local transport	$ 70	$ 700	$ 700	$ 800
Miscellaneous	$ 2 378	$ 2 700	$ 2 700	$ 3 200
Utilities	$ 2 194	$ 3 000	$ 2 500	$ 3 000
Total Administrative	**$ 5 392**	**$ 9 400**	**$ 7 900**	**$ 9 500**
REPRESENTATION				
Representation	**$ 1 365**	**$ 4 000**	**$ 4 000**	**$ 4 000**
FINANCING				
Expenditures exchange (gain)/loss	$ 23 460	$ 11 500	$ 16 000	$ 15 000
Host Country Payments exchange (gain)/loss	$ 22 184	$ 4 800	$ 6 500	$ 5 000
VAT Refunds net (gain)/loss	$ 10 760	$ 7 700	$ 7 500	$ 7 500
Total Financing (gain)/loss	**$ 56 404**	**$ 24 000**	**$ 30 000**	**$ 27 500**
SUBTOTAL EXPENSES	**$ 1 368 145**	**$ 1 370 679**	**$ 1 378 897**	**$ 1 398 456**
FUND APPROPRIATIONS				
Working Capital Fund	$ -	$ -	$ -	$ -
Staff Replacement Fund	$ -	$ -	$ -	$ -
Staff Termination Fund	$ 29 592	$ 29 108	$ 33 620	$ 30 951
Involuntary Separation from Service	$ -	$ -	$ -	$ -
Translation Contingency Fund	$ -	$ -	$ -	$ -
Total Fund Appropriation	**$ 29 592**	**$ 29 108**	**$ 33 620**	**$ 30 951**
TOTAL EXPENSES & APPROPRIATIONS	**$ 1 397 737**	**$ 1 399 787**	**$ 1 412 517**	**$ 1 429 407**
Surplus / (Deficit) for the period	**$ (17 571)**	**$ (18 190)**	**$ (27 920)**	**$ (45 310)**

FUND BALANCE

	Prov Statement 2022/23	Forecast 2023/24	Budget 2023/24	Forecast 2024/25
Working Capital Fund	$ 229 952	$ 229 952	$ 229 952	$ 229 952
Staff Replacement Fund	$ 50 000	$ 50 000	$ 50 000	$ 50 000
Staff Termination Fund	$ 126 489	$ 153 728	$ 160 109	$ 191 060
Involuntary Separation from Service	$ 81 495	$ 80 291	$ 83 858	$ 83 858
Translation Contingency Fund	$ 30 000	$ 30 000	$ 30 000	$ 30 000

Contribution Scale FY 2024/25

Party	Cat.	Mult.	Variable	Fixed	Total
Argentina	A	3.6	$ 36 587	$ 23 760	$ 60 347
Australia	A	3.6	$ 36 587	$ 23 760	$ 60 347
Belgium	D	1.6	$ 16 261	$ 23 760	$ 40 021
Brazil	D	1.6	$ 16 261	$ 23 760	$ 40 021
Bulgaria	E	1	$ 10 163	$ 23 760	$ 33 923
Chile	C	2.2	$ 22 359	$ 23 760	$ 46 119
China	C	2.2	$ 22 359	$ 23 760	$ 46 119
Czech Republic	D	1.6	$ 16 261	$ 23 760	$ 40 021
Ecuador	E	1	$ 10 163	$ 23 760	$ 33 923
Finland	D	1.6	$ 16 261	$ 23 760	$ 40 021
France	A	3.6	$ 36 587	$ 23 760	$ 60 347
Germany	B	2.8	$ 28 456	$ 23 760	$ 52 217
India	C	2.2	$ 22 359	$ 23 760	$ 46 119
Italy	B	2.8	$ 28 456	$ 23 760	$ 52 217
Japan	A	3.6	$ 36 587	$ 23 760	$ 60 347
Republic of Korea	D	1.6	$ 16 261	$ 23 760	$ 40 021
Netherlands	C	2.2	$ 22 359	$ 23 760	$ 46 119
New Zealand	A	3.6	$ 36 587	$ 23 760	$ 60 347
Norway	A	3.6	$ 36 587	$ 23 760	$ 60 347
Peru	E	1	$ 10 163	$ 23 760	$ 33 923
Poland	D	1.6	$ 16 261	$ 23 760	$ 40 021
Russian Federation	C	2.2	$ 22 359	$ 23 760	$ 46 119
South Africa	C	2.2	$ 22 359	$ 23 760	$ 46 119
Spain	C	2.2	$ 22 359	$ 23 760	$ 46 119
Sweden	C	2.2	$ 22 359	$ 23 760	$ 46 119
Ukraine	D	1.6	$ 16 261	$ 23 760	$ 40 021
United Kingdom	A	3.6	$ 36 587	$ 23 760	$ 60 347
United States	A	3.6	$ 36 587	$ 23 760	$ 60 347
Uruguay	D	1.6	$ 16 261	$ 23 760	$ 40 021
Total Pledged					**$ 1 378 097**

Salary Scale FY 2023/24

Schedule A

SALARY SCALE FOR THE EXECUTIVE STAFF

(United States Dollar)

2023/24		STEPS														
Level		I	II	III	IV	V	VI	VII	VIII	IX	X	XI	XII	XIII	XIV	XV
E1	A	$ 141 315	$ 143 943	$ 146 573	$ 149 203	$ 151 833	$ 154 461	$ 157 090	$ 159 721							
E1	B	$ 176 642	$ 179 929	$ 183 216	$ 186 504	$ 189 791	$ 193 077	$ 196 363	$ 199 652							
E2	A	$ 118 995	$ 121 233	$ 123 471	$ 125 707	$ 127 945	$ 130 181	$ 132 417	$ 134 655	$ 136 893	$ 139 130	$ 141 366	$ 141 620	$ 143 828		
E2	B	$ 148 743	$ 151 540	$ 154 339	$ 157 134	$ 159 930	$ 162 725	$ 165 521	$ 168 319	$ 171 118	$ 173 912	$ 176 708	$ 177 025	$ 179 785		
E3	A	$ 99 229	$ 101 386	$ 103 545	$ 105 704	$ 107 864	$ 110 022	$ 112 181	$ 114 340	$ 116 498	$ 118 656	$ 120 815	$ 122 110	$ 123 404	$ 125 534	$ 127 662
E3	B	$ 124 035	$ 126 733	$ 129 432	$ 132 131	$ 134 830	$ 137 527	$ 140 226	$ 142 926	$ 145 622	$ 148 320	$ 151 019	$ 152 637	$ 154 255	$ 156 918	$ 159 577
E4	A	$ 82 280	$ 84 278	$ 86 280	$ 88 274	$ 90 276	$ 92 272	$ 94 268	$ 96 270	$ 98 270	$ 100 266	$ 102 266	$ 102 823	$ 104 794	$ 106 765	$ 108 736
E4	B	$ 102 850	$ 105 348	$ 107 851	$ 110 343	$ 112 845	$ 115 342	$ 117 835	$ 120 336	$ 122 837	$ 125 331	$ 127 832	$ 128 528	$ 130 992	$ 133 456	$ 135 920
E5	A	$ 68 218	$ 70 007	$ 71 793	$ 73 583	$ 75 368	$ 77 155	$ 78 945	$ 80 727	$ 82 518	$ 84 306	$ 86 089	$ 86 669			
E5	B	$ 85 272	$ 87 509	$ 89 742	$ 91 978	$ 94 211	$ 96 445	$ 98 680	$ 100 910	$ 103 147	$ 105 382	$ 107 613	$ 108 335			
E6	A	$ 54 004	$ 55 721	$ 57 438	$ 59 158	$ 60 874	$ 62 591	$ 64 311	$ 66 028	$ 67 744	$ 68 789	$ 69 464				
E6	B	$ 67 503	$ 69 652	$ 71 796	$ 73 947	$ 76 092	$ 78 239	$ 80 390	$ 82 535	$ 84 681	$ 85 986	$ 86 829				

Note: Row B is the base salary (shown in Row A) with an additional 25% for salary on-costs (retirement fund and insurance premiums, installation and repatriation grants, education allowances etc.) and is the total salary entitlement for executive staff in accordance with regulation 5.1.

Schedule B

SALARY SCALE FOR THE GENERAL STAFF

(United States Dollar)

		STEPS														
Level		I	II	III	IV	V	VI	VII	VIII	IX	X	XI	XII	XIII	XIV	XV
G1		$ 67 667	$ 70 823	$ 73 982	$ 77 138	$ 80 428	$ 83 858									
G2		$ 56 389	$ 59 019	$ 61 650	$ 64 281	$ 67 024	$ 69 882									
G3		$ 46 989	$ 49 181	$ 51 375	$ 53 567	$ 55 853	$ 58 237									
G4		$ 39 159	$ 40 986	$ 42 813	$ 44 640	$ 46 544	$ 48 531									
G5		$ 32 349	$ 33 859	$ 35 368	$ 36 879	$ 38 454	$ 40 097									
G6		$ 26 516	$ 27 752	$ 28 989	$ 30 227	$ 31 518	$ 32 863									
G7		$ 14 334	$ 14 953	$ 15 574	$ 16 194	$ 16 841	$ 17 516									

Decision 3 (2023)

Renewal of the contract of the Secretariat's external auditor

The Representatives,

Recalling the Financial Regulations for the Secretariat of the Antarctic Treaty annexed to Decision 4 (2003), and specifically Regulation 11 (External Audit);

Conscious that the Secretariat of the Antarctic Treaty ("the Secretariat") conducts the majority of its financial transactions in Argentina, and that the detailed rules of book-keeping and accounting are country-specific;

Noting Argentina's proposal to designate the Sindicatura General de la Nación ("SIGEN") as the external auditor of the Secretariat;

Decide:

1. to designate the Sindicatura General de la Nación as the external auditor of the Secretariat for Financial Years 2021/22 to 2024/25, in accordance with Regulation 11.1 of the Financial Regulations for the Secretariat of the Antarctic Treaty; and
2. to authorise the Executive Secretary to negotiate a contract with the Sindicatura General de la Nación to carry out annual external audits for the above-mentioned years in accordance with Regulation 11.3, the Annex to this Decision (which lists the tasks to be carried out) and the budgetary limits set by the Antarctic Treaty Consultative Meeting.

Decision 2 (2023)

Renewal of the contract of the Secretariat's external auditor

Tasks to be carried out by the external auditor

To provide external audit reports covering the financial years 2021/22 to 2024/25 in accordance with Regulation 11.3 of the Financial Regulations annexed to Decision 4 (2003).

The audit report shall address:

- Implementation of regulations adopted by the Antarctic Treaty Consultative Meeting ("ATCM");
- Internal controls - Regulations and Procedures;
- Internal oversight of administrative processes, payments, custody of funds, and assets;
- Budgeting;
- Comparative budget reports;
- Expenditure efficiency analysis;
- Budget execution oversight;
- Analysis of the establishment of new area units;
- Control and reporting of contributions;
- Establishment and oversight of the General Fund, the Working Capital Fund, the Future Meeting Fund, the Staff Replacement Fund, the Staff Termination Fund and any other Funds held by the Secretariat of the Antarctic Treaty ("the Secretariat");
- Income and expense accounts;
- Trust funds;
- Custody of funds - Investments;
- Accounting oversight in accordance with Regulation 10 of Decision 4 (2003);
- Drafting an external auditor report;
- Other matters which may be necessary to ensure sound financial management of the Secretariat.

The provisional financial report for each Financial Year should be submitted by the Executive Secretary to the Sindicatura General de la Nación ("SIGEN") no later than 1 June of the year in which the Financial Year concludes and the final audited report should be submitted by SIGEN to the Executive Secretary no later than 1 September of the year in which the Financial Year concludes.

Tasks to be carried out by the external auditor

[illegible]

[illegible]

[illegible]

[illegible]

[illegible]

[illegible]

[illegible]

[illegible]

[illegible]

[illegible]

[illegible]

Decision 4 (2023)

Updated requirements for information exchange

The Representatives,

Noting Articles III(1)(a) and VII(5) of the Antarctic Treaty;

Conscious of the obligations within the Protocol on Environmental Protection to the Antarctic Treaty ("the Protocol") and its Annexes to exchange information;

Conscious also of decisions of the Antarctic Treaty Consultative Meeting ("ATCM") in relation to the information to be exchanged by Parties;

Desiring that the exchange of information by Parties be conducted in the most efficient and timely manner;

Desiring also that the information to be exchanged by Parties be readily identified to maximise its utility;

Recalling Decision 4 (2012), which decided that the Parties would use the Electronic Information Exchange System ("EIES") to exchange information in accordance with the Antarctic Treaty and the Protocol and its Annexes and which specified that Parties would continue to work with the Secretariat of the Antarctic Treaty ("the Secretariat") to refine and improve the EIES;

Noting that Decision 4 (2012) decided that the Parties would update relevant sections of the EIES regularly throughout the year, in order that such information be made available and accessible to Parties as soon as practicable;

Desiring to make changes to the consolidated list attached to this Decision, on sections 2.1.1. *Forward Plans* and 2.1.2. *Science Activities in Previous Year* (category *Annual Report*), and to add a new section 3.5 *Cooperation Agreements* (category *Permanent Information*);

Decide:

1. that the Annex to this Decision represents a consolidated list of the information to be exchanged by Parties;

2. that the Secretariat shall modify the EIES to reflect the information contained in the Annex to this Decision; and

3. that the Annex to Decision 5 (2022) is no longer current.

Information exchange requirements

1. Pre-season Information

The following information should be submitted as early as possible, preferably by 1 October, and in any event no later than the start of the activities being reported.

1.1 Operational information

1.1.1 National Expeditions

A. Stations

Names of stations (giving region, latitude and longitude), seasonality, operating period (for seasonal), status, maximum population, and medical support available.
Names of refuges (giving region, latitude and longitude), medical facilities, and accommodation capacity. Other major field activities, *eg*, scientific traverse (giving locations).

B. Non-Military Ships

Name of non-military ships, ice strength, country of registry, number of voyages, planned departure dates, areas of operation, ports of departure and arrival to and from Antarctica, and purpose of voyage. Maximum crew, maximum passengers.

C. Non-Military Aircraft

Type of non-military aircraft, planned number of flights, period of flights or planned departure dates for inter-continental flights, purpose. Maximum crew, maximum passengers.

D. Research Rockets

Coordinates of the place of launching, time and date/period, direction of launching, planned maximum altitude, impact area, type and specifications of rockets, purpose and title of research project.

E. Military

- Number of military personnel (officers and enlisted) in expeditions.
- Number and types of armaments.
- Information on military equipment, if any, not included in Section 3.2.D below, including its site name, coordinates (latitude and longitude), type of equipment, and purpose of equipment.
- Ship: Name of military ship, ice strength, number of voyages, planned departure dates, areas of operation, ports of departure and arrival to and from Antarctica, and purpose of voyage. Maximum crew, maximum passengers.
- Aircraft: Type of military aircraft, planned number of flights, period of flights or planned departure dates for inter-continental flights, and

purpose. Maximum crew, maximum passengers.

1.1.2 Non-governmental Expeditions[i]

A. Vessel-based Operations

Name of operator, name of vessel, maximum crew, maximum passengers, country of registry of vessel, number of voyages, expedition leader, planned departure dates, ports of departure and arrival to and from Antarctica, areas of operation including the names of proposed visited sites and the planned dates at which these visits will take place, type of activity, whether these visits include landing, (optionally) duration of landing and the number of visitors that participate in each of the specific activities.

B. Land-based Operations

Name of expedition, name of the operator, method of transportation to, from and within Antarctica, type of adventure/activity, location/s of activities and/or routes, dates of expedition, number of personnel involved, contact address, web-site address.

C. Aircraft Activities

Name of operator, type of aircraft, number of flights, period of flights, departure date per flight, departure and arrival location per flight, route per flight, purpose per flight, and number of passengers.

D. Denial of Authorizations

Name of vessel and/or expedition, name of operator, date, reason for denial.

1.2 Visits to Protected Areas

Name and number of protected area, number of people permitted to visit, date/period and purpose.

2. Annual Report

The following information should be submitted as early as possible after the end of the austral summer season, but in all cases before 1 October, with a reporting period of 1 April to 30 March.

2.1. Scientific Information

2.1.1. Forward Plans[ii]

Details of strategic or multi-year science plans, or a link to the corresponding Key Science Priorities section of the ATS website, or contact point for printed version. List of planned participations in major, international, collaborative science programmes/projects.

2.1.2. Science Activities in Previous Year

List of research projects undertaken in previous year under science discipline, giving location(s), principal investigator, contact details of the responsible institution, project name or number, discipline, main activity/remarks, (optionally) up to five keywords defining the project, and international cooperation (if any), providing country and institution involved in each case.

2.2. Operational information

2.2.1. National expeditions

Update of information given under 1.1.1.

2.2.2. Non-governmental expeditions

Update of information given under 1.1.2 plus, for section 1.1.2.A and B: total amount of passengers transported in each journey, total number of crew members on board in each journey and combined activity for section A, B and C. Information on unusual incidents for sections A, B and C, including type of unusual incident occurred (affected people, environment and/or materials/assets), date, place, from whom assistance was received and contact point for more information on the incident (operator or a member of the National Programme or whoever the competent authority considered).

2.3. Permit Information

2.3.1. Visits to Protected Areas
Update of information provided under 1.2.

2.3.2. Taking and harmful interference with flora and fauna
Permit number, permit period, species, location, amount, sex, age and purpose[iii].

2.3.3. Introduction of non-native species
Permit number, permit period, species, location, amount, purpose[iv], removal or disposal.

2.4. Environmental Information

2.4.1. Compliance with the Protocol[v]
Description of measure, date of effect.

2.4.2. Contingency Plans
Title of Contingency Plan(s) for oil spills and other environmental emergencies, copies (PDFs) or contact point for printed versions.

2.4.3. List of IEEs and CEEs[vi]
List of IEEs/CEEs undertaken during year giving proposed activity, (optionally) period/length, location, level of assessment and decision taken.

2.4.4. Monitoring activities report[vii]
Name of activity, location, procedures put in place, significant information obtained, action taken in consequence thereof.

2.4.5. Waste Management Plans
Title, name of site/vessel, copy (PDF) or contact point for printed version. Report on implementation of waste management plans during the year.

2.4.6. Measures taken to implement the provisions of Annex V[viii]
Description of measures.

2.4.7. Procedures relating to EIAs
Description of appropriate National Procedures.

2.4.8. Prevention of marine pollution[ix]
Description of measures.

3. Permanent Information

The following information can be updated at any time.

3.1. Science Facilities

3.1.1 Automatic Recording Stations/Observatories

Site name, coordinates (latitude and longitude), elevation (m), parameters recorded, observation frequency, reference number *(eg,* WMO no.).

3.2 Operational Information

A. Stations

Name of stations (giving region, latitude and longitude), status, seasonality, date established, accommodation and medical facilities.
Names of refuges (giving region, latitude and longitude), medical facilities, and accommodation capacity.

B. Non-Military Ships
Name of non-military ships, country of registry, ice strength, maximum crew, maximum passengers.

C. Non-Military Aircraft
Type of non-military aircraft, maximum crew, maximum passengers.

D. Military
- Number of military personnel (officers and enlisted)
- Number and types of armaments.
- Information on military equipment, if any, not already reported in the EIES, including its site name, coordinate (latitude and longitude), type of equipment, and purpose.
- Ship: Name of military ship, ice strength, maximum crew, maximum passengers.
- Aircraft: Type of military aircraft, maximum crew, maximum passengers.

3.3 Environmental Information

3.3.1 Waste Management Plans
Title of Plan, site/vessel, copy (PDF) or contact point for printed version.

3.3.2 Contingency Plans
Title of Contingency Plan(s) for Oil Spills and other environmental emergencies, copies (PDFs) or contact point for printed versions.

3.3.3 Inventory of Past Activities
Name of station/base/field camp/traverse/crashed aircraft/etc., coordinates (latitude and longitude), period during which activity undertaken, description/purpose of activities undertaken, description of equipment or facilities remaining.

3.3.4 Compliance with the Protocol[x]
Description of measure, date of effect.

3.3.5 Procedures relating to EIAs
Same as 2.4.7.

3.3.6 Prevention of marine pollution
Same as 2.4.8.

3.3.7 Measures taken to implement the provisions of Annex V
Same as 2.4.6.

3.4 Other Information

3.4.1 Relevant National Legislation
Description of law, regulation, administrative action or other measure, date of effect/enacted, giving copy (PDF) or contact point for printed version.

3.5 Cooperation Agreements

Existing formal Antarctic (or polar) cooperation agreements with other Parties. If any, indicate for each case: a) title of the agreement; b) subject matter of the agreement (general, science, logistics, environmental management, other); c) description (optional); d) year of signing (optional); e) duration of the agreement (optional); f) copy (PDF) or link to the document (optional).

---

[i] provision of information on Non-governmental expeditions will be allowed for it to be provided as soon as possible after completion of national processes, with the relevant timing description being: 'as soon as possible following completion of national processes, preferably by the pre-season target date of 1 October, and no later than the start of the activity'.

[ii] optional provision of information on Forward plans will be allowed at any time, for example when domestic plans are completed or updated.

[iii] purpose with reference to Article 3 of Annex II to the Protocol.

[iv] purpose with reference to Article 4 of Annex II to the Protocol.

[v] new measures adopted during past year in accordance with Article 13 of the Protocol on Environmental Protection to the Antarctic Treaty including the adoption of laws and regulations, administrative actions and enforcement measures.

[vi] information on IEEs and CEEs is encouraged to be provided 'as soon as domestic processes are concluded, while maintaining the existing deadline for Parties to submit the information'.

[vii] Monitoring activities connected with activities subject to initial and comprehensive environmental evaluations (referred to in Protocol Annex I, Art. 6.1 c).

[viii] Information on measures taken to implement Annex V including site inspections and any steps taken to address instances of activities in contravention of the provisions of ASPA or ASMA management plans.

[ix] Measures to ensure that any warship, naval auxiliary or other ship owned or operated by a State and used, for the time being, only on government non-commercial service acts in a manner consistent, so far as is reasonable and practicable, with the Annex.

[x] Measures adopted in accordance with Article 13 of the Protocol on Environmental Protection to the Antarctic Treaty including the adoption of laws and regulations, administrative actions and enforcement measures.

Decision 5 (2023)

Multi-year Strategic Work Plan for the Antarctic Treaty Consultative Meeting

The Representatives,

Reaffirming the values, objectives and principles contained in the Antarctic Treaty and its Protocol on Environmental Protection;

Recalling Decision 3 (2012) on the Multi-year Strategic Work Plan ("the Plan") and its principles;

Bearing in mind that the Plan is complementary to the agenda of the Antarctic Treaty Consultative Meeting ("ATCM") and that the Parties and other ATCM participants are encouraged to contribute as usual to other matters on the ATCM agenda;

Decide:

1. to adopt the Plan annexed to this Decision; and

2. that the Plan annexed to Decision 3 (2022) is no longer current.

ATCM Multi-year Strategic Work Plan

	Priority	ATCM XLV (2023)	Intersessional	ATCM 46 (2024)	Intersessional	ATCM 47 (2025)	Intersessional	ATCM 48 (2026)
1.	Consider coordinated outreach to non-party states whose nationals or assets are active in Antarctica and states that are Antarctic Treaty Parties but not yet to the Protocol	ATCM to identify and reach out to non-party states whose nationals are active in Antarctica	Coordination to be considered within Competent Authority online forum	ATCM to identify and reach out to non-party states whose nationals are active in Antarctica				
2.	Contribute to nationally and internationally coordinated education and outreach activities from an Antarctic Treaty perspective	WG1 to consider the report of the ICG on Education and Outreach	ICG on Education and Outreach	WG1 to consider the report of the ICG on Education and Outreach				
3.	Share and discuss strategic science priorities in order to identify and pursue opportunities for collaboration as well as capacity building in science, particularly in relation to climate change	Parties, Observers and Experts encouraged to report on activities relating to promoting the implications of climate change in Antarctica		Parties to consider to assess progress against the recommendations and priority actions identified by the 2022 ACCE Decadal Synopsis and the 2023 joint CEP/ATCM session on climate change				
4.	To bring Annex VI into force and to continue to gather information on repair and remediation of environmental damage and other relevant issues to inform future negotiations on liability	ATCM to evaluate progress made towards Annex VI becoming effective in accordance with Article IX of the Antarctic Treaty, and what action may be necessary and appropriate to encourage Parties to	Australia to coordinate an informal intersessional process on the ATCM forum	ATCM to evaluate progress made towards Annex VI becoming effective in accordance with Article IX of the Antarctic Treaty, and what action may be necessary and appropriate to encourage Parties to approve				

	Priority	ATCM XLV (2023)	Intersessional	ATCM 46 (2024)	Intersessional	ATCM 47 (2025)	Intersessional	ATCM 48 (2026)
		approve Annex VI in a timely manner ATCM to consider the implications of liability limits in other relevant international instruments for the potential future amendment of the limits in Article 9 of Annex VI ATCM to take a decision in 2025 on the establishment of a timeframe for the resumption of negotiations on liability in accordance with Article 16 of the Protocol on Environmental Protection, or sooner if the Parties so decide in light of progress made in approving Measure 1 (2005) – see Decision 2 (2022)		Annex VI in a timely manner				
5.	Assess the progress of the CEP on its ongoing work to review best practices and to improve existing tools and	WG 1 to consider advice of the CEP and discuss the policy considerations of the	Exchange EIA best practices	WG 1 to consider advice of the CEP and discuss the policy considerations of the review of				

	Priority	ATCM XLV (2023)	Intersessional	ATCM 46 (2024)	Intersessional	ATCM 47 (2025)	Intersessional	ATCM 48 (2026)
	develop further tools for environmental protection, including environmental impact assessment procedures	review of Environmental Impact Assessment (EIA)		Environmental Impact Assessment (EIA)				
6.	Advance in the implementation of Resolution 4 (2022), including issues related to the development and/or strengthening of research activities and the dissemination of their results	Update from COMNAP on its work with national programmes to use consistent methods to quantify and publish savings made by energy efficiencies and which contribute to both (a) reducing carbon footprint and (b) reducing fuel consumption		Parties to share information on their experiences on Infrastructure vulnerability, Biosecurity protocols, ways to increase energy efficiency and waste and emissions reductions.				
7.	Modernisation of Antarctic Stations in context of climate change	Parties to continue sharing information and experiences on the environmental, safety and cultural aspects of their construction activities		ATS to provide a summary of documents submitted on the modernisation of Antarctic stations from 2016 to 2023 Parties to continue sharing information on modernisation of Antarctic stations Parties to assess the performance of this priority				

	Priority	ATCM XLV (2023)	Intersessional	ATCM 46 (2024)	Intersessional	ATCM 47 (2025)	Intersessional	ATCM 48 (2026)
8.	Contribute to strengthening the consistent implementation of the Polar Code	Parties to share documents on the national experiences at implementing the Polar Code. A dedicated session will be organised to enhance and support harmonised implementation of the Polar Code		Parties to continue sharing documents on the national experiences at implementing the Polar Code Parties to submit papers on how they promote implementation of the Polar Code to different stakeholders in their national maritime clusters. Parties to discuss possible ways to cooperate with the Arctic Council States and other major Flag States for sharing information and best practices in implementing the Polar Code.		Parties to assess the progress of this priority		
9.	Promote enhancement of hydrographic surveying in Antarctica	Parties to discuss ways and means to implement existing resolutions on Hydrography (refer to ATCM XLIII - IP 4 (2021)) Parties, IAATO and IHO to report on		Parties to inform their geographical priorities to map unchartered areas Parties, IAATO and IHO to report on progress in hydrographical products		Parties to assess the progress on this priority		

	Priority	ATCM XLV (2023)	Intersessional	ATCM 46 (2024)	Intersessional	ATCM 47 (2025)	Intersessional	ATCM 48 (2026)
		progress in hydrography		Parties to assess progress on this priority				
10.	Develop a strategic approach to the management of Antarctic tourism to ensure it is conducted in a safe and environmentally responsible way	Consider implications of increased tourism activity for search and rescue burdens, including on national Antarctic programs	Consider options to assist and encourage implementation and entry into force of Measure 4 (2004) and Measure 15 (2009)	Review progress on implementation and entry into force of Measure 4 (2004) and Measure 15 (2009) Consider any relevant outcomes arising from the COMNAP Antarctic SAR workshop relating to tourism activity				
		Discussion on how the ATCM can best identify monitoring strategies, including indicators that might suggest tourism trends which could increase risks to effective management or present a risk to the Antarctic environment	Interested Parties to consider options for ATCM post visit report forms for land-based tourism activities and air-supported tourism activities Informal intersessional discussions on possible applicability and use of tourist fees	Assess any growth in tourism or non-governmental activities conducted by non-IAATO operators				
		Parties and other participants to provide updates on progress with tourism-related environmental monitoring activities they are sponsoring or conducting, as well as		Request advice from the CEP on the design of a strategic tourism environmental monitoring program, to support a discussion of implementation options		Assess whether the suite of Site Guidelines and other tools adequately cover the locations in which tourism		

	Priority	ATCM XLV (2023)	Intersessional	ATCM 46 (2024)	Intersessional	ATCM 47 (2025)	Intersessional	ATCM 48 (2026)
		compliance monitoring of tourism activities				activities occur		
				Consider whether guidance for Antarctic operators on the collection and provision of evidence of suspected non-compliance should be developed				
11.	Enhancing compliance with ATCM regulations relating to non-governmental activities including tourism activities	Working Group 1 to provide advice on how those operating in Antarctica can most effectively gather and share evidence of suspected non-compliance	The Secretariat will develop a best practice guide on how to gather and share evidence of suspected non-compliance	Parties will approve such a guide	Request feedback on utility of guide	Further enhance the guide		
12.	Address equality, diversity and inclusion issues, by promoting full participation of underrepresented groups in Antarctic science and operations activities across all Antarctic issues, including science, operations, policy and law	Parties, Observers and Experts to share information on their plans on these issues		Parties, Observers and Experts to share information on their plans and policies on these issues		Parties, Observers and Experts to share information on their plans and policies on these issues Parties to assess progress on this priority		Parties, Observers and Experts to share information on their plans on these issues
13.	Strengthen coordination on the management of	Review and discuss how Parties can adequately deal with these events in	Parties to continue exchanging information on seismic stations through the	Parties to continue exchanging plans to manage hazardous natural events in		Parties to discuss where		

	Priority	ATCM XLV (2023)	Intersessional	ATCM 46 (2024)	Intersessional	ATCM 47 (2025)	Intersessional	ATCM 48 (2026)
	hazardous natural events in Antarctic facilities	Antarctic facilities COMNAP to inform on the work of this group at ATCM XLV SCAR to inform on seismic activities in Antarctica	EIES	Antarctic facilities Parties to discuss where to consider these plans Invite COMNAP to report on the work of its Technical Collaboration Group		to consider these plans Parties to assess progress on this priority		

Note: The ATCM Working Groups mentioned above are not permanent but are established by consensus at the end of each Antarctic Treaty Consultative Meeting.

Decision 6 (2023)

Dedicated process for the development of a comprehensive and consistent framework for Antarctic tourism and other non-governmental activities

The Representatives,

Noting that in Article 2 of the Protocol on Environmental Protection to the Antarctic Treaty ("the Protocol"), the Parties committed themselves to the comprehensive protection of the Antarctic environment and dependent and associated ecosystems and designated Antarctica as a natural reserve, devoted to peace and science;

Acknowledging that the concerns arising from, *inter alia*, the growth, diversification and compliance in relation to Antarctic tourism and other non-governmental activities in Antarctica require the Antarctic Treaty Consultative Meeting ("ATCM") with urgency to take responsibility and strengthen international governance action;

Decide:

1. to start a dedicated process to develop a comprehensive and consistent framework for the regulation of tourism and other non-governmental activities in Antarctica;

2. that the Special Working Group on the Development of a Tourism Framework established pursuant to Rule 11 of the Rules of Procedure of the Antarctic Treaty Consultative Meeting (2016) in Agenda Item 18 of the ATCM XLV Final Report will have its first meeting of two days during ATCM 46; and

3. to invite all Consultative Parties to develop proposals prior to the convening of that first meeting, to be exchanged through the normal means of diplomatic communication and other means, such as the ATCM Forum, in order to ensure due preparation of discussions. Parties may decide to organise one or several informal and voluntary virtual or hybrid workshop(s) to support their preparation for the first meeting.

3. Resolutions

Resolution 1 (2023)

Consideration of Mitigation Measures in Environmental Impact Assessment

The Representatives,

Recalling the Environmental Principles contained in Article 3 of the Protocol on Environmental Protection to the Antarctic Treaty ("the Protocol"), and specifically paragraph 2(c) of Article 3 which states that 'activities in the Antarctic Treaty area shall be planned and conducted on the basis of information sufficient to allow prior assessments of, and informed judgments about, their possible impacts on the Antarctic environment and dependent and associated ecosystems and on the value of Antarctica for the conduct of scientific research';

Recalling also the requirements under Article 8 of the Protocol and its Annex I regarding environmental impact assessment for proposed activities in the Antarctic Treaty area;

Recalling that under Article 8 of the Protocol that proposed activities shall be subject to the procedures set out in Annex I for prior assessment of the impact of those activities on the Antarctic environment or on dependent or associated ecosystems according to whether those activities are identified as having a less than a minor or transitory impact; a minor or transitory impact; or more than a minor or transitory impact;

Recalling specifically paragraph 2(g) of Article 3 of Annex I to the Protocol, which requires a Comprehensive Environmental Evaluation to include 'identification of measures, including monitoring programmes, that could be taken to minimise or mitigate impacts of the proposed activity and to detect unforeseen impacts and that could provide early warning of any adverse effects of the activity as well as to deal promptly and effectively with accidents';

Recognising that Article 1 of Annex I states that Parties shall consider, in accordance with appropriate national procedures, environmental impacts of proposed activities before their commencement;

Recognising that Parties are also encouraged to apply the appropriate level of environmental impact assessment commensurate with the level of environmental impact;

Noting that under Resolution 1 (1999) the Antarctic Treaty Consultative Meeting ("ATCM") adopted Guidelines for Environmental Impact Assessment in Antarctica;

Noting also that under Resolution 1 (2016) the ATCM adopted revised Guidelines for Environmental Impact Assessment in Antarctica ("the Guidelines"); and

Desiring to ensure that, consistent with the Guidelines, all environmental impact assessment for proposed activities in Antarctica include mitigation measures, commensurate with the nature of the activity and the level of environmental impact;

Recommend that their Governments encourage that Initial Environmental Evaluation and, where appropriate and practical, Preliminary Stage levels of environmental impact assessment include identification of measures, commensurate with the nature of activity and the level of environmental impact, to minimise or mitigate the impacts of the proposed activity.

Resolution 2 (2023)

Helsinki Declaration on Climate Change and the Antarctic

We, the Consultative Parties of the Antarctic Treaty and the Members of the Committee on Environmental Protection (CEP) having met at the 45th Antarctic Treaty Consultative Meeting (ATCM) and the 25th Meeting of the Committee for Environmental Protection in Helsinki, Finland from 29 May to 8 June 2023;

Reaffirming our firm commitment to combat the adverse impacts of climate change in Antarctica;

Recognising the critical role of Antarctica and the Southern Ocean in the global climate system, and the implications of Antarctic cryospheric and oceanographic changes for global climate and sea-level rise;

Further recognising that observations, modelling and global assessments describe significant changes in Antarctic physical and living systems, both marine and terrestrial, and that changes in Antarctic and Southern Ocean environments are linked to, and influence, climate impact drivers globally;

Deeply concerned that further irreversible change is likely to occur without accelerated efforts to reduce greenhouse gas emissions in line with a trajectory consistent with holding the global temperature increase to well below 2 degrees Celsius above preindustrial levels and pursuing efforts to limit warming to 1.5 degrees Celsius;

Acknowledging that by further delaying concerted global action on climate change mitigation and adaptation, we risk missing the window of opportunity to secure a liveable and sustainable future for all;

Underscoring the need to improve the scientific understanding of climate change in Antarctica and the implications globally, as well as for the Antarctic environment, and the need for adaptive management and conservation;

Highlighting the continuing work of the ATCM and CEP on climate change response, including, for example, through the Climate Change Response Work Program (CCRWP) Resolution 4 (2015), and Resolution 8 (2021);

Acknowledging the important contribution of the Subsidiary Group on Climate Change Response to the implementation and follow-up of the CCRWP adopted by the CEP;

Highlighting that in 2022, the ATCM welcomed the report of the Scientific Committee on Antarctic Research (SCAR) on Antarctic Climate Change and the Environment: A Decadal Synopsis and Recommendations for Action (ACCE), and adopted Resolution 4 (2022) and Decision 4 (2022) on the subject, including welcoming SCAR's advice that urgent action is required to prevent irreversible changes to the Antarctic environment and consequential implications for the planet;

Recognising the objectives and principles of the UNFCCC and the on-going work to tackle climate change by strengthening the full and effective implementation of the Paris Agreement, adopted under the UNFCCC;

Recalling the ATCM Paris Declaration in 2021 and *reaffirming* their commitment to better understand changes to the Antarctic climate and to implement actions with a view to limiting the adverse impacts of climate change on the Antarctic environment and dependent and associated ecosystems, protecting ecosystems and improving Antarctica's resilience to climate change;

Acknowledging that scientific evidence clearly shows that with the current trajectory of CO_2 emissions, the atmosphere and oceans will continue to warm and the oceans to acidify, atmospheric and ocean circulation patterns will continue to alter and the cryosphere will continue to lose ice in all forms, and sea levels will continue to rise;

Deeply concerned that multiple meters of sea level rise resulting from ice-sheet loss that is irreversible for centuries to millennia would have devastating to catastrophic impacts, particularly on millions of people living in low elevation coastal zones;

Taking into consideration the best available expertise and scientific findings on climate change and including the IPCC's AR6 Synthesis Report: Climate Change 2023, published on 20 March 2023;

Aware of the tools that the Parties to the Antarctic Treaty have at their disposal for action, such as research, monitoring, management, environmental protection, advocacy and communication, in accordance with best available science;

Hereby:

1. Commit to substantially increasing our efforts to communicate the global implications of climate change in Antarctica within our own countries and in international forums, and the need to prevent the irreversible changes to Antarctica and consequential implications for the planet;
2. Reaffirm the importance of the ongoing work of the Committee on Environmental Protection to support efforts within the Antarctic Treaty system to mitigate, prepare for, and build resilience to, the environmental impacts of a changing climate, and commit as a matter of priority to continue the implementation and regular review of the Climate Change Response Work Programme;
3. Give strong support to the 5th International Polar Year (IPY) 2032-33 by championing its objectives, and seek to provide sufficient means to support the scientific endeavours of those planning IPY projects and logistics, and encourage SCAR and COMNAP, together with its IPY partners, to use the occasion to take a further step forward to understand the impacts of climate and environmental change on the Antarctic environment and dependent and associated ecosystems, as well as the global implications of these changes;
4. Encourage all Antarctic operators, including national Antarctic programs, tourist and non-governmental operators to continue to reduce their carbon footprints and investigate pathways and move towards carbon neutral ('net zero') operations, as well as to reduce their impacts on the Antarctic environment and its associated and dependent ecosystems and to continue deliberations on possible policy recommendations to this end;
5. Intensify working together, including with SCAR and COMNAP, to plan and implement large scale internationally coordinated field-based research and information exchange efforts to make leaps in knowledge with respect to understanding the impact of global climate change on Antarctica, as well as the global role of Antarctica and the Southern Ocean in regulating global climate and future sea-level rise, under a range of future global temperature rise scenarios;

6. Invite SCAR to continue to provide annual updates to its ACCE report and reconfirm our commitment to take account of the best scientific and technical advice available in taking appropriate measures to deliver our commitments made in the Protocol on Environmental Protection for the comprehensive protection of the Antarctic environment and dependent and associated ecosystems;

7. Reaffirm efforts to increase knowledge on the Antarctic environment and dependent and associated ecosystems, including better assessment of the risk of invasions by non-native species, to effectively inform the decision-making process;

8. Aim to assess the risks of climate change to Antarctic Infrastructures and Historic Sites and Monuments and include mitigation, adaptation and management measures in Conservation Management Plans for Antarctic Historic Sites and Monuments, as appropriate;

9. Work towards developing a systematically coordinated Antarctic climate and environment observation and monitoring network with an optimal spatial distribution, comparability and/or complementarity between observations where input can be used in key global observation and modelling systems and processes;

10. Commit to strengthen and implement all management tools under the Environment Protocol, including *inter alia* area protection and management, in light of the effects and projected changes to Antarctic environments resulting from climate change, to provide enhanced protection of the Antarctic environment and dependent and associated ecosystems; and

11. Reaffirm our commitment to Article 7 of the Protocol on Environmental Protection to the Antarctic Treaty, and stress that Antarctic mineral resource activities other than scientific research, including the extraction of fossil fuels, remain prohibited, in accordance with the Protocol on Environmental Protection to the Antarctic Treaty, which does not have an expiry date.

Resolution 3 (2023)

Reaffirming ongoing commitment to the prohibition on Antarctic mineral resource activities, other than for scientific research

The Representatives,

Recognising that the Protocol on Environmental Protection to the Antarctic Treaty ("the Protocol"), which has been in force for more than two decades, is an essential element of current efforts to protect the Antarctic environment;

Noting that Article 7 of the Protocol prohibits any activity relating to mineral resources, other than scientific research, in the Antarctic Treaty area;

Taking into account that, outside the Antarctic Treaty system, many hold the mistaken belief that the Protocol expires in 2048;

Recalling that the Protocol contains no expiration date and that Article 25 relates solely to the possibility of a review conference at the request of any Antarctic Treaty Consultative Party after the Protocol has been in force for 50 years;

Recommend that their Governments:

1. commit to dispelling the myth that the Antarctic Treaty or the Protocol expire, either in 2048 or at any other time;

2. acknowledge the benefits to the Antarctic environment and dependent and associated ecosystems that have resulted from the prohibition on activities relating to mineral resources, other than scientific research, under Article 7 of the Protocol;

3. reaffirm their commitment to Article 7 of the Protocol; and

4. declare their firm commitment to continue to implement this prohibition as a matter of highest priority to achieve the comprehensive protection of the Antarctic environment and dependent and associated ecosystems.

Resolution 4 (2023)

Urgent measures to be taken with respect to certain tourist and non-governmental activities

The Representatives,

Concerned about the continuing and substantial increase in the numbers of tourists and diversification of tourism and other non-governmental activities in Antarctica;

Acknowledging that the concerns associated with the growth, diversification, monitoring, compliance and governance in relation to Antarctic tourism and other non-governmental activities in Antarctica prompt the Antarctic Treaty Consultative Meeting ("ATCM") to take urgent action;

Acknowledging the desire for National Competent Authorities ("NCA") to improve harmonisation of assessment and standards, and to address issues arising from new activities or those seldom conducted, and potentially risky activities, as expressed in the NCAs discussion forum and reported in IP 91 (2023);

Recalling Resolution 2 (2022), which adopted and updated lists of sites subject to Site Guidelines for Visitors ("Site Guidelines");

Recalling Measure 15 (2009) and the "General Principles of Antarctic Tourism" adopted by Resolution 7 (2009);

Recalling also Resolution 2 (2004) "Guidelines for the Operation of Aircraft near concentrations of birds in Antarctica";

Recommend that their Governments:

1. recommend operators organising or conducting tourist or other non-governmental activities in the Antarctic Treaty area, for which advance notification is required in accordance with Article VII(5) of the Antarctic Treaty, to discontinue except in case of emergencies and for the purpose of enhancing human safety:

    a. any off-ship activities in Antarctica from vessels carrying more than 500 passengers to clarify the purpose of Measure 15 (2009);

    b. the use of helicopters for recreational purposes in areas with concentrations of wildlife; and

2. engage in further discussions on these and other specific actions in the context of future discussions regarding tourism.

Heads of Delegation picture

May 29 – June 8, 2023
XLV ANTARCTIC TREATY CONSULTATIVE MEETING
Helsinki ~ Finland

www.ingramcontent.com/pod-product-compliance
Lightning Source LLC
LaVergne TN
LVHW060029210926
848481LV00013B/3822